PENGUIN BOOKS

LOVING MEN MORE, NEEDING MEN LESS

Judith Sills, Ph.D., is the author of the #1 national bestseller *Excess Baggage*, as well as *A Fine Romance: The Passage of Courtship from Meeting to Marriage* and *How to Stop Looking for Someone Perfect and Find Someone to Love*. A clinical psychologist in private practice in Philadelphia, Sills is also a contributing editor to *Family Circle*, and has been widely quoted in leading publications including *The New York Times* and *The Washington Post*. She appears regularly on such national television shows as *The Oprah Winfrey Show* and *Sally*. She is currently the host of her own radio talk show on WPHAT in Philadelphia.

A Penguin reading group guide is available while supplies last

Call (800) 778-6425 or write to:
Penguin Books, Marketing Dept. CC,
Reading Group Guides
375 Hudson Street, New York, NY 10014

Loving Men More, Needing Men Less

Judith Sills, Ph.D.

PENGUIN BOOKS

PENGUIN BOOKS
Published by the Penguin Group
Penguin Books USA Inc., 375 Hudson Street, New York, New York 10014, U.S.A.
Penguin Books Ltd, 27 Wrights Lane, London W8 5TZ, England
Penguin Books Australia Ltd, Ringwood, Victoria, Australia
Penguin Books Canada Ltd, 10 Alcorn Avenue, Toronto, Ontario, Canada M4V 3B2
Penguin Books (N.Z.) Ltd, 182–190 Wairau Road, Auckland 10, New Zealand

Penguin Books Ltd, Registered Offices: Harmondsworth, Middlesex, England

First published in the United States of America as *Biting the Apple* by Viking Penguin,
a division of Penguin Books USA Inc. 1996
Published in Penguin Books 1997

3 5 7 9 10 8 6 4 2

Portions of this work first appeared in *Cosmopolitan*, *Good Housekeeping*, and *Redbook*.

THE LIBRARY OF CONGRESS HAS CATALOGUED THE HARDCOVER AS FOLLOWS:
Sills, Judith.
Biting the apple/Judith Sills.
p. cm.
Includes bibliographical references and index.
ISBN 0-670-85846-3 (hc.)
ISBN 0 14 02.4223 6 (pbk.)
1. Love.   2. Love—Religious aspects.   I. Title.
HQ801.S5825   1995
306.7—dc20   95-42698

Printed in the United States of America
Set in New Caledonia

First, for my mother and my daughter

Then, for Pamela Dorman, Joni Evans, and Patti Kelly

Finally, for each of my girlfriends

and each of yours

Acknowledgments

Pamela Dorman is the editor of this book. Joni Evans is its literary agent. Separately they are as good as publishing gets. Together they were the heat and light that made this book possible. My own would never have been enough.

Patti Kelly, director of publicity at Viking, is godmother. Pam and Joni took care of the book. Patti, a unique combination of creativity and kindness, took care of me. I am deeply grateful.

And Dr. Michael Adams, dean of the College of Design Arts at Drexel University, took care of the manuscript. He arranged it, formatted it, printed it, and once, when the computer stole a chapter, he rescued it. Dean Adams provided this continuous support over two and a half years, as an act of friendship.

Two others made significant contributions to *Loving Men More, Needing Men Less*. Graphic designer Toby Schmidt Schachman, at the top of her profession, donated her design concepts, including the apple/heart logo that is a perfect visual expression of what I have tried to write. And Susan Adams made me a recipient of her particular genius for easing and improving the lives of those around her. Toby and Susan are those rarest of life's essentials: true friends. Thanks are inadequate for the gift.

Also I am grateful to the following people, whose assistance made an especially difficult project easier: Paul Buckley, Denise Drummond, Dalma Heyn, Dr. Patricia Ondek-Laurence, Carole Ivy, Rochelle Kinzel, Larry Teacher, and Sharon Wolmuth Teacher.

Last, my thanks to my beloved husband, Lynn Hoffman, particularly for the phrase, "biting the apple." It is only fitting that a key concept for this book came from him. He is, after all, its laboratory and its inspiration.

If I am not for myself,
who will be for me?

If I am for myself alone,
then what am I?

If not now, when?

—Rabbi Hillel
Pirke Avot 1:15

Contents

Preface

This is a book about a path. We are all—every one of us—somewhere on it. The path ends up at love, and getting there is our whole point.

You knew that.

At least, you knew it couldn't all be about getting thin, getting married, getting rich, or just getting by. Many of us sense a purposefulness to our lives, a direction in which we are heading, even if it is hard to stand apart from our daily rituals long enough to grasp it. We do not move from twenty to seventy and beyond simply for the chance to experience aging. We are hoping to gain something along the way.

We hope to be wiser, more compassionate, freer in our spirits, with a greater capacity for joy. We want to be rid of the fears that limit us, closer to the harmony we sense in some of those around us. We move forward, striving to acquire more of whatever it is that we think will make us stronger: a healthier body, perhaps, with an enhanced capacity for physical pleasure; more money, with its promise of both security and opportunity; a record of achievements to mark our progress and establish our worth; more risk for some, more shelter for others; more good deeds done for credit in heaven, or right here on earth. Each goal promises to enrich us; each turns out to have its own element of illusion.

Eventually, we recognize that these outer accomplishments, while comfortable and comforting, are limited in what they can do for us. Any of them can make our lives broader in experience, but none can make it deeper. They can get us down the path to success, but they cannot get us to a path on a higher level.

Love is our only access to that higher level, because only love moves us beyond ourselves, beyond our personal limits. To put it simply, we are here, first to develop ourselves, then to be ourselves, and finally to extend ourselves to each other. Our highest purpose is to connect the dots between us with love, and to cherish those connections.

The idea that love is a higher level of experience is not a new one. Religions preach it. Ethics teach it. Love is that piece of God, that chip of enlightenment, which we are all able to experience first-hand. If you have touched love yourself, you already know why it is the prize at the end of the path.

The view of love as a higher order of experience may be an old concept, but it is not necessarily a reassuring one, at least not for me. It has been tainted by the spiritual Muzak that drones louder and louder lately, trivializing our very genuine longings to see our lives in a bigger context. *Loving Men More, Needing Men Less* describes an inner path whose prize is love. It suggests a fundamental change in your thinking that may enhance your progress. But it is not meant to be a form of quick and dirty Zen, or a one-minute guide for busy people who want relationships. Instead, it outlines a new choice for women, a forward step we can now take, towards the love we have always envisioned.

This book is written so that you—single, married, divorced, widowed—whether you are hoping for love or remembering it, living in it or recovering from it—can see this choice, and the road that leads to it, as a possibility in your own life.

Sit back, relax, and take a slow look. What follows is not a formula, a strategy, or an exercise. The path is an emotional direction, a marker for your spirit, and an opportunity to develop in yourself that higher level of awareness that is love. And this book is simply meant as a spotlight on that path, because we all struggle less when we see more clearly.

Loving Men More, Needing Men Less

CHAPTER ONE

Temporary Blindness

"This is strange, but it happened and it made a difference in my life. James and I had been married about a year. You know what he's like, so you can imagine how much we had to work out that first year.

"We were taking a little day cruise with my family. I have a clear memory of walking up a bumpy gangplank, with him walking next to me, snapping at me: 'Watch where you're going.' 'Where's the camera?' 'Do you have everything?' 'Don't you ever look where you're going?' I clenched inside, not wanting to scream back at him in front of my parents.

"I turned away from him and met the eye of a woman standing right behind us. She was a very old lady. Actually, she looked like one of those wrinkled apple dolls in white tennis sneakers. All of a sudden, she smiled at me and reached over to touch my hand. 'I would give everything I have left,' she said, nodding towards my husband, 'to have mine back, looking out for me just like that.'

"I can't explain why, but all at once it was as if I were being sent a message, as if she were behind me in line because she was supposed to tell me something and I was meant to pay attention to it. My anger vanished—totally vanished. Out of nowhere I felt an overwhelming love for James and a sense of pure, calm happiness. I turned back to him and took his hand and we kept going."

"My father, I swear to you, is the most difficult man in the world. He is the kind of person who would leave a glass of water in the re-frigerator and not let anyone throw it out for three weeks. He used to drive my mother up a wall and they argued all the time. In recent years, though, she's changed. She reacts to him so differently. I still get irritated every time I open the refrigerator and see that stupid glass of water. But when I say, 'Ma, how can you stand to live with him?,' she just chuckles and answers, 'Oh, you know, honey, that's just your father.' "

A woman is holding hands with her husband at a party. She is a woman of great physical impact, widely regarded for her style and polish. After complimenting her appearance, an admiring friend gestured to the husband and asked the woman warmly, "What does he say to you when he sees you dressed to go out for the evening?" "Oh, that's easy," said the woman, smiling affectionately at her hus-band. "He always says the same thing: 'How do I look?' "

"A girlfriend and I are leaving for a weekend woman's retreat. As she's walking out the door, her lover hands her a package of tissues, saying, 'You know you always forget tissues and you always need some.' I bristle a bit, hearing the reminder as the kind of thing one might say to a not-very-bright seven-year-old. But my girlfriend seems to hear it differently. 'You are so sweet,' says my friend, giving her lover another quick kiss before she leaves. When we're in the car, she puts the tissues in her bag, right on top of two other packs of tissues. Seeing me notice, she explains, 'True, I didn't need the re-minder. But if it makes Frankie happy, why spoil it?' "

D o you remember love, before it became work? Your vision of love, that is—love, apart from any lover; love, before you knew what it could cost you or what kind of power it gave you?

Do you remember your girlhood Saturday-night anticipation of love, when the best parts were the before and after, with your friends? Then the body-driven sweep of love, when your friends were no longer the best part?

Do you remember sensing there was more to love, that love went past movie plots and into actual homes? Happy homes. Whatever it was, some people's parents had it, living at the center of their family. It made all the difference. You didn't know exactly what you were seeing, but whatever it was, you called it love and knew that, someday, *you would have it, too.*

Do you remember knowing, knowing with complete conviction, that love was a reason, in and of itself? In fact, you thought it was the reason, the necessary condition for your happiness, the feeling for which nothing else can substitute? You know what? You were right.

We see the proof of this belief when we are in the presence of a couple who love each other. Then we know love, if only because we have been in the same room with it. It's something we sense, some pleasure they take in one another, some basic regard. It may be nothing we can pin down—just an aura of kindness, or an absence of tension that signals the alchemy that transports two people to another level of experience.

We see it in the way he listens when she comments, or in the way she shows him off. It is the glance exchanged in passing, the cheek brushed, the mentioning of each other's names. It is a responsiveness. One moves to leave; the other rises. In shadow, their bodies curve inward, as if love literally inclines each towards the other.

We see it, and we say to ourselves, That's it. That's what I want. That's how I want to feel. That's how I want us to be. What do those two have that I don't? How did they get that way? That lucky? Or that smart?

If you have ever felt love yourself, if you have known firsthand its power to transform, you will probably require no further explanation. Those of us who have met the elves know that they make some of the cookies, no matter how many factories we tour.

. . . .

Love is not a woman's only purpose, nor is a relationship what our whole lives are about. There is so much more to want, so much more to work towards, so much more we have to work against. But no matter what else has been on our agenda—from political power to personal freedom, from self-development to social improvement—*we never intended to trade any of it for love. And there is no reason why we should.*

We have, however, temporarily blinded ourselves to our female image of love, because it was blotting out our ability to see ourselves. Now, after more than a generation of work, having developed a much fuller portrait of ourselves, of our abilities, entitlements, and contributions, women are ready to reclaim our dream of love. It is an essential part of our strength and of our spirit. In the circle of life, love is how each of us gets her bearings.

Reclaim our old dream of love? What could that possibly mean? If we look backwards, across the last two generations or just across our own lifetimes, we see ourselves harnessed by that old fantasy of love, placing men firmly at the center of our lives. We remember dressing up in pleasing personalities, dancing around the Maypoles men constructed. There was a time we were taught to call this love, and we believed it. We danced around as best we could and were rewarded accordingly.

Eventually, enraged by the arbitrary confines of this dance of devotion, dulled and diminished by the same old cha-cha, we burned the Maypole. It's hard to believe we could poke through those ashes and find anything of value.

Why would we look backwards to reclaim a vision of love, when backwards is what we are moving away from as fast as we can? Because we left something important behind.

Honoring Both Gods

"one's not half two. It's two are halves of one. . . ."
—e. e. cummings

Why turn to the idea that love, romantic love, is necessary to a woman's happiness? Why not cling to a newer and no less truthful position, that only *she* is essential to her happiness—her self-respect, her goals, her proven support system, and her own stock portfolio?

Because it's not the whole truth.

Yes, our capacity to be self-sufficient is the more palatable half of the truth today. And, because it was a long-neglected half of the truth, it deserves to be shouted in order to be heard. Self-esteem *is* the course required before any of us can sign up for love. (Even if we have used it as the universal substitute for self-awareness. "I've got low self-esteem," we announce matter-of-factly, as if it were something you could get from a public bathroom.)

Besides, self-reliance is the half of the truth that feels better. The whole "fish without a bicycle, who the hell needs him, I could do better on my own if only he'd get out of the way" attitude is not just invigorating, it's utterly true. As far as it goes.

Here is the other, less comforting, but nonetheless accurate half of the truth: there is a step further to go. That step is towards attachment—the other piece of the human heart.

Every one of us has two contradictory pulls, one towards separation and the strengthening and satisfaction of the self, and the other towards attachment and the loving relationships that take us beyond our small selves into a grander connection with the world. Thomas Moore calls these pulls "two valid claims of the heart" and gives the only advice there is, "Honor both Gods."

Yes, separation is essential, because it is the only way to be strong enough to know ourselves, and to be ourselves. Separation is the foundation of self-respect and self-reliance.

But attachment is what makes us even stronger. Loving attachment is what takes us beyond ourselves, to double our strength. It is the power of two connected, of pooled resources, of a whole far greater than the sum of its parts.

Women's next step forward is the step that gets us from here to love. I don't think we've been in a position to get there before, and I don't think we've been ready to learn how. We are ready now. The fuel for this step is the new strength we've developed over the last thirty years, the strength that has won us opportunity, autonomy, and the courage to take advantage of both. But the direction of the step is as ancient as our first bite of the apple. Because the heart of our female vision is the vision of love.

Our old vision is of attachment. Our new power results from separation. We need them both.

Seeing Through to You

"Look into the pond, Wart," said Merlin. "Look deep into the pond. What do you see?"

Arthur peered in the pond. "I see myself reflected," he said.

"No, no, no," said Merlin. "Look deeper. Think, Wart. Think."

It was then that Arthur was able to look past himself to see the hawk. And finally to see that he was the hawk.

This is what women, too, need to do, in order to retrieve the piece of ourselves left behind. We need to look past parts of ourselves, not to overlook our experiences, but to look deeper into them. We need to clear our palate, to get past our own static about loving men, in order to see through to ourselves.

To retrieve our original picture of love, we need to see it purely, without the distorting shadows of what we have been taught to expect, or what we have come to believe we can't have. We need to look past the politics of gender, and past the rescue fantasies bred deep into our Cinderella bones. We need to look beyond our anger with men—be it mild irritation, affectionate contempt, or consuming rage. We need to stop for a moment, to take a step back so that we can see the bigger picture. That picture has not been easy to grasp.

Of the several factors that have temporarily blinded us to this bigger picture of ourselves, the single greatest shadow has been cast by our avalanche of analysis of The Relationship. That avalanche buried our ideal of love.

To a large degree, this burial was deliberate, a conscious female resistance to the seductions of love, while we examined its consequences in our lives. And it was absolutely necessary, because our minute analysis of relationships has been a critical survival tool in the emotional hurricane of social change. As women changed, romantic relationships had to change. So, individually and collectively, from one girlfriend to another, we took on the huge, uncertain job of figuring out how to change them.

We have worked to define The Relationship, torturing it into shape and torturing ourselves in the process. We have struggled both to make him fall in love with us, and to make him into a man worth falling in love with. We've read about each of his ten secrets, translated each of his obscure signals, studied owner's manuals, astrological charts, and male confessionals. We have puzzled together over the tea leaves of relationship minutiae—*What do you think he meant by . . . ? If he cares about me, don't you think he'll . . . ?*—all this and more, in our ferocious attempt to Make The Relationship Work.

We have also attempted to override our brutal inner chorus of feminine self-criticism (toofattooflattoobossytooneedytoo in de pen dent . . .) with an increasingly keen awareness of the shortcomings of men. We have educated ourselves about men who will never grow up, about men who must leave at the mere threat of love. We have warned each other about the early signs of abuse, and have come to accept that there are men who truly hate women, men for whom marriage is a license both to possess and to punish.

Our voracious analysis of relationships has been essential. Essential, but exhausting. Essential, but at a price. Minute scrutiny of The Relationship has crowded out our image of love. That's why we need to look backwards; why we need to retrieve what was lost in the rush of female rebellion. In our necessary examination of men and relationships, we have momentarily lost touch with ourselves and with our own hearts.

What was new in our intense analysis of relationships was that it took us a step beyond our passive dreams of romance, towards an active appraisal of what we get, in return for what we give. And we developed the strength to insist we get our fair share. That was even newer.

What was old, however, was that we were thinking new thoughts about the same old someone. About *him*. Focused on *him*. Helping *him* to change, insisting that he stretch himself, pushing *him* to give more, to "get it," to become more of what we believe (on our better days) he can be: A better lover. A fairer partner. A closer husband. A sweeter boyfriend. We've done our very best with his part. Now it's our turn.

Analysis made us strong, because it made us smart about men and smarter about relationships. We are ready now for the next step forward towards love: the leap from smart to wise. That step forward is the step inside.

Only by turning our attention inward can we see through to ourselves, to some essence at the core of every relationship we enter, every lover we analyze, every man we turn away from or turn towards. That essence is, quite simply, the feeling of love. It is a feeling for someone else, a feeling from someone else. And the feeling was always what mattered, first and last. Remember? The whole point of The Relationship was to achieve that feeling—without selling our souls to achieve it.

It made sense to bury our old image of love. We believed we had to leave it behind, in order to become who we knew we could be. Not forever, of course. We would reclaim our dream when we were powerful enough to love without losing ourselves as the price. Now is that time. Now, before we lose ourselves in a different way.

Of a Woman, By a Woman, For a Woman

When I say "we," I mean women. This book is written for women, and it is about women. It is about ourselves and where we might go from here.

It's not about men. It has no findum, catchum, keepum strategies. It has no tips on how to tell the good guys from the bad, not even any "Here's how to get him to . . ." hints. It's just about us.

You may find that frustrating at first. I have noticed that, when I suggest to a woman a romantic option she may not have considered, quite often her first response is "Why? Do guys like that?" If, for example, I suggest a firmer boundary between a woman and her lover, she frequently interprets it as a secret strategy. "So you think, if I don't say another word about picking up the check, he'll realize himself that his friends think he's cheap?" No, I explain. I don't know what effect it will have on him. I'm just pointing out that what his friends think of him is his own issue. You don't have to make it your problem. "Oh. But what do you think the chances are that he'll pick up a check, say, in my lifetime?"

If I assert that women are some particular way, you may agree or disagree. But it's just as likely that you will find yourself thinking, "Well, aren't men that way, too?" If I recommend a change in your approach to a problem, you may or may not find my reasoning persuasive. But you may also veer off into thinking, "For once, why can't he be the one to change?"

As best I could (hey, I'm conditioned, too), I have resisted answering all of these questions about men. They are not addressed, even when I felt you'd want to ask, even if I thought I had an answer.

It's not that these questions are unimportant. On the contrary, our searching inquiries and commentaries have been our one indispensable source of information and support, the source that has made possible a new balance between ourselves and our lovers. It's just that we've been asking these same questions over and over, struggling to answer them correctly, passing along what worked, comparing and refining our answers. We have tried out all the solutions, too. Tried confronting him, enduring him, refusing him, coaxing him along, and turning our backs in frustration.

We have asked it all, tried it all, and you know what? It's enough!

We need a break. We need to get back to ourselves. We need to hear our own voices, to see ourselves as the locus of our own desires. Focusing on men has taken us as far as it can. This book is written directly to women, and just about women, so that we can turn the corner.

The way we turn the corner is that we let go of the idea of getting to love by helping men to change. In our all-too-understandable obsession with getting more of what we need and what we are reasonably entitled to in a relationship, we have overlooked a key psychological truth: **relationships depend far less on whom we choose than on who we are.**

What matters most in your experience of love is who you are, and how far you've come in the path of your own development. *You* are the single most important factor in whom you choose to love, and in what you experience in return. Love is a measure of your own inner stretch—a stretch both in what and to whom you are able to give, and a stretch in what and from whom you are able to receive.

We can get closer to our old vision of love as we balance it with a new vision of ourselves. To all the ways we've been strengthening ourselves, we can add a new permission to release ourselves.

This is the forward step we can take towards the love we have always envisioned. It is the step beyond the face-off we've come to, as a group, in our cold war with men.

More important, it is a step forward for you, one woman, no matter where you happen to be in your lifelong circumnavigation of love.

- Retain the strong sense of self you have been working to develop.
- Reclaim your old vision of love.

Together, these are our payoff for two generations of struggle. For God's sake, don't forget to cash in.

The Dirty Little Secret

One thing stands in the way of our profiting from this new opportunity to love from a position of strength. We've allowed ourselves to become ashamed of our desire for men. When sex came out of the closet, love went in. Quite simply, our focus on men is embarrassing to us. We feel we ought to be beyond it, ought to let them worry about us for a change.

Let's be absolutely clear on one point: you can get to romantic love without a man. There are lesbian women for whom men seem as irrelevant as debutante balls—pleasant enough diversions, but no one you know actually has one. Whoever your choice of partner, the sense of vulnerability, the faint innuendo of weakness, clings to the longing for love.

How did we let this happen? How did we let our dream of love become a symptom of weakness? Why did we allow wives to become punch lines and anxious single women to become objects of ridicule, even in our own eyes? When did our deep appreciation for connection become the subtly demeaning "need for attachment" (as we mental-health professionals call it, with our genius for making everything human sound like a symptom)? Why did our open desire for love become feminine stigmata?

Easy. Love involves an emotional yielding that is somehow not submission, an acceptance that has nothing to do with the dreaded "settling." *Yielding. Submission. Acceptance.* What could be more risky for women?

So dangerous is this swoony feeling that we have learned to drown it out, shouting warnings to ourselves and to each other.

Watch out! He's going to hurt you! See? I knew he wouldn't call. I told you he wouldn't leave her. You don't have to put up with that, honey. Don't let him get away with it. Don't be a fool.

Longing on the one hand, fearful on the other, we fight against that part of ourselves that looks for love. Or, alternatively, we are overwhelmed by that desire and suffer for it. We sometimes end up working against ourselves, canceling ourselves out, hoping for love but trying to barricade that vulnerable *wanting* piece of our heart.

Few of us are proud to acknowledge that a deep and permanent romantic relationship is essential to us, and that we would give up a great deal to have one and to maintain one. Far from admiring or respecting women who need love, today we are planning recovery programs for them. We see our longing for a relationship as a sad sign of weakness, *and so do so many "experts."*

From Freud through Erik Erikson and beyond, there is general consensus: normal, healthy psychological development has been described as progressing from the dependency of a baby to the independence of an adult, or, to put it another way, we grow from being attached to someone else to being separate, self-sufficient entities. In other words, the male pattern of going off to conquer the world, while regarding women as a prize of victory, has been defined, largely by male social scientists, as healthy and right. Women are seen as less mature, clutching from behind, longing to be attached, to be returned to, attended to. Of course, goes the thinking, without a penis, what can you expect?

Social science hasn't helped, but we don't need the opinions of experts in order to feel disgusted by our own hunger for love. "It's like I deflate," mourned one woman, noting her descent into anxious obsession the moment she begins to care for a man. Another described this same disheartening fading of her sense of self by saying, "When I get into bed, I'm my own woman. But if we make love, I get out of bed feeling like his woman. Is there something in sperm that makes me collapse on contact?"

So we may wonder, devastated when a man who was exciting for four dates fails to call for a fifth, or clinging frantically to the arm of a husband who yesterday called us "bitch." *What happened to me?* we wonder. *Is my self-esteem so shaky, am I so desperate?*

I hear this self-recrimination from women frequently, women who view themselves with scorn for how easily they are hurt or mislead, or for how much they will tolerate; women filled with hatred for men and shame at themselves, some because the last three boyfriends didn't become husbands, some because of the dreadful man who did. These women tell me how weak they are, or how flawed their sense of self must be, because men and love have overwhelmed them.

I hear about women's weakness, but I don't often see the supporting evidence of it. I see these same women holding down jobs, dealing with landlords, acting as decent friends, dutiful daughters, and, when necessary, as auto mechanics to their cars and construction engineers to their bookshelves. I see women who do all this with one hand, while raising a child or two with the other—children who do get their bedtime stories read, their green vegetables forced upon them, and their homework reviewed.

I watch women carry these loads without breaking, through the ravages of a love affair that dissolved, through the writhing disillusion of divorce negotiations or the sometimes equally torturous load of staying married, through the relocation of the friend who made life possible, through their own illnesses and financial upheavals.

In the end, what is the truth about the emotional strength of women? Do we ever long to collapse? You bet. Do we wish we were rescued? Of course. Do we ever paint a man into a prince to give flesh to our daydreams? Yes, we do (and a very pleasant painting it is, for all its brief life span).

Does any of this mean we are too weak to be ourselves and love another? Not at all. What it means is that we are strong, our vision is true, and it's time we stopped holding love against ourselves.

Ah, but that is not so easy to do. Not so easy, when you are in the midst of the pain that accompanies attachment—the hurtful remarks, critical byplay, anxious moments, infuriating compromise. Not so easy to stop fearing love, when you've asked him to account for his mean comment, his cold withdrawal, and he offers one firm explanation: It's because of *you.*

Because you are such a drag. A nag. Just like your mother. Or all your girlfriends. And if he's yelling it's because you provoked him. And if he's silent it's because you made it scary to talk. Or because you got fat. Or old. Or boring. Or because he's turned off and he wishes he weren't. Or because he knows that what he has to say will hurt you, so what is the point of saying it? So, instead of saying it, he stops calling. Or, married, he stops coming home much. Or, home, he stops connecting and lies on the couch thinking dog thoughts in front of the television.

Until you find yourself pursuing him around the house trying to make contact. Hoping for feeling and getting dead eyes. He's angry and he knows why. It's you. You and marriage and monogamy and your family and your spending habits and your smug critiques and impossible expectations; you and all women—all, that is, except the one he still dreams of meeting.

Oh, it's easy to feel humiliated, easy to fear the cost of reclaiming your vision of love.

Since the post-Friedan sixties, some women have come to believe that we shouldn't want men at all, or, at the very least, not unless certain terms are met. And for once, *we will be the ones dictating the terms.* This profound shift in attitude feels so good and so right that we never want to retreat from it. The problem is that we haven't figured out how to go forward—to get to love. And we've come to feel ashamed if we want to.

It's the shame I'm angry about, the sense of a dirty secret that prevents so many single women from smiling across a bar, for fear of smelling needy; the shame that makes it so much tougher for a married woman to forgive an affair, or to love a failure.

I'm angry at the man who, sensing a woman's love, her hope, her basic desire to connect, has caricatured her as a bomb about to explode in his life unless he is careful. How dare he let her carry the weight of his own need for love, and then belittle her for toting his load!

And I'm angry at the women who've made us ashamed, too, the ones who have made men into such villains that, as Naomi Wolf says, we can no longer distinguish between a rapist and a man who sits while the table is being cleared.

Well, I have news for you. Frankly, though I wouldn't pause for breath if the rapist were exterminated, **I want the table sitter. And I refuse to be ashamed of it.**

I want him even though I will spend half my life trying to get him to do the dishes, and the battle alone will make it tough for me to tolerate him. I want him, not because I have some masochistic desire to serve, not because I need his money, his sperm, or the social security that having him conveys. I want him because I want a shot at getting to love, and none of us get there on our own.

I want us to get past the shame in our way, past our consuming anxiety over whether and for how long some male will want us; past our fantasies that must make men into gods of sex and success, in order for us to want them; and past our disappointment, disapproval, our outrage when we see them clearly.

Past each of these aspects of a relationship, past our own temporary blindness to ourselves—is our own vision of love. Love is the elevated kingdom set beyond reason's requirement that we wrestle with things as they are. Love is how things should be. Everyone, female and male, acknowledges that such a state exists. Love is at a woman's center because we are wise enough to want to live there. With men. And without apology.

But how?

CHAPTER TWO

Loving Him More
and
Needing Him Less

"As William Faulkner's aged hero and narrator in Knight's Gambit *explains how he has earned a second chance in the game of love: 'I improved.' "*

—Andrew Sarris, in *The New York Observer*

T he path to love is not about finding the right person, the person who would be so effortlessly, so automatically easy to love. It's not about fixing the person you have found, either, or enduring that person, or trading him in for a better person. It's about overcoming the inner obstacles—the fantasies, the wishful thinking, the fear that make us look away, the rage that freezes us in place, the sense of being so special that we are entitled to receive, or so lowly that no one could love us at all—that trip us on our paths to love.

The path to love is finally more about us, and less about him.

We have been moving towards that path for some time now. We hear it in the new public acknowledgments of the value of love to women, acknowledgments from women who, a decade ago, were more likely to have warned us away. Faye Wattleton, former head of Planned Parenthood, noted the shift of emotional spirit in women when she said, "I do believe that we have crossed the threshold, where it is not assumed that if women are for women, they hate men. It has to do with the reality of ourselves as women but also

16

recognizing that our attraction for others is an important part of the fullness of who we are as human beings."

We sense the change reflected by the new voice in which some women speak of their sexuality—neither as victims nor aggressors nor canny marketers but, rather, as comfortable appreciators. We note it in a new generation of women who are neither especially belligerent nor cloyingly deferential towards men. These women, and many of their mothers, are more apt simply to be themselves.

These are not new strategies for handling men. These are not women who have eliminated the frustration and pain of relationships by eliminating the relationships themselves. This is a more subtle yet more pervasive shift in our view of ourselves, of men, and of love. This is a sea-change.

Getting to Love

A compelling force blinds us to our own power over love: the myth that love is utterly out of our hands. We believe firmly that the magic of love is not just in the feeling itself. The magic is also in how this feeling comes about. Love must find us. We can't seek it. Love happens to us, we fall into it—if we are lucky enough to meet a person, *the* person, who will cast the spell that makes us feel love; *and* if we are ourselves bewitching enough to make that person love us in return.

We cannot cause ourselves to love, or so they say. We can, however, make ourselves more likely to attract it. So we do, investing massive amounts of time, attention, and effort in making ourselves more lovable. As we polish, we dream; when we are ready, we are either found or we are forced to hunt.

"I look for him everywhere," one woman said to me. In that small confession, she expressed the intensity and exhaustion of so many women who, believing more in the myth than in themselves, search everywhere to find that sorcerer, and do everything they can to make themselves attractive to him. Some few never find him.

Others—most of us, in fact—do find something, someone, some face or form or version that feels close enough to love.

You know what happens next. It all works, to a point. Then . . . smash. You've hit the stone wall of your own anger, frustration, or disappointment with the man you've found. Early in your relationship, and in the spell of romance, this man is worthy of your love just because of what you believe about him and because of how he makes you feel. Over time, you've moved from what you believe about him to what you know about him, and that is a very different feeling.

You begin the work of making him more lovable—confronting, cajoling, suggesting that he change whatever it is about him that gets in the way of your loving him or feeling loved by him. Yes, you resent the process, and its disappointing outcome. But you haven't known what else to do.

There is something else you can do, something every one of us can do. We can put all that energy into creating a new path for love. The new path to love begins with this step: quit struggling to make him easier to love; instead, overcome your own obstacles to loving him.

Get to love by being loving. It's almost as simple as that. Instead of making yourself more pleasing to a man, put your energy into making yourself more pleased by him. Learn to abandon the beliefs that determine what he should be, what he must be, in order for you to love him. In other words, learn to love him more.

Love him more! But isn't the problem that we already love him too much, that we are giving more than we get, and to men who fail to appreciate it or deserve it?

I don't think so.

I don't think most of us love him too much. Instead, I think we need him too much, depend on him too much, look to him for too much support and too much attention.

Need is in direct competition with love. It smashes us straight into the wall of our anger (*What's wrong with him?!*) or our anxiety

(What's wrong with me!?). Therefore, the essential corollary to "love him more" is: "need him less."

Need men less? The very issue of needing men at all is such a hot button that we sometimes dismiss any discussion before we've even heard it. "Need him less" is not an indirect criticism of women as "needy." Nor does it mean that our own needs must come second. After all, no matter how generous the spirit, we don't have much to give away if we haven't gotten enough for ourselves. "Need him less" assumes that women's needs are human and reasonable, but that, to realize our vision of love, we must look beyond men to satisfy many of them.

It is so easy for us to confuse need with love, because both put men at the center of our lives and turn us urgently towards them. But love is about giving, whereas need focuses on receiving. What we need most is to learn to tell the difference.

> **Loving Him More**
> **Needing Him Less**
> **Learning to Tell the Difference**

Loving Men More, Needing Men Less will describe these three principles in detail, from their origin, through their application in your specific situation, to the experience of those women at the vanguard, women who have followed this new path and who find themselves closer to love. First, though, we need to clear the air.

Total Woman Meets Amazon Woman

Here is what I am afraid of: Instead of disagreeing with what I am proposing, you will disagree with what you assume I'm proposing. Worse, what you may assume I am proposing would be anathema to me, whether you agreed with it or not.

So let me spell it out. "Loving him more" is not a code phrase for that good old-fashioned man-pleasing, iron-fisted, velvet-gloved Total Woman, to whom we have so often been urged to revert. Likewise, "needing him less" is not a disguised feminist attack on the puny penis and its inflated sense of its own value.

In fact, extremists at both poles of women's thinking are the first to be instantly irritated by the idea of loving more or needing less. Need him less? Some feminists may resent the concept, thinking, *"Who needs him at all?,"* while traditionalists, equally resentful, reply, "I don't want to need him less and I am oh-so-tired of being pushed towards this mythic independence you've decided I should want."

"Love him more" is subject to the same misunderstanding, and the same instant resistance, though in an opposite direction. Women who prefer not to need men at all may say an automatic "No, thank you," to loving him more. Those women who know what it is to need a man desperately can't imagine loving him more, either. After all, how much more is there?

Loving more and needing less are easy to distort in these ways, because each raises the specter of the earlier model of love from which it is adapted. (We will discuss these two earlier models—the Traditional Path and the Women's Revision—in detail, later in this chapter). "Loving more" echoes the sentiments of its roots in the traditional view of love, where love is at the center of a woman's life and she shapes herself around it. "Needing less," on the other hand, immediately reminds us of the feminist repudiation of that traditional model.

Pull "loving more" and "needing less" apart from each other and you will take two giant steps backwards, though in two opposite directions. Put "loving more" and "needing less" together, finally, and you have a whole new ball game, a new path to love.

If they are taken together, "loving more" and "needing less" each mean something very different from when they stood alone. For example, both the traditional view and this new model define love as giving, and both appreciate the value of being a giver. But that is where the similarity stops. In the traditional model, a woman has only a child's opportunity for power. She needs to be hooked to a strong parent, in order to be truly safe or effective in the world. This woman is a giver who is advised to please her dominant partner, on the theory that, if he is happy, he'll be good to her and she'll be happy, too.

In the new model, "Love him more" also means giving, but it is giving from the strength of the emotionally rich. It does not mean pleasing a man or being submissive, in the hope that he will love you. On the contrary, give love because all the power, most of the joy, and, frankly, a good deal of control, is in the giving.

The same is true of needing him less. "Needing less" could be confused with the traditional mother-to-daughter gettaguy advice: Be the first to look away. Make sure he loves you a little bit more than you love him. Keep some money in a secret stash, and, for God's sake, don't let yourself go. In other words, *act* as if you need him less.

Let's be perfectly clear. When I suggest that you shift inwardly towards needing a man less, I am not referring to any ploy. Playing hard to get is a technique to increase your desirability in someone else's eyes. "Needing him less" is about how you appear in your own eyes.

But, further, "need him less" is not an endorsement of the idea that love is delusion and separation is a woman's only source of strength. Both the contemporary model and the new path I am describing value independence. That makes it easier to confuse them, but there is a key difference.

The contemporary, cynical relationship view is *Who the hell needs men?* I say, if you are heterosexual, the answer is simple: Who needs men? You do. We all do. We need men to get to love. "Need him less" only suggests that we reduce the number of other things we need from men, because those are the ones that get in the way of love.

Our knee-jerk reactions to loving more or needing less are the inevitable result of the huge political and social gender upheaval of the last forty years. "Love" and "need" are words so loaded, at least as they refer to women and men, that it is difficult to hear them with fresh ears. But that's what I'm asking you to do.

Think about loving and needing as they play a role in your life today. Are you as loving as you could be? Do you feel as loved as you might be? Do you have the calm that comes from knowing that most of what you need you could get for yourself, rather than through someone else? Are you at least on your way there?

As we'll discuss in the next chapter, loving and needing are inseparable threads of a knot, whose tangling and untangling mark our progress on our path. "Loving more, needing less" is the combination that finally reconciles our old image of attachment with our new sense of self. This combination depends on the emotional, intellectual, financial, and physical strength we have acquired in the last thirty years, with two steps forward and damn the backlash.

Loving him more and needing him less is the step forward. Don't confuse it with those who are always urging women to take a step back.

It is an effort to free ourselves from our old assumptions about love and need, or even to push these assumptions aside enough to make room for a new focus. Your attention needs to return to you, but not with the old attitude of ruthless self-criticism aimed at evaluating how lovable you are. Instead, you will be focusing on your spirit, with the goal of strengthening your own capacity to love and your willingness to take the risk of loving.

I feel very sure of one thing. The time is right for women to focus away from the obstacles men have created, and towards our own inner lives. Everything that has come before is pushing us to take a leap upward in our relationships with men, by taking a further leap forward within ourselves.

Whatever other difficulties we might encounter in this process, *we* are our greatest obstacle in our progress along this inner path. At the moment, our attitudes towards love and our feelings about men have calcified. You could sum up our current feelings in four words: *I won't!* and *We shouldn't!*

I Won't!
(I AIN'T MARCHIN' ANY MORE....)

I hear you. You are arguing back: *O.K. Maybe I could go along with you about love, about the importance of being loving and feeling loved, and maybe even about a man being crucial to the mix. But as much as I might intellectually understand the idea of being generous with love, I don't feel like it!*

I don't want to stop being angry. I don't want to have to do the work anymore. Why do I always have to give in, make things better? Why the hell can't he be the one to budge, just, say, every hundredth time?

I don't want to make one more concession, change one more thing about myself. I am so tired of you self-improvement jockeys flogging me and my girlfriends to the gettaguy, havaguy, keepaguy finish line. I'm tired of being the one who gets to ask what's wrong and of him getting to decide whether to tell me or not.

I will not conceal, distort, or in any other way reshape my personality, my body, or my spirit in order to win a man. Here I am. Take it or leave it. And the hell with you if you leave it.

As we've noted, it's easy for you to hear what you've always heard, even if I'm saying something different.

It's easy to assume that, when I say we should take a step towards love, it has to be a step away from ourselves. But it doesn't.

It's easy to assume that, when I say to take a step towards men, it must be on our knees. It's not. And that's a very tired insult.

It's easy for you to assume that, when I suggest you focus on changing yourself, it will be for the purpose of pleasing him. It isn't.

This book is not written in defiance of our anger. It is written in response to it. Our communal wave of exhaustion and frustration *is* the signal of a sea-change in our attitudes about love. It is the loud, firm statement that we are done with what we've been doing about love.

We are done because the effort to fix relationships has not been equal, because we've tried it all and it hasn't taken us far enough. Mostly, though, we are done with fixing him and fixing relationships because there is something inescapably demeaning about the process. Yes, maybe sometimes we can "get" him to make a commitment, "get" him to be faithful, to be a better communicator, to be separated from his remote control. Some of our strategies work, though at a cost to our sense of self. Sometimes we get him, but the price is us.

We are done with what we've been doing about love, but we are not done with love. We're just getting started.

Here is the foundation of our sea-change: Change in order to bring yourself closer to the person you want to be, not to become the person he wants you to be. Focus more on yourself and less on him. Move down your own inner path, in ways that you may never have considered. Your purpose is not to win him, please him, nor get more of what you want from him—although it's true, some of your changes are likely to have this effect. Believe me, some won't.

The purpose of loving more and needing less is simply this: become what it is in you to become, and, as one of many rewards, you will move closer to your vision of love.

March. Just make sure you're going in your own direction.

We Shouldn't!
(NOT NOW, NOT YET. MAYBE NOT EVER?)

Some women feel strongly that whether you can or cannot love a man more is beside the point. What matters is that we *shouldn't,* at least not yet. The fear is that loving a man more will mean letting go of legitimate anger, and that anger is the essential force to create the changes that are essential to our well-being. We still only earn seventy cents for every dollar a man earns. Many of us still do two jobs to his every one, without decent child care, with no real protection against domestic violence, at the mercy of ruthless divorce laws, not to mention divorce lawyers. But we finally have some momentum going. Now is not the time to back out.

Besides, these women might argue, an effort towards loving men more, at this moment, can only be read as a gesture of appeasement. Men are angry now, and full of the power of a conservative backlash. Any move a woman makes in the direction of love will sound like we're saying, *Oh, my dear, I'm so sorry if I focused for a moment on me and what I wanted. Naturally you're mad. Wait. I'll go right back to focusing on you and how wonderful you are.*

These are powerful arguments against a move towards love—but only if you view a step towards loving men as a step against women. This perspective is certainly understandable in light of what we have been willing to tolerate in the name of love. But, as we have discussed, it is not the whole truth about love, nor are we the same women we were.

Give us credit for our strengths. Our appreciation of love was never a sign of our weakness, no matter how many men took it that way. It was never love but, rather, what we allowed ourselves to do in the name of love, that made us vulnerable. When "I love you" meant "I'll serve you," squelching love was a step forward. As "I love you" comes to mean "I adore you, I'm thrilled by you, and don't let it get your hopes up, darling, I'm still not going to let you take advantage of me"—then we don't have to be so fearful of love.

It is quite true that many of our toughest political and social campaigns are ahead. Loving a man does not mean sweetly tolerating his policies. (Remember when Julia told Lillian Hellman, "I've always liked your anger. Don't let people talk you out of it. It may be uncomfortable for them, but it's valuable to you."? We all knew she didn't mean Lillian should give up Dashiell Hammett.) Loving a man does not mean ignoring abuse, or overlooking injustice. It could mean inviting him to be a partner in correcting those social ills. It will probably mean standing apart from him, on these and other issues. But we are strong enough to stand on our own now—to separate ourselves from men, without denying ourselves the feeling of love.

The Road We've Traveled

The good news is: none of us has to reinvent completely a way to get to love.

Generations of others have gone there before us, at least gone as far as they could. When our turn comes, we look for love where we've been told we are likely to find it, and the path we choose is the one we've been told is most likely to get us there.

No matter what the situation with which you wrestle—*If I really loved him, would his job bother me this much? How can I get him to feel the way he did in the beginning? Why is he so mean to me one day, and so nice, so normal, the next? How long can I put up with this? And should I?***—your response will be fundamentally influenced by one or both of the two basic paradigms you've absorbed about men and love. Each of these is, in effect, a road map for love.**

These two models of heterosexual love—which I am calling the Traditional Path and the Women's Revision—make very different assumptions about power, dependency, femininity, masculinity, about our dream of love itself. Their content will not be news to you.

Most of us, however, don't appreciate the profound degree to which these basic maps shape our day-to-day reactions. When assumptions are so basic, we don't notice them any more. They are simply the ground we stand on. We don't look down very often to ask if it's good ground, or if it's really there. We just stand, and that points us in a direction.

The problem is: what happens if you've outgrown the map?

It happens every so often—sometimes every century, sometimes in only a generation—that the model of how things should work just doesn't work anymore. Small improvements in the map, minor adjustments of the model, won't do it any more. We have to make a fundamental change in our thinking.

Easy to say. Profoundly disruptive actually to consider. Yet essential for women to move towards—because this change in our thinking incorporates our new knowledge about what is possible between men and women.

Loving Men More, Needing Men Less describes a new map to love. This map is drawn from women's new wisdom about ourselves and our evolving relationships with men. We need this new map for one reason: the two older ones, which we've learned and used and believed in and stood by, don't get us to love.

The Traditional Path: Live to Give, and Give to Get

Like any working social model, the traditional paradigm is described in sweeping strokes. It's an economic deal and an emotional pact; a division of labor and a distinction in gender identities; it's both a soothing social philosophy and a naked statement of power balance. In the same way that the Constitution lays out the broad strokes of democracy and then leaves every generation to interpret it, our traditional model of the relationship between men and women lays out a basic path to love and leaves each couple to work out the details.

In the traditional model of male-female romantic relationships, women realize their dream of love by giving to men. "Live to give" refers to women's "natural" need to be pleasers and nurturers, to be both submissive and accommodating. (Surely whoever dreamed this up had never met our great-grandmothers or any of their immigrant girlfriends.)

"Give to get" is a natural corollary to "Live to give." "Give to get" advises women to get love by giving, because what is given will be so valuable and so appreciated that it will inspire love in its recipients. That is, give love to get love. "Give to get" has another, associated meaning: Give to a man and he will take care of you. Give because you need him, because you are not able to take care of yourself. Give because you are softer, weaker, and in need of protection. And men will show their love for you by offering that protection.

Each of the models of love also makes certain basic assumptions about the proper relationships between power, need, and love. In the traditional model, women's core vision of love is seen as right and natural. In fact, "love" is a woman's only real option. Because she is shut off in the private world of women and children, she needs a man for access to the basic tools of survival: food, clothing, and shelter. And, as her mother carefully explained (if it even needed an explanation), with the right man, you could do a lot better than the basics.

Therefore, according to the Traditional Path to love, love a man because you need him so much. Relinquish any claim to power, and in return you'll get his love and care. Some women have made this deal and swear by it. Many more made this deal and lived to swear about it.

The Women's Revision: Give Less, Take More

If you think of the traditional model's themes of "live to give" and "give to get" as a thesis, the Women's Revision, "give less, take more," is its antithesis. It is a relationship paradigm born of outrage at the inequities of the traditional deal. It says, in effect, that women are only needier than men because men set it up that way.

Give less because men don't give back. Instead, they use our services, decide on our lives, and then, if someone more useful— sexually, socially, financially, or emotionally—comes along, men are free to dump us and our children. After all, they can always make more babies, and quite often they do.

Give less because, when we give a great deal, each gift is less appreciated and you, the giver, are less valued. Your many loving acts become his baseline expectation, while his own few sacrificing gestures stand out in his inner landscape as colossal evidence of his magnificence. Give less!

And take more! You don't need to sit by sweetly, practicing smiles in the mirror and oral sex on a banana, in order to become so alluring that someone will give you what you need. You can go and get your own money, your own lover, your own career, insurance policy, car, even your own baby. You can stand up, be independent, become more person, less possession, when you begin to take care of yourself.

In this revision, the path to love is blurry, because love is what women have focused on at the expense of self-esteem, opportunity, and power. At the extreme of the Women's Revision, love is synonymous with fool's gold or servitude. *Don't look to him for love. He's too selfish, too emotionally underdeveloped, perhaps even too brutal to understand love.*

Or, more moderately but no less emphatically, *Love him, but don't let him get away with anything. Love him, but only if this time he does the changing, the accommodating. Don't twist yourself into a pretzel to make him happy. That's what got us into trouble in the first place. Love him, as long as you remain powerful and in control.* Love him, but only if certain conditions are met. And this time we'll be the ones dictating the conditions.

Well, I don't have to tell you that the shift from *Oohhh, I hope he likes me* to *Who the hell needs him?* was the social high of the century. And the psychological, political, and economic consequences of this attitude shift have changed every first date, every marriage, every secret love affair or public courtship, forever. Often (but not always) for the better.

Our opportunities got better, just by virtue of our having more of them. Our education is better, our financial opportunities have improved. Our status improved, too, as our clout increased. Inevitably, the more we insisted we do, the more respect we won (grudgingly, yes; hard-won, yes; but won), and the more respect we felt for ourselves. The Women's Revision was pure payoff in terms of female self-esteem—and that was true whether you endorsed the new model or you reviled it.

The great reward of the Women's Revision was that we liked ourselves a lot more. But we liked men a lot less.

Three Models of Love for Women

	TRADITION	REVISION	RESOLUTION
Our Dream of Love Is . . .	Positive, natural, in fact the only option for a woman	Negative, poisonous because: • it keeps us dependent on and vulnerable to men • men are too immature, brutal, or self-serving to fulfill the dream of love	Positive, because love is a higher order of experience. But love is the step beyond self-development, not an alternative to it.
The Connection between Love and Need:	Love him because you need him	Who needs him? Love him, but only if he meets your terms Don't let him get away with anything	Need him less, so you can love him more
The Connection between Love and Power:	Trade power for love	Fight for power, at the expense of love	Use your newly won power to reach our old goal of love
Advice to Women on Giving:	Live to give and Give to get	Give less, Take more	Give, because the power is in the giving, and because giving gets to love
The Life Stage Best Suited to This Model Is:	Childhood: Daddy's Little Girl	Adolescence: The Defiant Rebel	Adulthood: The Strong Woman

Backlash in Our Hearts

We have our regrets. We may hate ourselves for them, refuse to admit them, or polarize around them. But an awful lot of us see the Women's Revision as a mixed blessing, because we sense that all this self-focus has pushed us further away from heterosexual love. Some of us are happy about this tradeoff. ("Hangin' up my coil, I'm in love with a goil. . . .") But many of us can't make peace with it. We worry that revising our traditional paradigm has cost us happiness by making us so profoundly angry with men and so consciously and unconsciously challenging to them.

We think of women we know like thirty-five-year-old Christine, who could be the poster child for *WHY ISN'T A NICE GIRL LIKE YOU MARRIED?* Christine wonders, too, although she has had so many romantic disappointments it's almost easy for her to believe that there are no decent men. Almost.

Christine does not know it, might not even recognize herself in this description. But she brings an edge of defiance to every interaction with a man. It is as if her unspoken agenda is to compete with him and win, as if she has to put him in his place before he thinks he's conquered her. It shows in very small interactions: He fixes a bookshelf and she says, "I can't believe you used a number-four wrench." He offers a political opinion and she explains to him why he's wrong. Or she kindly gives him driving pointers, professional tips, sexual suggestions.

Does she have a right to her own opinions on each of these topics? Oh, yes. Should she withhold her thoughts and feelings just to make him feel good? No. But does she have to make every conversation a contest in order to prove her equal worth? And would you be drawn to a man who was always subtly besting you? (Actually, some women are, confusing a critic with "a man I can look up to." Men are less likely to get a hard-on for a critic. Some say their egos are too weak, but I can't help thinking it's often to their credit.)

We are not the only angry ones. Men are mad, too—and who wouldn't be, when the help quits and calls you names *and* insists on having the right to run the company? Men have retaliated by saying, *Fine. You want some of my power? You insist on the right to do all the great things I get to do? O.K. Go to it. Work yourself to death, stop having fun, let someone else raise your kids while you get deep personal satisfaction from selling insurance.*

But, they continue, *if you take some of my power, I'm going to take away some of my love. You know what? I used to love you, desire you, admire you. I thought you were a better person than me. I thought you were kinder, softer, more . . . I don't know, more moral than I am. But you're not. You are just a ball-breaking bitch who wants it both ways.*

So I'm not going to rush to marry you, or rush to make your life any better. Sometimes I'm not even in a great rush to fuck you. I'm certainly not going to feel any obligation to stay married to you, like I used to. You think you don't need my protection? Great. Go it alone.

Which has only proved to us that they are worse jerks than we thought—name-calling, child-molesting, wife-beating, deal-making, self-interested jerks. Which only proves to them that we are hypocritical and money-grubbing, always whining, sneaky, and manipulative. Which has hurt us and hurt them and turned us away from each other as groups, even while we try—each of us, one by one—to find a way back. Back to each other and back to love.

That's why, for so many people, "back" has become the operative fantasy. It's an undercurrent, a whisper all around us. "I just want my daughter to meet a nice boy and get married soon," confided a fifty-year-old politically and socially liberal mother.

"Why? She's only twenty-three!" I said, shocked to hear this woman, of all women, sounding so much like both our grandmothers.

"Because I see what happens to women in their late twenties and early thirties who haven't married. I see how desperate they get, and how many of them miss their chance for children. And I don't want my daughter to suffer that."

There, wrapped in a mother's love, is the fantasy: Let's go back!

Let's re-embrace tradition. Maybe the traditional deal wasn't so great—but is our revision any better? *My daughter wants a man and a home and a family and love. If she has to pretend, if she has to be a little coy, a little clever to get it, what is the big deal?*

Let's go back! is the fantasy of so many women who fought their way into the world of work, only to experience the soul-rending tug-of-war between professional achievement and personal relation-ships, between office and child, or between being a good person and being a successful one. So many of us have been exhausted by our effort to keep a foot on both paths, stretching ourselves to im-possible lengths when the paths inevitably diverged.

The path to professional achievement and financial indepen-dence can be harsh. The work is often unsatisfying; the opportunity and salary, though improved, are still unfairly biased against us; and the subtle and not-so-subtle aggression, directed towards women who go unprotected into the public arena, is an irritating and some-times absolutely intimidating reality. True, women are gaining on each of these fronts, but the battles leave their marks. With the price of progress so high, it's only natural that a part of us should dream of going back, romanticizing the joys (one's children, for ex-ample, are always so much better company in one's mind than in one's bathroom), and minimizing the liabilities. (Even when women worked only in the home, we still dealt with poor pay, aggressive bosses, and emotional exhaustion.)

Whether you dream of going backwards or are still clinging there yourself, sweetly submissive to your wise and happy husband, and hoping that your daughters will be smart enough to do the same, the fact of the matter is, the days of the traditional model are done. It was buried under a social, an economic, and a psychological cave-in.

The social cave-in, of course, was the Women's Movement. You have your own opinions about that.

The cave-in was also economic, and it looks to continue indefi-nitely. The world population is growing, resources are diminishing, and the cost of things we want, need, and expect is therefore increasing. We are in "two-income families" because *we need the money*.

It's not just that the economy won't let us go backwards, it's that we are too self-aware to see ourselves in the old ways. We are too educated to pretend incompetence, too smart to enjoy long idleness, too wide-ranging in our talents to tolerate unnecessary limits on our opportunities. We can not put the genie of our sexuality back into the bottle. We are not adjuncts, happy to serve. We are separate people, heading towards love from the strength of self-respect.

No, much as we might fantasize about it on a bad day, we can't go backwards.

And we can't stay where we are, because it doesn't feel as good as it could. We have heard the argument that a loving man or a man worth loving is as much a fantasy as *The Brady Bunch*. Maybe. But maybe not. It just might be that, beyond any divorce horror, corrosive marriage, or heartbreaking betrayal, we have, deep inside us, a sense of a path. We turn towards men because so many of us see them as our partners on this path; we head towards love because that's where our spirits know to go. If neither of our models can get us there, the solution is simple: we need a new one.

Resolution: The Move to the Middle

Jack and Jill went up the hill
To fetch a pail of water;
Jack fell down and broke his crown,
And Jill came tumbling after.

Where do they go from here? Back up the hill, some new way. Only this time they must find a way to make room for both of them at the top. Believe me, without the crown it will be easier.

Recently a woman described to me an all-female dinner party she gave in the late seventies. This woman is at the top of her profession, and has been since the days of the dinner she was reminiscing about. As is so often the case with such people, all the other guests at this dinner were stars in their own right—women who had achieved enormous professional and financial success through their own efforts, and who were therefore very much the role models of their day.

Describing the party, she said, "We were so proud of ourselves, and having such a great time in our lives. At this dinner, we talked about how we couldn't get over how much money we were making and how fabulous it was and how we didn't need men anymore and it was fantastic.

"I remember one woman, Diane Von Furstenberg, was the only one who disagreed. 'But what about our men?' she kept asking. 'What's the point of it all if we don't have our men?' Do you know, we all felt sorry for her. It was as if she was so unenlightened, so dependent, that we thought she needed help.

"It took me twenty years to come around to thinking that she was right. At the time, and for a long time after, I was pretty smug. I thought I was on a higher plane because, unlike most of the women I knew, I didn't need men. Now I see that what I thought was strength was really just dodging. I was avoiding relationships because I was avoiding conflict. The bravest thing is to be strong in yourself and then to risk loving someone else."

The new solution this woman is describing is an evolutionary step beyond the two that came before it. It is a psychological shift, but it is made possible by the social changes for which we have fought. We are ready to build on our past. We have come to synthesis, to the moment when we can begin to re-examine the classic paradox of loving:

THESIS: attachment is exalted.

This has been a traditional social premise, the premise of many of our religions and social institutions, of our parents and teachers. In fact, it is the basic premise of all of us who seek love, believe in love, and hope to fall into love. Love is unity and joy, security and closure. We are the parts; love is the whole.

ANTITHESIS: attachment is our weakness.

This revisionist position has powerful adherents. It is one of the Four Noble Truths of Buddhism *(desire is the root of all suffering)*, a basic premise of some parts of feminism, and the shameful truth to any of us who has ever begged for one more chance, called just to hear his voice on the machine, or taken him back even though we knew he was still lying.

SYNTHESIS: the problem is not in attachment itself; it is in the self we bring to attachment.

Weak selves make desperate attachments; hungry selves make cloying, annoying ones. Frightened selves withhold love. Dependent selves make demands, and use their very helplessness to insist these demands be satisfied. Again, relationships depend less on whom you choose, more on who you are.

The secret to making an attachment that provides the satisfaction and the support we hope for, without the suffering we've experienced, is in the strength of the self that makes the attachment. Love him more—because that is the source of the joy. But need him less—because that will keep you strong.

The Bottom Line

In a television interview some years ago, Esther Williams told a story about her marriage to Fernando Lamas, in answer to a question about what marriage to a traditional Latin male was like. "We'd be sitting by the pool and he would ask for a tuna-fish sandwich. He would want me to get up and get it even though he was sitting just as close to the kitchen and he was perfectly capable of making his own tuna fish. And," she continued, smiling, "if I could make it for him, I did. Not because I was afraid he'd be mad at me. And not because I thought it was my job as a wife or anything so rigid as that. I made it for him because it made him happy and I loved to make him happy. I knew he thought being a Latin male made him king of the world. I wasn't willing to be his full-time subject. But I wasn't out to prove he wasn't king, either."

Loving is giving. Part of giving is serving. That doesn't make either of you a servant. Increase your capacity to love, not in order to serve men, but in order to serve yourself. Need less from a man, because, the more you can get directly for yourself, the more secure your life, and the more serene your spirit. From this base of satisfaction, you are more apt to love and be loved.

Serve yourself—in what way? More apt to be loved—why? What exactly do you get if you follow this third path?

Simply stated, the shift of focus, away from him and towards yourself, will change your experience of love. Some of the payoff is easy to itemize. For one thing, you'll spend less time trapped between those pincers of anxiety that so frequently accompany real-life romance. Loving more and needing less makes you less desperate to find a relationship, and less apt to be disappointed when you do.

You'll reduce your own sense of frustration. Men take up a lot of space on our hard drive. The ongoing struggle to find the right one, or to tenderize the one you've got, is pure, energy-sapping stress. How much more time do you want to spend grinding your teeth?

Loving more and needing less means you won't be angry so often, and that's just an easier way to go through your days. You'll be angry less because, when you need a man less, you can set better limits to protect your feelings, and you will have developed more and better ways to react to disappointment.

Outer events may remain the same, but what once gave you stomach knots no longer scares you. What once hurt begins now to roll off your back. *How* to go about making this kind of change in your reactions is the subject of the next chapter. The reward for being in charge of your emotional life is obvious: it feels better.

Your improved reactions are not just sweeter for you. They are a gift for your children. Every inch that you are able to reach beyond your anger or your numbness, every moment that you can stretch beyond your feelings of anxious depression or dismissive contempt, eases something inside your child. Loving more and needing less is not easy. Your efforts, though, will be repaid by the strength of your child's spirit.

In these and other ways, loving more and needing less will improve the quality of your relationships with men. When you are no longer dependent on a man's protection, his status, or his approval, you will seek him out, or stay, only when you two give each other the respect, affection, and fair play that are the foundation of every solid relationship. When you need a man less, you are strong enough to insist on that kind of relationship.

And when you are able to overcome your own inner barriers and love a man more, you are far more likely to find it. The inevitable irritations and disillusionments of even the most solid of relationships will be easier to bear. So many of us push for intimacy without having first created within ourselves a spirit loving enough to tolerate it.

A more serene spirit, a sweeter romance or a stronger marriage, a solid framework for your kids to grow on, are all great rewards for a change in your approach to love. But there is a deeper level of reward that is important to recognize, though it is more difficult to itemize.

When we ask, "What do I get if I make this change?," often we mean, "Will I get more of what I want *from him?*" And it's true, any change in one of you is likely to cause some degree of change in the other. You are, after all, attached. Even if you are without a particular relationship at the moment, any change in your attitude towards men as a group is very likely to influence the way individual men respond to you.

Yes, you may get more of what you want from men, or from one particular man, by taking this new path. As you allow yourself to be more loving, less easily upset, or more personally satisfied, the atmosphere of your relationships is likely to warm up. You've become a person who is easier to be nice to, easier to come home to, easier to make love to, easier to love.

It's also true that, when one person goes to a higher level of interaction, the other person sometimes then dares to follow along. If you risk admitting you were rude last night and you're sorry for it, the man who was just accusing you sometimes has the courage to admit he wasn't so nice himself. Sometimes.

But there is no guarantee that he will. You might be easier to be nice to, but that doesn't mean he'll be nicer. You may be willing to see his side, but that doesn't mean he'll see yours. Loving more and needing less may help you get more of what you want from him, but that's not the point.

Loving more and needing less is not a change in strategy, it is a change in spirit. This new path is not a better way to get him to be different. It's entirely about you.

In a way, the question *What do I get if I do this?* is perfectly appropriate. After all, this step will require effort, like every other forward step we have undertaken. It is only reasonable to have a clear sense of the rewards you can expect for your effort.

Yet, in another sense, the question *What do I get?* is the wrong question. It reflects the underlying biases of our culture—our veneration of "the deal," our ever-present whiff of competitiveness, the bedrock of me, *moi*, myself, and I on which our social philosophy is built. These values, positive in many parts of our lives, have worked very much against us in love. Chapter seven, "The Limits of Love," discusses this in detail.

The most important question is not *What do I get?* but *Where does this take me?* The greatest payoff of loving more and needing less is in what you will come to feel about yourself. Stretch to love him more, not to make him feel good, but to become what you yourself can be. Stretch yourself in the direction of love. Risk being your higher self, your wiser, most generous, richest self.

Don't deny yourself this reach just because he isn't willing or able to match it. Don't work so hard to make him just right, in the hope that he will evoke just the right feelings in you (spiced passion, served on a bed of total security). Love not because he's earned it, not because he's worth it, and not because you've made an even trade for it.

Love the way you imagined you could, because you've pushed past your own barriers to loving and to being loved in return. Love more and need less, not to be who he wants you to be, but because it will bring you closer to who you want to be.

Here is the bonus: In the process of using this new path to get to love, you will come to find yourself again. As you need him less, you will rediscover the strong, clear self who may have been temporarily submerged by your hunger for love. As you love him more, you will rediscover the tender, generous self who may have been driven underground by your fear of love or by your anger towards your beloved. You will have found your power, found your freedom, and found that you could have yourself and love, too.

Women began by focusing on love at the expense of our own needs. We moved on when we focused on what we needed, what we were entitled to, and what we were going to insist upon—even at the expense of love. Now we can balance both.

I know, I know . . . *but how?*

CHAPTER THREE

Clearing Your Path

My friend Linda was disappointed that I was writing a book about love, when what she wanted was advice about living with her "controlling" husband, Michael. ("Linda," he'll scream, if she's engrossed in a book, "get down here and see the sunset. Jesus, don't you even know how to enjoy a vacation?")

I told her that this book about love was exactly on the point of controlling husbands, and that her own exasperation, ridicule, and struggle for power were not helping either of them to find an easy harmony together. "Well, what am I supposed to do," she asked, "when he acts like such a jerk?" Love him, I said, love him anyway.

Take a new look at your reaction to his demands and his rigidity. You don't have to heave your book aside and march martyr-like off into the sunset; neither do you have to clash with him head-on, shouting back in retaliation that sunsets are not best enjoyed on command; nor do you have to ignore him, all the while turning your thoughts away from the pleasures of your book and towards your internal catalogue of his idiocies. You have other choices.

You might hear his abrupt command as a clumsy request for your company, instead of as a tyrannical assertion of control. You still would not necessarily put down your book simply because he has asked for your company. But you wouldn't ruin your own relaxation with anger, either. You'd just shout down something like, "I love you honey, and I love sunsets. But I'm into my book." And dive right back into the story.

Alternatively, you might recognize his shouted order for exactly what you believe it to be—a direct assertion of his need to control your every move—and still not get caught up in it. You can't allow yourself to be controlled, but nowhere is it written that you have to be furious with him for trying. You might come to feel compassion for his constant inner tension, instead of raging against his know-it-all attitude. You might love him into a greater calm, help him get comfortable enough to relax into life, just by maintaining your own composure in the face of his upset. When he begins to hustle you down to a sunset, you remind him, "It's all right to miss something once in a while, Steve, even something wonderful. You don't need to push so hard."

Or you might not. But surely you will enjoy your new, unruffled reaction more than your customary anger.

You will, of course, have a battle with yourself over doing any of this. "Why should I have to make this effort?" you'll ask. "I'm not his doctor. I'm not his mother. And he sure as hell is not doing the same thing for me. I just shouldn't have to put up with it."

Linda, you're right. You shouldn't have to, and no one will make you. But this is the path towards love. Each of us is stuck somewhere on the path. Instead of focusing on where Steve is stuck, and all the things that make him so difficult to love, look inside. And ask yourself: What are the bad things that would happen if I just looked at him with loving eyes?

"I can't!" you'll say. "Not when he's like this."

Why not? What're you afraid of? What power would you lose, what abuse would you be vulnerable to? Why do you believe that you can't love him until he is less moody? Or less brash? Or more intellectual? Or more socially savvy? Or a more sensitive lover, a softer dad? Or any of the other things you have on your list of Things That Are Wrong with Steve?

In order for Linda to love Steve more, and to feel his love for her more fully, she will have to do the one thing she has not yet tried. She will have to become more of a lover, less of Steve's critic. How to do that? Well, in a sense, she'll have to detach from Steve, or at least from her investment in Steve's being some particular way. She will have to need him less.

Yes, but how?

How do you need a man less when you are newly lovers, only barely a couple, and he hasn't called in five days?

How do you feel loving towards a man who becomes a twelve-year-old on the weekends his kids visit—excluding you from their magic family circle, yet expecting you to provide full wife, mommy, cooking, and cleanup services?

When a man is so independent that he makes his own plans, allocates his own time, maintains his own separate friendships, and never complains when you do the same—how do you keep from needing constant reassurance that he cares?

The one time *you* have the crucial business dinner, and he forgets to pick up the kids—how do you keep from killing him, much less loving him more?

How can you feel more loving towards a man who refuses to change his sexual technique one iota to please you, no matter how directly or tactfully you ask? Especially if you've met a man who will? The question is not only can you love the first man more, but should you?

Should you risk loving a man who is the perfect boyfriend, with a long list of ex-girlfriends to prove it? Should you need less from a man for whom you do so much? *How* do you need less from a man who does a great deal for you?

How do you love a man more who not only won't apologize for his belittling remark, but insists he never said it, you heard it wrong, and your very anger is proof that you are insecure, neurotic, or demanding?

How do you continue to love the man who makes the racist joke, the sexist comment, or the insulting observation about your family? Marry him? Sometimes. Stay with him? Often. But love him?

And—having pointed these things out to him, having argued with him, confronted him, sweetly pleaded with him, and, on occasion, even kicked him under the table when he was verging on complete disaster—having tried everything you know to get him to change and found he's still the same, *how do you get yourself to stop needing him to be different?*

She Who Feels It

Here is the dilemma. In order to stop needing a man to be different, we need to feel comfortable with him as he is. And, of course, we don't, at least not entirely. Even worse, our negative reactions don't feel under our control. They feel like unavoidable responses to something he said or did.

Any woman can explain this reasoning to her lover quite bluntly:

Look, if you and I haven't made love in four months, and you haven't looked me in the eye for two, you know what? I'm going to feel anxious, sickeningly anxious. Any woman who wouldn't be made anxious by these signals either doesn't care or doesn't care to think about what they might mean.

If your visits to me in the hospital were perfunctory, and your explanation was that work was busy and, besides, you knew I would live, I am apt to be more than angry. I am very close to hating you. That rage has nothing to do with my being needy. It is an outright response to an outright son of a bitch.

If you mention the coffee I spilled on my blouse, the book it would do me some good to read, or a better way to shift into second, I am going to flee. No, I am not oversensitive to criticism, no matter how much you may try to convince me that I am. I know a dictator when I date one.

I do dream that someday you'll say, "What can I do to help?" instead of waiting for me to write down a list of seven chores in the hopes that you'll do two of them. Call me overbearing, call me crazy, call me a wild-eyed idealist. But when you fail to meet these expectations, when I am forced to see the huge gap between who you are and the way I hoped you'd be—I can't help how I feel!

In other words, if what you do makes me mad, *stop* doing it. If your behavior makes me anxious, *cut that out.* If you are not what I expected, hoped for, or deserve—*change.*

The force of this emotional logic is so powerful, it can make you forget all your experience to the contrary.

For one thing, no matter how just your complaint, he frequently does not (won't, can't, meant to but forgot to) change. Does this leave you stuck with your anger or anxiety? No. It doesn't have to. If you look more closely, you'll see why.

The fact is, for different women, or even at different times in your own life, the very same experience can evoke vastly different feelings in you. Perhaps you once interpreted a man's open sexual interest as a promise of long-term commitment. If you did, then a man who pursued you vigorously probably made you feel reassuringly cared for (assuming you returned his interest).

You have since learned that sexual interest does not necessarily imply interest in a relationship. Now, instead of reassuring you, a man who comes on strong may make you wary. He didn't change—but you did. What was at work to change your feelings?

Or perhaps you once felt that a lover who did not bother to ask about your day was cold and uncaring. Then you spent six years married to a man who wanted to know how you spent every minute. After your divorce, those men whose distance once made you feel unloved, now make you feel comfortably respected. The very same behavior that once made you feel bad, now makes you feel good. Your feelings changed. How?

The fact is, **feelings do not depend entirely on the person or the situation that evokes them. They also depend on the person feeling them.** This truth, which we all know and we all tend to forget, is the key to bringing ourselves closer to the love of our earliest vision.

Our image of love is simple: love, we tend to believe, either is, or is not—because someone either does or does not move us to feel it. The reality, however, is anything but simple. Love is far less a reaction to our lover than it is the result of a finely tuned balance of some of our deepest drives and desires.

A particular lover is surely a significant element influencing this balance. But he is only one of several elements, whose interplay moves you towards love or keeps you from it. To appreciate the difference you make in your own experience of love, it helps to examine the ways in which *you* influence your own emotional reactions to someone else.

We are most likely to realize our vision when we stop seeking love's simplicity and start appreciating its complexity. Love is not the one perfect pearl; rather, it is the miracle of the oyster.

How You Take It

Do you know the expression *"Life is 10 percent what you make it, 90 percent how you take it"*? Nowhere is that more true than in your experience of loving and feeling loved. Love is not just about what he does, how he acts, and how you feel in reaction. It is also about how you interpret what he does, and how you respond to that interpretation.

Love is less about what he does to offend than about what you take offense at; less about how he takes care of you, more about how you take care of yourself; less about what he does to provoke anger, more about what kinds of things make you mad, and how you handle it when you are. Whom we choose matters less than who we are.

Consider, for example, Rita and Jayne.

Rita screams threats at a husband who is regularly late for dinner. "You son of a bitch" is a standard greeting for this sin of omission. "I'd like to drive a knife through your heart." He laughs and she snickers, he makes excuses for his absence and she rolls her eyes at every one. In the meantime, she is dishing out his dinner, he is going through the mail, and in a short while conversation turns to other things.

Jayne is more deeply affected by having a husband who lingers at work in the evening. She may scream or remain silent, and she, too, will serve the dinner. But the difference is that Jayne's every anger simmers for days. She accumulates disappointments, stores slights. When they reach some particular weight, Jayne shuts out her husband emotionally.

She stops speaking to him, withdraws into herself. Sometimes her silence is coldly disapproving. More often it is empty of any feeling at all, as if she herself has left the marriage, though her body is physically present. Jayne continues to see to all her family responsibilities, but she is just going through the motions.

Jayne's anger is a solid boulder. Loving feelings are not possible as long as that angry mass is blocking them. It can drag on for days or even weeks. Comfortable with this familiar weight on her spirit, Jayne rarely takes a second look at the situation that infuriated her. She makes no effort to dislodge her anger, because she sees it as a protection against pain. "I see my husband as he is," she explains. "There's no point in talking to him, because people don't change. But when he hurts me, I put myself far enough away so that he can't do that to me again soon."

Rita's anger doesn't linger, whereas Jayne's is a slow daily trip. Rita vents, while Jayne broods, and brooding tends to hover like a low-hanging cloud. These women have different styles of handling anger for any number of reasons, ranging from temperament to family tradition. But one significant and rarely noted reason they handle anger differently is that each interprets the offense differently.

Rita the screamer believes that her husband often misses dinner because he is overly anxious about his work. She knows he's never totally sure he is good enough. He comes home late because he needs to check and recheck what he has done, and he feels relaxed only when he is there to oversee things. Yes, she does resent the time away from her and the children. But at heart she assumes that he puts work first because of his own needs and anxieties—not because of anything to do with her.

This thinking allows Rita to let go of her anger. In Rita's interpretation, her husband is not trying to take advantage of her. Even though the effect of his anxiety may be to inconvenience Rita, that is not his intent. Rita knows that her husband's anxiety sometimes gets in her way, and when it does, she screams. After she screams, she loves him.

Jayne needs more from her husband in order to feel loved. She needs frequent reassurance and continuous displays of attention and "respect" in order to feel valued. Unaware of her own fragility in these areas, Jayne tends to trust her feelings more than they merit. When her husband is late for dinner, she feels unappreciated. If Jayne feels unappreciated, she assumes she *is* unappreciated. Then, she reasons, how else could she feel towards her husband except angry?

It is far more difficult to forgive a man you interpret as taking you for granted than a man you believe is simply too anxious to love you properly at the moment.

Both these women share the same outward experience: a husband who is frequently late for dinner. But each woman perceives the event differently because she processes it through a different inner filter. *That inner filter is a product of any woman's unique internal balance between loving and needing.* What she thinks about the event changes what she feels about it and, ultimately, what she feels about him.

Here is the most important point: Unlike so many of the cards you are dealt and must play as best you can, you can deliberately adjust that inner filter. When you do, it will change your experience of love.

Between Stimulus and Response, There Is YOU

A cat is not self-aware. She cannot evaluate a particular reaction and decide whether it bespeaks the kind of cat she wants to be. If catnip sends her into a frenzy of delight, the cat cannot say to herself, "Well, the last time I lost myself in catnip, I was sick as a dog the next day. Even though it looks delicious, I know I'd hate myself in the morning." Catnip is her stimulus, and a delighted frenzy is her response.

You, on the other hand, can stand between the stimulus of your particular catnip and your customary "I can't help how I feel" response. You can, in fact, change how you feel.

Changing how you feel actually means two things:
• You can change what you do with a feeling.
• You can change the feeling itself.

Let's say your boyfriend asks you to change your dress to one he likes better, and the implied criticism hurts your feelings. You change your dress, but your evening is ruined. Changing your emotional response means that, given the same stimulus ("Oh, honey, not that baggy brown dress again"), you could reinterpret his remark in a way that doesn't hurt your feelings. ("He thinks my body is great and he's telling me he wants me to show it off tonight.") This interpretation may make you feel either complimented by his appreciation, or resentful of his sexist possessiveness. But, either way, your new interpretation of his remark has changed your emotional reaction from just feeling hurt.

Alternatively, you might feel hurt but change how you handle those hurt feelings—that is, you might respond differently. Instead of changing your dress and ruining your mood, you might say, "Hey, that hurt my feelings." Then give him a chance to make you feel better.

These two examples of emotional change techniques are accurate enough in theory. But they do not begin to convey the effort required to get ourselves to use them. It can be a herculean battle to stop and make a new interpretation of a hurtful remark, or to respond to something negative in a new or better way.

Making these changes is difficult partly because we aren't taught how to achieve them. The rest of this chapter describes three psychological tools that will make the process easier. But the greater obstacle to changing our feelings is not our ignorance of technique. We don't shift our own feelings because often we feel that even if we could, we shouldn't.

We have been taught to revere the genuineness of our emotional reactions. It is as if our feelings are some uncensored part of our spirit, some personal truth with which we must not tamper. Changing a feeling might imply faking, masking our real self for something more expedient.

In fact, feelings are not a pure expression of our souls. Our emotional reactions both influence and are influenced by how we think, how we act, how we are socially conditioned and genetically programmed. Though our emotions may feel like personal truth, they can also be as much a reflection of the times in which we live as they are a reflection of our unique personalities.

Twenty-five years ago, when my boyfriend told me that no wife of his would be allowed to work, I burst out laughing. It didn't make me mad, because it had not occurred to me that it should. It didn't scare me, because I never took it seriously. Instead, since I believed then that I would marry this man, what I felt was some sympathy for him. I could see he was in for a bit of a letdown. I recall worrying about how I could make marriage to me less of a shock for him. I had no intention of being different once I married, but I thought I could kind of break me to him gently.

What! What was I thinking? Ten years later, if a man even hinted at such a parochial attitude, I would slay him with a speech so furious, it *was* sex. What had happened to my compassion for his misguided belief in his own power? Which reaction was my "true" feeling?

These days, I've noticed a new emotional reaction. When I hear a man speak of his wish to have the woman he loves out of the work force, I start my old speech, but it has lost its fire. I still hear all the old male undertones of dominance and control that are so damaging to women, no matter how sweetly they are packaged. But I also hear his version of love, his urge to cherish and protect and ease the path of a beloved. I have felt that urge myself, when I was feeling most loving. I can no longer wholeheartedly condemn it.

I do not report this change of heart with pride. In fact, I think there is a danger in it—a danger that, like so many of us, I am tired, and the old programmed longings to collapse into dependency are sneaking up on me. If so, I will need to remember that this mellowing should not entirely dictate what I do, any more than I let a boyfriend dictate to me years ago. All feelings matter. But those feelings that accord with one's values and thoughtful judgments matter most.

Of course, you must rely to some degree on your feelings and intuition as a guide to choices and to your interpretation of events. Just keep in mind that emotions are not an especially objective guide. Rather, they are apt to be biased in some particular direction, and your emotional reactions will be more distorted in some situations than in others.

We all have areas where our intuition is acute, our emotional sensors accurate. You may, for example, be able to tell when your teenager is lying or when your best friend's feelings are hurt, to within a .999 margin of accuracy. But we all also have highly reactive areas, areas of great vulnerability where we tend to overreact, and to distort. These are the feelings that cannot be trusted, the ones that cause us excessive pain or distress, which create unnecessary conflict or disrupt our peace of mind. If you can learn to identify those emotional triggers that lead you off course, you are far less likely to be solely guided by them.

Consider this difference: When your gut tells you a lover is losing interest, chances are great that you are right, even if you cannot exactly say how you know. Chances are great, that is, unless you are a person for whom any separation triggers the irrational threat of permanent loss. Then your intuitive sensor is like a smoke alarm on the fritz. It rings every time he wants to have lunch with a friend. It flashes a warning at every business trip, or at his every grumpy Sunday evening. If you rely only on your automatic feelings to guide you through a relationship and towards love, you'll find it far more difficult to get there.

One woman might be especially sensitive to criticism, whereas another panics at any hint of competition. Some of us overreact every time we get "No" for an answer; others lose all respect for people from whom we win a "Yes" too easily. You may be someone who unravels when your careful plan is unexpectedly interrupted, or, by contrast, any planned obligation may instantly turn you into an adolescent rebel. Between stimulus and response there is *you*.

True, you are not the whole story. We cannot create love where none exists. But so often there *was* something there to begin with, something that got lost along the way; or there might have been a great deal of feeling there, if only we had allowed it, if only we hadn't been afraid of being hurt, being a fool; if only we hadn't been lavish with the permission we give ourselves to judge, but miserly with permission to accept.

Where love is concerned, there is often a great deal of underground feeling, damned up, clouded over, plowed under. We cannot create love, but what we can do, if you will, is to clear our emotional underbrush in order to make room for love.

You can nurture a spark of feeling, or let it die. You can take active steps to overcome an anger that is threatening to suffocate your feelings of love. Or you can let that anger overtake you, and follow in its wake to whatever unhappy, self-righteous, unloving place it leads.

The same is true of fear. Any of us can learn to face fear, to fight fear. We can learn, through risk and survival, to take the edge off our own anxiety. We can force ourselves beyond the threats that relationships pose—threats of betrayal, rejection, obligation, and all the other miseries that love may entail. Or we can sit back and let fear decide who and what and how much we will know of love.

Both our belief in love as a purely reactive experience, and our belief that our feelings are the one wholly untouchable piece of ourselves, have made it hard to believe that we could exercise any influence over love. You may become more of a believer if you recognize the tools we each have available to insert ourselves with authority between stimulus and response: Refocusing, Reframing, and Responding Differently.

The How-To

Needing less and loving more is the newly balanced emotional center towards which women are heading. Refocusing, reframing, and responding differently are broad strategies to help get us there.

Refocusing shifts *where* you define the locus of the problem; **reframing** shifts *what* you define as the problem; **responding differently** focuses on *how* you might react to the problem.

In effect, these are techniques to tilt your attitude towards the optimal angle for love. Their purpose is to tone down negative feelings, or to bring up the volume on the ones you'd rather experience. Considering how frequently we are led around by those feelings, don't you think we should have some say in where they're going?

Refocusing

"Things got better when I stopped sniping at him for being a pushover with the kids, and started wondering why I needed to be so strict."

"If Allen was reading a book, or working at his computer, I was magnetized to him. I justified it to myself by saying, 'Hey, it's my turn. What am I—a body that turns into a six-pack and a pizza when he's done with it?' I'd be so mad because I didn't come first. Since I've gone back to graduate school, everything is in reverse. I'm so busy, I wish he'd sit down to read a good book. Now, when I'm at the computer, he's the one who starts to talk to me. I realize that what I thought was a relationship problem (actually, what I thought was his problem) was just a difference in our circumstances. I could have saved us both so much unhappiness."

The worst thing about clichés is that they tell a truth we can no longer hear, because we've heard it too often. Refocusing dances around the most ho-hum of psychological clichés: you can't change him, you can only change yourself. Lily Tomlin's Edith Ann would sign off on this piece of tired wisdom with "and that's the truth . . . splat."

You may also be tempted to sigh past it. Slow yourself down, if you can. Sometimes the most obvious point is also the most diffi-cult. Since, in fact, we can only control ourselves (and that only barely), relationship problems are often, ironically, solved by focus-ing on ourselves—even if we did not cause the problem. Consider these examples:

His cool distance is not a problem, in and of itself. It is a prob-lem if it makes you feel insecure about the depth of his love.

His impatience is not your problem, per se. It is your anxious ef-fort to match his pace, your irritation at always being pressed, or your embarrassment for the rudeness that accompanies his rush, that interrupts your feeling loved or loving.

His continued need to please and placate his mother is his own issue to live with or resolve. Your problems might be jealousy, an outraged sense of privacy, or just an increased level of tension be-cause you don't share that need to please. His problems may stem from his attachment to Mom. Yours, though, come from your reac-tions to that attachment. Your own feelings are the barrier between you and feeling love.

Refocusing means that you attend less to his provocation and more to your own reaction. It begins when you stop asking the two old questions: *"What's wrong with him?"* ("Why does a grown man throw a tantrum if he's going to be late?") and *"What's wrong with me?"* ("Uh, I didn't make him late, did I? I mean, it's not my fault. Right?") Instead, turn your focus away from his tan-trum and towards your own reaction ("Why do his temper outbursts upset me so? What am I afraid of? If I find them so unpleasant, why can't I walk away?"). Refocusing asks: *What is it that I need? Why do I need it? Can I get it another way? Or at another time? Finally, can I live without it?*

It is important to note that self-focus is not self-blame. **Focus on yourself, not because you caused the problem, but be-cause you have the problem.** Along the way, if you discover that some aspect of your thinking or behavior contributes to the problem—so much the better. Now you have something to work on that is under your control. But the purpose of refocusing is not to discover how you are to blame. Its purpose is to help you examine what hurts from a different point of view, so you can find a way to make it hurt less.

Consider, for example, the struggle to "get" a man to make a commitment—whether to marriage, to a home purchase, to having a child, sometimes even to a date for a joint vacation. You already know that he's half in and half out. When he cannot or will not act, stop pushing on him. Push on yourself instead. You need a change of focus. Why do you need the commitment so much? Could you do without it? Assuming he remains undecided, what are your choices? Could you get what you need in some other way? From some other person?

Facing your own options in this difficult situation is very hard, because usually none of them is completely desirable. Do you stay, and abandon your tension-filled push towards your goal, knowing in your heart that if you don't push he will probably never get there on his own, yet knowing that it won't feel good to you if he agrees only because you push him? Or do you just walk away, refusing to tolerate this slow death by rejection for one minute longer, though you know, clearly and solidly, that you don't want to start over, you want *him*? Him—but different. Yes, of course you keep hoping he'll change, so you'll never have to confront impossible choices like this one.

The same impossible choices come up at every impasse in the course of a relationship. Your choices may be wrenching ("How long can I live with a person who throws a tantrum if I disagree with him on the least little thing? He has revoked my freedom of speech! Still, he's a good dad, a good person, and when he's not going nuts, he's perfectly nice"), or merely frustrating ("He constantly complains that he misses me. But when I get home, he doesn't even look up from his laptop. Just wiggles his fingers in the air to say 'Hi, I'm busy' "). Either way, it is far easier to keep your focus on him, and on the fantasy that he'll be different, than to face your own painful choice.

Difficult and deflating though it is, refocus on you. Take back your own power to act. You'll go so much further. On the simplest level, turning your focus towards yourself gives you new options. If you need a change and he won't be different—well, you are pretty much left with either changing yourself or staying unhappy. Impossible as changing your own feelings may seem, you might as well give refocusing a try. The alternative—staying unhappy—is stuporously safe.

Beyond generating new possibilities for old problems, refocusing has a broader impact. It strengthens us in the two directions we hope to go: inward and upward.

Refocusing is the logical step to take when you understand that your feelings depend at least as much on you as they do on the person for whom you feel them. Actually, since feelings are an inner experience, they are a lot more about us than we've realized. Women are quite accustomed to looking inward for the cause of problem. ("It must be something about me"; "It's all my fault"). But we are new to looking inside ourselves for powerful solutions. Focusing back on ourselves reawakens this overlooked source of power.

Then refocusing takes us a step further. It shows us how to use this power, if we so choose. Refocusing points us up.

When we keep our focus on his need to change, we are saying, in effect, "There is the obstacle he has placed in my path towards love. It doesn't belong there. I don't deserve it. How can I make him move it?" Refocusing directs us towards a higher emotional level, a higher spiritual level—because it asks that we stretch ourselves towards love, *despite the obstacles in our path.*

If we look inward long enough and far enough, we will eventually see past our own public selves. We get past our own complaints, our frail uncertainties, past our secret, superior pride, and past the walls we've built to mask our own fears. We can see beyond everything that has to do with ourselves and social relationships, and get a glimpse into the part of us that has to do with love.

It is the part of us that has to do both with self-love and with our passionate affection for someone else. Some teachers call it our higher self (though something about that phrase makes me want to stick up for the rest of me). Whatever you call it, it is a far more profound source of the feeling of love than any improvement in your man could ever be.

Think of it as simply the best of who you are. Refocusing—away from him and how he makes you feel, and towards yourself and what it is within you to feel—sets you on that path.

Reframing

"Judith," said a friend's husband as we were cleaning up a kitchen together, "look at what you've done with the ice cream." Since he spoke in tones I usually reserve for life-threatening situations, I did look.

"Look at the lid," he commanded. "You put the lid on all wrong. Christ, if you leave it like that, you'll get freezer burn." I was teetering on the edge of issuing a few commands of my own when suddenly I saw the world as it must appear to him. I saw the detail he cannot escape noticing, the frustration that he experiences, because casual people like me are oblivious to that which is obvious to him.

When I looked at him from that perspective, I felt a surge of affection for him that eased me past the judgment in his voice. *Gee,* I thought, *I guess I do get freezer burn. This man is trying to teach me something.* As soon as I stopped hearing his remark as a foolish criticism, and began hearing it as information, I was no longer annoyed. So I looked and I listened and I thanked him, and you know what? My frozen yogurt hardly ever has those little chips of ice at the sides anymore. Nor does my friendship with this man. It only required a little reframing.

Reframing works because, if you state a problem differently, that alone may suggest a solution. In fact, it may no longer be a problem at all, because the new way you think about it takes the sting out.

Over the last fifty years, psychologists, sociologists, biochemists, and an untold number of girlfriends have examined nearly every factor that influences our emotional reactions—from our birth order to our biology and back. But there is one significant factor in the cause of our emotional responses that we tend to overlook. **We often feel what we feel because we think what we think.**

This is the basis of the strategy of reframing. If you think about a problem from a different point of view, you may feel very differently about it.

Think of a relationship conflict, plus your reactions to that conflict, as a picture. It's a complicated picture, one that goes beyond the specific circumstances that upset you. The picture also includes both your personality and his, your history together and the ongoing dynamics of your relationship. Now think of your interpretation of that situation as a picture frame. Placing the frame has a lot to do with what the picture looks like.

To be free to reframe, you need to disengage a bit. It requires stepping back to think about how you feel, much as you'd advise a friend to reflect on her feelings from a different perspective. ("You know, maybe your boss didn't mean to insult you when he asked about the program for the third time. Maybe he's just one of those worriers who need constant reassurance.")

For example, picture the man who is leisurely reading his new issue of *Macworld*, ignoring everything that obviously needs doing, in the hopes that you'll get it all done without him. On first take, you might conclude that this man is obviously a passive-aggressive son of a bitch, who will exploit your hardworking, goodhearted nature at every possible opportunity. Him you would stay mad at a long time.

Or you might reframe. You look at that same man, still leisurely reading his new magazine and ignoring every chore that obviously needs doing, and say to yourself, "Now, there is a person who does what he wants to do, instead of what he should do." This new thought might be accompanied by any number of different feelings. True, you might be every bit as angry as when you just thought of him as lazy. ("Who is he? The prince who does as he chooses?")

But it's also possible that your new thought will free you of some anger. You might identify with him, recognizing that you, too, sometimes do what you want instead of what you should do. Rather than taking advantage of you, he might simply be taking his turn.

Your new perspective might help you recall that part of your attraction to him was his ability to set aside obligation long enough to ensure time for pleasure. He helps you leave time for your pleasures, too, and sometimes you love him for it. This new perspective might free you to sit down and enjoy your own magazine, reminding you that if the laundry doesn't get done you'll live. You'll be dirty—but you'll live.

Then again, your new perspective might not free you at all. Sometimes obligations must be met. Period. Reframing may help you to love him greatly, appreciate him deeply, and still rip that magazine out of his hands and put a vacuum cleaner in its place. As we'll discuss later, **loving him more means sympathizing with what he wants or needs. It does not mean that you always have to give it to him.**

Reframing makes a difference not necessarily in what you do, but in how you feel while you are doing it. It helps you have a different emotional reaction to a situation, because you see it from a less offensive point of view. The situation doesn't change. He is still lying on the couch reading, and there are still chores that should be done. But, because you think about it differently, your attitude shifts, your focus softens. You feel better, because you have less "reason" to feel bad.

But what about "the truth"? Why see Mr. Macworld as wonderfully spontaneous when the "truth" is that he's a lazy slob? Everything can't be solely a function of the eyes of the beholder, can it? Are there no objective measures by which we can steer?

Actually, not many. I don't know how we ever get to "truth" in these elusive questions of interpersonal perception. I don't know a single objective measure of laziness, no matter how many friends' opinions we can offer as evidence of support for our interpretation. (*And I'm not the only one who thinks so!* is how the argument usually goes.)

There is no one truth, no absolute measure in the complicated arena of human nature, much as we prefer to fix on one and only one point of view. How could sitting on the couch and refusing to clean up after dinner be both good and bad? In the same way that cleaning up night after night can be responsible and reliable, yet dull and imprisoning.

You can end up doing most of the work in your marriage because your husband is a lazy, unambitious slob. *And* you could end up with an unfair share of the burden because you are a martyr who allows lazy slobs to get away with doing no work. *And* what you call lazy, another woman might interpret as the capacity to slow his pace, something she criticizes her hyper-driven, perfectionist husband for being utterly unwilling to do.

If every situation, every lover, can be understood from so many different points of view, how do you know which to believe? If there can be ways of understanding your own behavior that you had not considered, how do you know the true perspective? You don't.

But this opens up a new guiding principle. Free yourself to see the possibilities. Pay attention to the interpretation that brings you closer to your vision of love, without ignoring your own separate self-interest. Translated, this means you can give him the benefit of the doubt, think of him as "spontaneous" rather than "lazy," and still tell him that if he doesn't do his share of the laundry you will dye all his underwear pink. Choose to see with a loving eye, not to blind yourself to exploitation, but simply so you yourself can enjoy a better view.

Let's say, for example, that your husband starts to get impatient with you whenever you aren't feeling well. In fact, his temper keeps pace with your temperature. This is not pleasant. Still, the way you think about the situation could strongly affect your experience of it.

You have a coughing spasm and he slams out of the bedroom in the middle. You see him as a cold, uncaring brat, who resents your illness because it threatens his health—and, besides, who is going to make dinner?

Alternatively, if you have a coughing spasm and he slams out of the bedroom in the middle, you might react to that slam as a reminder that he can't tolerate your illness because there is nothing he can do to make you feel better. You interpret his every angry outburst as an expression of his attachment to you and a measure of how scared he gets when anything is wrong with you. Between coughing bouts, you reach out to reassure him.

Which interpretation is accurate? A little of both, probably. Which should you attend to? My simple rule of thumb is this: Make your thinking as flexible as possible. Allow yourself to think about an upsetting situation from your side, from his, from the way a friend might see it, and from the way his mother might interpret it. Reframing means that you stress the interpretation that would best serve your own overall goal of loving him without its costing you.

If what you are aiming towards is to love him and to feel loved by him, seeing him in a softer light might get you there sooner. Actually, it may be the only thing that gets you there at all.

Responding Differently

Three husbands stand in three different bedrooms, opening three different underwear drawers. In unknowing unison, each turns to his wife, looks accusingly, and states the obvious: "I have no clean underwear."

One woman automatically problem-solves, though perhaps not as her mother might have. Mom would have gone to the dryer, fished out a clean pair, and delivered them dutifully. This wife has neither the time nor the inclination to fetch underpants. Instead she says, "You know, the kids had the same problem yesterday. From now on, let's make Thursday night wash night and stick to it." She smiles and adds: "For today, just turn a dirty pair inside out."

A second woman is considerably more tart-tongued. "What do you think I am, your maid? You know where the washer is." Her husband snaps back in return, and they are into a morning fight— she with the righteous sense of setting him straight; he with the bitterness of a man who has been unexpectedly attacked while wearing no underwear.

The third woman receives her husband's accusation softly. She doesn't try to solve his problem, but she doesn't get mad because he wanted her to. He lashes out: "I have no clean underwear." "Gee, honey," she says, "that must be awful for you."

The first solution is perfectly acceptable, because both wife and husband seem satisfied with it. This woman and her husband both expect her to be underwear captain, and both are comfortable with that expectation. It stems from the great tradition of women as caretakers and domestic problem-solvers, who serve the needs of the family they love. This solution does have one unavoidable drawback, however. You always end up organizing someone else's underwear.

For others, the fury of the second woman is infinitely more gratifying—at least for the moment. She and her husband have very different domestic expectations, and she finds his offensive. Naturally, she's angry—she feels insulted. Her anger is exhilarating, and she may respect herself more for expressing it. Still, though she feels good about herself, she feels ugly about him. And he's not liking her much, either. Both were hoping for affection. Instead, what each got at that moment was anger. And each blamed the other for the loss.

The third woman sees a choice that the other two have yet to identify: **you don't have to run and get his underpants, but you don't have to be angry that he expected you would, either.** In other words, the third woman knows about love. You don't have to choose between giving in and being angry. The best choice may be neither.

This third woman is able to bypass both. How did she do it? She responded differently. Instead of responding to his expectation (Either "How dare he think of me as his maid!" or "Uh-oh, I forgot to do the wash"), this woman overlooked it. She responded instead to the fact that he had a problem. She is able to respond with sympathy because she has learned that, just because he has a problem, *she* doesn't necessarily have to solve it—even if he expects that she will.

Why hold a person's expectations against him? Hey, didn't she once expect that marriage would mean constant companionship? She remembers how angry she was in the early years, sitting home waiting for him after work, only to have him call to say he was going to the gym. She was hurt, outraged. Husbands shouldn't act like single men! They are supposed to be with wives whenever possible! She remembers the fights, the hours of angry silence, when her husband made it clear that it didn't matter what she expected of "husbands," he was still going to go to the gym with his buddies from time to time and she should feel free to do the same.

She has come to believe that he was right, although it took her a long time to see it. Neither of them should be entirely bound by what the other expects. Each of them must act according to what he or she feels is right and comfortable. And the disappointed other should be given time to have a snit fit about it, as disappointed partners usually do.

What is important is not so much what her husband expects as what this woman chooses to do, or not do, in response to those expectations. She loves him, so, as often as she can, she tries to give him what he wants or needs or what will make him happy. (Hasn't she put up with his antique-tool collection, which is currently handsomely mounted over the couch? Believe me, that is love.)

The point is, she can't always make him happy. She can't always meet his expectations, nor he hers. It never feels good to be let down by your lover, no matter how outrageous your hope. When she looks at it from his point of view, she's less angry that he expected her to be responsible for his laundry, more sympathetic that this will be yet another expectation to bite the dust.

This woman found the third option: Focus on your response, instead of on his demand. You don't have to do the laundry, but you don't have to be angry that he wanted you to, either. She is able to love him more—that is, love him even though sometimes he thinks like his great-grandfather. And she is also able to need his approval less, to placate his anger less, to please him less.

Will he be angry when she makes her choice known? Probably. He might go into his silent pout and leave the house without talking to her for the rest of the morning. He might be more explosive—slamming drawers, stamping feet, even sending a withering remark or two her way. Though she would not tolerate name-calling, or a personal attack, she doesn't get too ruffled by a rude outburst or two. After all, she reasons, aren't most of us usually angry when we expect something and we don't get it? Why should he be any different?

She is allowed to say "No." He is allowed to feel angry. His anger, in fact, is apt to be less intense, because she is not angry right along with him. She doesn't get caught up in the battle, doesn't defend her decision to abandon his underwear, doesn't retaliate by telling him how wrong he was to expect what he did in the first place. She keeps a bit of a distance, maintains an even temper, and goes on about her business.

Eventually, they will make comfortable contact again, on some common ground. The laundry issue will probably come up a few more times before he really believes she means it. But each new instance will be less of a shock to him. If he is seriously troubled by her choice, he will need to let her know his point of view. ("I thought laundry was a job you were willing to do. If that's supposed to change, don't I at least get a say in it?") On those occasions, she makes a real effort to hear him out and to consider his feelings. He is, after all, speaking not in the heat of anger, but after careful consideration.

Alternatively, she might raise the issue herself in a calm moment, clarify what she is and is not willing to do, or even negotiate a bit, if her decision is open to negotiation. The purpose of her discussion is not to win his approval of her decision, not to soothe his anger or argue away his disappointment. It is simply to say that, if the situation is looked at from his point of view, she understands his annoyance. She didn't make a decision *in order to disappoint him,* and she's not changing her mind *in order to make him happy,* but she acknowledges his right to be momentarily mad. An open acknowledgment of someone's right to be angry can go a long way towards helping him let that anger go.

. . . .

Responding differently is not limited to your reactions to him. It also includes responding differently to your own emotional signals. By way of example, the following describes how you might decide to respond differently to a very upsetting stimulus—the feeling of jealousy.

Say your lover is having a long and apparently intimate conversation with his former girlfriend at a party. Maybe this kind of thing has always made you jealous, and guess what—it does this time, too. In the past, though, you have handled your jealousy by pretending not to notice him off in the corner. That protected your pride, but it didn't make you any less upset. (In fact, you probably ended up picking a fight later on some irrelevant subject, and that didn't get the two of you anywhere.)

This time you choose to respond differently. Seeing their ongoing conversation, you walk over, wrap your arm around his waist, and pleasantly introduce yourself. After all, he's always said they were friends. Surely he'll want to share that friendship with you, right?

Yes, it's difficult to do. Yes, it makes you roil with apprehension. Yes, you are worried that you might embarrass yourself, or that he will be mad at you or other people will notice. But you know what? It's hard and you can do it. Keep telling yourself that it's just one foot ahead of the other. Pretend you are Katharine Hepburn and do what she would have done. Or remind yourself that we only go around once and you promised yourself you would have tried it all—remember?

You can decide to respond differently—because your customary response doesn't make you feel good; because you don't need his approval or the approval of an audience as much as you once did; even because it seems so different from anything you would ever do that you dare yourself to try it out. You can push your own envelope, and you don't need a better reason than that you didn't think you had the guts and now you know you do.

Then, perhaps, instead of the anger or embarrassment you were anticipating, he may put his arm around you and invite you into the conversation. In fact, it may turn out that he welcomes your support. Your jealous anger evaporates, because you see that, far from the longing you'd imagined, your lover is stuck being polite to an old girlfriend whose feelings are still hurt. He has no idea how to turn his back on this conversation without triggering a scene or being a bastard. And he welcomes your help.

On the other hand, you may discover something entirely different. He may look unduly pleased, and you realize that this whole public conversation was an attempt on his part to stir your jealousy. He may have needed reassurance, needed to know you care. At first that makes you angry, as if somehow he'd laid a trap that you were foolish enough to fall into. When you rethink it, however, you are able to reframe the incident. If he set up the situation, whether consciously or not, he did so because he needed to know your feelings. When you walked over, you gave him what he needed. If you want to go towards love with him, that's a very fine thing to do.

Finally, what if you walk over and your worst fear is realized? As you approach the two of them, he looks up irritated and his ex stands smirking, because she sees right through you. You feel humiliated: she sees your jealousy and knows you care. Well, the fact is—you do care. Why let that embarrass you?

There is no need to be ashamed of your jealousy. It may not present you in your most flattering light, but it shows you in a very human one. Besides, there really is little use in pretending. Most of us recognize jealousy in someone else, no matter how much that other person tries to deny it. You command so much more respect and feel so much better about yourself when you are able to say, "Yes, I did feel uncomfortable." "Yes, that did bother me." "Yes, I did get jealous." Remember, no one can make you feel bad about something you recognize and accept in yourself.

When you do allow your feelings to show, you give yourself options that were simply not available when you were pretending to be indifferent. You have a chance to take the relationship deeper, because you are connecting on a different and more private level of truth. You may get a more realistic (albeit possibly more painful) assessment of his feelings for you, and of his degree of attachment to his old girlfriend. You may now communicate clearer limits on what you will or will not tolerate, because you have faced, rather than sidestepped, a sensitive issue. You gave yourself all these additional options, and all these possible outcomes, by deliberately responding differently to the same old provocation.

Refocusing changes your feelings by changing where you locate the problem—that is, inside yourself. Reframing changes the way you interpret a situation, and therefore how you feel about it. Responding differently adds to this mix the idea that you can change how you feel, by first changing how you behave.

Does changing your own emotional reactions mean that you are supposed to accept whatever he does, whoever he is, and just learn to tolerate it? NO! None of this implies that you have to stifle your outrage, have to be nicer, sweeter, or more accommodating in order to win him. These strategies are not about winning love or wooing lovers. They are strategies for enjoying a fundamental shift of attitude, from woman as reactor to woman as actor. And for experiencing a certain zest while doing it.

Though we have discussed refocusing, reframing, and responding differently as distinctly separate techniques, unblocking some bottleneck in your experience of love usually calls for the interplay of all three. The following story about Helen, and her efforts to be at peace with the conflict between her fiancé and her family, is an example of how all three strategies might work together in a highly emotionally charged situation.

Helen's socially withdrawn boyfriend, George, did not make a particularly dazzling impression on her family. (Her brothers have taken to calling him Mr. Potato Head.) Every subsequent family gathering has become a tense opportunity for Helen to get George to participate, so her family will see him as she does.

Helen throws George conversational openings, and resents him for failing to take advantage. She brags about him, and her brothers roll their eyes. And she worries. Does George hate being there? Is her family possibly more astute about him than she is? Maybe

George is not Mr. Right? But she loves him. And her family has never thought anyone she brought home was Mr. Right. Round and round she goes—"gerbil thinking," she calls it.

To get off this circular track, Helen's first step was to refocus, away from George or her brothers and towards herself. Having seen that George and her brothers are an awkward fit, Helen realizes that she has been asking, essentially, "How can I get George and my brothers to like each other?" Apparently, the answer is that she can't. Now she needs to figure out why she needs to, and how strongly attached she is to that need.

What does she need? ("One big happy family," she sighs.) Why does she need it? (Eventually, Helen works her way past "Wouldn't anyone?" and arrives at "Because I feel the tension between George and my brothers and I can't stand the feeling.") Could Helen ease her tension in any way other than by relying on George and her brothers to change? ("I don't know," she says. "I haven't really thought about it.")

Focusing away from George and towards herself has helped to redefine Helen's problem. Helen has always been a peacemaker, because she finds conflict between people she cares about absolutely intolerable. Making peace is all well and good, and every family benefits if the person in this role is skilled. But sometimes, despite the peacemaker's best efforts, the others will not back off. Helen needs some other way to ease her own anxiety; otherwise other people's relationships will always hold her emotionally hostage. Helen needs social harmony in order to feel happy and relaxed. But she will have to need it less.

It is no simple matter for Helen to become less anxious in a situation where she is automatically on guard. She will need to make a conscious effort to stretch her comfort zone, so that conflict around her does not become conflict within her. That effort would be considerably eased if she could somehow see the conflict between George and her brothers in a less threatening way. She needs a way to reframe the dilemma.

But she hasn't been able to think of another way to see the situation. To Helen, conflict in relationships is catastrophic. She doesn't believe people's feelings for each other ever change for the better. She fears that the current underground tension between George and her brothers will escalate into something very ugly. Besides, she feels guilty. George is her boyfriend, these are her brothers, and it is therefore her responsibility to make things nice.

Driven by this guilty sense of responsibility, Helen frequently defends George to her brothers, or her brothers to George. Unfortunately, her defense has the effect of making each more intensely aware of a conflict that he had previously been minimizing. It has not made things better.

Finally, friends challenged Helen's reading of the situation. One, hearing about a testy interchange between George and Helen's youngest brother at a recent family birthday, started to laugh. "I can't believe you call that conflict," she said. "That sounds like every Sunday dinner my family ever had."

A second friend agreed. "I don't see what's so awful here," he said. "Looks like the normal cockfight that always goes on for a while when a new male threatens to join the pack. What are you so worried about?"

Once she is buoyed by these reframed perspectives, Helen's anxiety began to ease a bit. This was normal? This was not catastrophe? She slowly realized that it was possible she was overly sensitive to conflict. What was she so afraid might happen? Perhaps George and her brothers might "be mean" to each other. Maybe they would even break the surface politeness and yell at each other. Though Helen wasn't comfortable with open conflict, even she could see (eventually) that this is not the very worst thing that can happen in a family. Perhaps she doesn't always have to put herself in the middle to make things go smoothly.

Helen's deepest worry was that George would leave her because everything wasn't perfect. The fact is, he might. He might be a man still caught in the fantasy that the right person should come with no freight at all. The other fact is that Helen cannot make everything perfect—not her family, not herself, not even George—no matter how hard she tries. If George is going to leave because the situation makes him too anxious, that still doesn't mean that Helen can fix things. It is out of her hands.

Finally, Helen decided to risk responding differently, even though she imagined it would be impossible. She would give up trying to make George more presentable to her brothers, and her brothers more tolerable of George. Helen gritted her teeth and decided to step back. She had tried her best, and now it was up to them.

Helen stopped trying to get George to talk more. If he wanted to participate, he'd do it on his own. She forced herself to ignore any derogatory remarks her brothers made behind George's back. She no longer defended him or discussed him. She forced herself to smile sweetly and move on. (Amazingly, when her brothers could no longer get a rise out of her, they stopped trying, and took up some new family target. By that time, Helen had ceased to notice anyway.)

George continued to be quiet, and Helen came to accept that social situations, which were a great source of pleasure for her, were less fun for him. He tended to go into a shell, because that was where he was most comfortable. Helen saw that she would have to accept that part of him. She did so only slowly, over time. It helped to remind herself that he shed his shell when the two of them were alone and, after all, that was more important to her. Her brothers would either see that part of George or not, as they got to know him. George would have to accept her brothers' teasing as part of her family's style. He would either grow accustomed to it over time, or he would not.

Assuming George did stay (he did), and assuming Helen did marry him (she did), Helen might have to come to accept a situation that was less than desirable for her. Although she wants her family to be enthusiastic about her choice of husband, she might have to live without their support. Ideally, George would enjoy her family as she does, but she is not responsible for his good time.

"One big happy family" is maybe how things should be, or what she always envisioned. But it's not how they are.

Helen needed to stop trying to get things to match her original picture, and focus on that one point: this is how the family relationship with George *is*. Yes, it may improve later. Or it may not. Instead, her questions must focus back on herself: Is their relationship cordial enough for Helen to live with it? Can she satisfy her need for that feeling of group harmony in some other way? Can she do without it? Refocusing, reframing, and responding differently are tools to help Helen ask and answer these questions.

As we've noted, each of these three strategies overlaps with the others. Seeing a situation differently influences how you understand that situation, which changes how you might react to it, which affects how you see it, and so on. The mixture of these approaches is more artful than scientific. The art, of course, is the art of loving.

Who You'll Need to Be

Imagine you call a friend and leave an important message for her with her husband, who swears to tell her as soon as she comes in. When you get no response from your friend, you eventually call back. She confirms that she never got the message.

This is the kind of selfish thoughtlessness that makes you explode at your own husband. You are almost embarrassed to have stirred those troubled waters for your friend. So you are surprised by her comment, which perfectly demonstrates the spirit in which she faces life with an absent-minded, sometimes thoughtless mate. "That's us," she says, "separated at marriage."

On paper two horses are equal, yet on the track one is the consistent victor. Why? Well, it is explained, the winning horse has "heart." Two patients with a similar disease course are given the same prognosis. What separates the one who recovers from the one who does not? Her doctors' explanation is more spirit than science: "She's a fighter," they say. Statistically two athletes are evenly matched, but on the field only one is a proven champion. Why? Well, it is explained, there is an "X factor."

An X factor—some quality of the person, some energy or attitude, some sense of joy or depth of grit—makes the difference between success and failure in so many parts of life. Clearly, it is not just what we do but the spirit with which we do it that affects an outcome. Some of us do, others do well, and some few do well— plus. Plus X.

Nowhere is X more influential than when you are pressing yourself towards love. The three techniques just described—refocusing, reframing, and responding differently—are neither more nor less than tools. None of these tools will change your feelings: *you* shape your own thoughts and feelings. These techniques are merely tools that might be useful to you in the process. Those who use them best, use them with *heart.*

There's no way around it. Not everything can be concretized, not everything can be tested and measured, because somehow, when we break some things into pieces, they lose their essence.

We cannot wholly analyze what it takes to have heart, but we have a sense of what contributes to it with regard to romantic relationships. Below is a description of attitudes, characteristics, or personality biases that enhance our capacity to love because they are components of that X factor in love. This is not a list of skills, complete with a program for personal development. Think of it instead as an emotional direction in which to point, in order to point towards love.

Willingness is the prerequisite for loving. You've got to be willing to take love as it really is, to love a person as he or she really is, even though the experience is so *other* than you imagined love would be.

The importance of this indefinable stance, this opening of attitude, might frustrate you. It is an *unquantifiable spirit,* out of sync with a data-driven world. Plus it sounds like the old light-bulb joke. (You know, it only takes one psychologist to change a light bulb, but the light bulb really has to want to change.)

Willingness may not be *quantifiable,* but its effect on the path to the love we've envisioned can certainly be described. Willingness is a spiritual and emotional tilt away from the safety of anger, towards the risky business of acceptance; away from the easy comfort of the known, towards the anxious and interesting world of possibility.

In addition to willingness, it helps to be on to yourself, to know your emotional hot buttons and your sensitivities. This is **self-awareness,** meaning that you know both what kinds of situations are likely to make you overreact, and that you also know what it is about you that is hard for other people to be around.

The step beyond self-awareness is **emotional discipline,** the ability to temper your emotional reactions with wisdom and judgment. Emotional discipline means that you are able to act according to what you *think,* at least as often as what you *feel.* You don't give way to every feeling, just because you feel it. Instead, if you know this is one of your sensitive spots, you judge your own reaction as much as you might judge the person who provoked that reaction. If judgment tells you that your reaction is excessive or self-defeating, emotional discipline helps you to put your efforts into modifying your own feelings instead of into changing someone else's behavior.

The ability to process your feelings, instead of just suffering through them, depends on yet another human trait that is elusive, but essential to love. Think of it as an **inner flexibility.**

Inner flexibility has both a thinking and a feeling component. The cognitive component is your ability to see a situation, particularly a conflict situation, from your own point of view and from your adversary's. It means that you may know you didn't mean that remark as an insult, *but you can see why your lover took it that way.* It means you may choose not to invite your husband's colleague to join your committee, *but you can see why he might prefer it if you did.* You may still be angry that a lover didn't take your side in the fight with his sister, *but you can acknowledge he had a good reason to sidestep it.*

Cognitive flexibility really means that you are able to disagree with someone without needing to dismiss his or her point of view totally. It is the simple ability to acknowledge the other side, to treat a partner's feelings with respect—even while you don't necessarily agree with the conclusions drawn from them.

The other essential aspect of inner flexibility is the emotional component. We touched on that earlier, when we talked about emotional discipline. Obviously, sometimes tempering an emotional reaction with reason requires a tremendous stretch. One's own instant feelings seem so singular, so inevitable. It's hard to pay more than lip service to the idea that, given the same circumstances, you could react some other way. The fact is that you could. But it requires flexibility even to envision another emotional option, and great discipline to nudge ourselves in that more productive direction.

Emotional flexibility is not just about the range of reactions we allow ourselves. It also determines what we are able to feel for the other person. It's not enough to see a problem from his point of view, though that in itself is further than most of us can go. Love requires that we *care* about how things look when we are looking from his point of view. That is known as **empathy,** and in a fight it's not easy to come by.

Melanie Wilkes had it. She could see the world through Scarlett's eyes and love her, even though Scarlett's view was radically different from Melanie's own.

Edith Bunker had it, squinting and stretching to understand Archie's twisted view of the world, as did Alice, when Ralph Cramden explained the world to her. Both women endured and indulged their men, long beyond the point where most of us would have made a strong argument for mercy killing.

Still, to my mind Edith and Alice were not the doormats they are too easily stereotyped as. It was love, and the ability to think like the aliens to whom they were married, that allowed these romances to endure. And, when each woman had reached a limit beyond which she could not go, she could set an iron boundary with only one word. *"Ralph,"* Alice growled. *"Aaarrchieee,"* Edith bayed. *"Heel!"*

. . . .

The qualities we've been discussing—self-awareness, emotional discipline, cognitive flexibility, empathy, and the will to push beyond easy anger and your old safeguards against anxiety—are more than just a list of independent traits that contribute to an X factor in love. Accompanying, or possibly even underlying these traits is a specific personal value system that tends to enhance its adherents' capacity for love. The lynchpin of this value system is **tolerance.**

To love someone—not just to love him or her more, but to love that person at all—requires tolerance. Think of tolerance as *allowing* and it will be easy to see what makes it so essential. Tolerance helps us assume the same stance as love: you can be the way you are and, though I might not like it, I will accept you, tolerate you, leave room for you, just because I love you. Unfortunately, this trait has fallen into disrepute, which has significantly reduced all of our chances for love.

Tolerance did not always have its current undertone of burden and endurance. It once had a more glorious and admirable connotation, a cachet of high-minded generosity. When did it become a sign of weakness? When did we stop admiring the woman who could tolerate her husband's moodiness, and start thinking a bit less of her for being willing to put up with it? How did refusing to tolerate abuse become refusing to tolerate crankiness?

My husband stood me up for our first date. When he asked me for a second, I told him he'd better not stand me up again, and off I went. At the time, a friend cautioned me that I was much too "lenient" with men. I do try for lenience—with men, with my girlfriends and my family, with my patients and neighbors, and with all the colleagues who don't scare me. God knows, I need them to go easy on me.

Lenient doesn't mean "no standards." It means clear boundaries between tolerable and intolerable. It's just that what is intolerable is specific and extreme, and everything else is pretty much O.K.

In that sense, maybe lenience is another word for love.

Marcia

"I can't get through to him. He is sealed in a tight little box, and no matter what I do, I can't make contact. It's just not enough for me. There is not enough talking, not enough feeling. When he is fully present, there is no one better. But he's not all here enough of the time. I don't want to leave him, I love him. But I don't want to live my life with a man who shuts me out."

Marcia and Jerry had been living together for the last two years, making picture-book progress from evenings at Houlihan's with friends, to evenings at dog-training class with their co-owned cocker spaniel. Marriage had been a comfortably shared assumption since the day he sold his CD player because they didn't need two. Jerry was rather excited about their coming engagement, dropping hints about jewelers and talking seriously to his dad about real estate. Marcia was more and more torn.

Marcia wanted to get married and she was deeply attached to Jerry. But she hesitated. There was an emotional flatness to Jerry that Marcia had slowly come to recognize as simply part of who he was. He was a man who didn't react much. He talked about his day, perhaps, but never about his private reactions to the events in it. There was some exchange of fact, little exchange of feeling. For Marcia, this silence was a void to which marriage would confine her forever.

Jerry was a third-generation member of a printing business that was the financial and emotional center of his extended family. The men of the family talked and thought business and very little else, except sports. The family women did not work in the business and were therefore excluded from much of the conversation, though they were welcome to listen. At twenty-eight, Jerry fit comfortably into this family pattern. He was the kind of man who knew he loved Marcia because he was happy to have her in the next room. Marcia would rather be sitting in his lap.

These differences in temperament revealed themselves in interactions as small as the drive home from a party. Either this drive was a monologue of Marcia's observations about the evening, or it was made in silence. Whereas Jerry was comfortable with the silence, Marcia was a woman suddenly stripped of social oxygen. She wanted to go home with a buddy, someone to talk to, someone to laugh with. What she had, she felt, was a handsome, loving, reliable Barcalounger.

Their day-to-day life had the same flavor as the car ride. "Jerry disconnects at the end of the day. He likes it that way. He comes home and watches television. Period. Or maybe works out and then hits the TV. Whatever it is, it doesn't involve much contact with me. I hate it. It's like I come home and no one's there."

She went on. "If I try to break in, I get the politely-listening-but-every-muscle-is-sort-of-straining-towards-the-tube reaction. Like, would I hurry up and get it over with. When I try to tell him I need more, it ends up in some colossal shouting match. All he says is 'Quit attacking me.' "

Marcia had made any number of attempts to get Jerry to appreciate her problem. She'd talked to him about it—more than once, actually. She believed she was calm and reasonable, asking him only to meet her halfway—say, an hour of dinner and conversation at the end of the day, and then the TV. Marcia explained patiently that she was not the only person who found Jerry unusually disconnected from people. She was even willing to speculate with him as to what it was about his family that could make a person so emotionally removed. From time to time, Marcia expanded on her theme by pointing out examples, reinforcing positive behavior, offering books that might present Jerry's problems more clearly—the whole arsenal of change techniques that sometimes work.

Sometimes, but not this time. The end result of all these efforts was pretty much the same as before. Jerry was self-contained. Marcia was just as angry, angrier perhaps, because she'd tried so hard to make Jerry see the light. "In the beginning, Jerry was just as unforthcoming as he is now. But then it was easier for sex to fill in most of the blanks. And I guess I read his silence more sympathetically. I wanted him to have the quiet he needed. Now I'm frustrated, thinking, What about my needs?"

Marcia would acknowledge that Jerry made something of an effort to accommodate her. He might remember to ask her about her day, or he might occasionally turn off the TV if she needed to tell him something. (Marcia especially appreciated this gesture because, as she explained it, "Otherwise I'd only get commercial time.") None of this added up to any substantive change. The easy intimacy of a close couple that Marcia had envisioned was just not to be.

Eventually, Marcia grudgingly accepted that Jerry could not be changed. This did not mean that she had accepted Jerry—that is, accepted this noncommunicative pattern as a part of him and loved him with it. On the contrary, Marcia disdained his inability to be reflective and his reluctance to discuss his inner life. "I'm not sure he has one, frankly," she said recently. "I think he's just one of those people who live on the surface."

This is an example of negative reframing, where a trait or a situation you once thought of in a way that made it tolerable, starts to appear worse and worse as your frustration with it builds. Once Marcia had thought of Jerry as "on the quiet side." She may even have seen his relative silence as an asset, a sign that he was more serene within himself and less socially needy than she. Jerry was no quieter these days, but Marcia no longer saw it as a strength. Because she needed him to be different, quiet became a sign of Jerry's inadequacy, of his withholding or his emptiness.

The more Marcia acknowledged Jerry's trait as a permanent feature, the more she was forced to face the fact that he either would not, or could not, provide something she had always believed was essential to her. Jerry would not be the deep emotional companion Marcia envisioned. The more clearly she saw this prospect, the less loving Marcia felt towards him. It was as if love were a bank balance and disappointment had cost Jerry some of Marcia's deposits.

Envisioning years of this kind of emotional deficit made marriage an unhappy prospect. But leaving Jerry and starting over was even worse. Though Marcia thought about leaving him—agonized over it, actually—leaving felt like more of a threat than an option. Marcia wanted to marry, and, moreover, she wanted to marry Jerry. Just—Jerry with a difference: a more open, more expressive, more introspective Jerry.

That was not to be. Or, more precisely, though Marcia could not read Jerry's future, she had to accept that nothing she could do would change him. This was Jerry. Take him, leave him, or take him and hold it against him. These were Marcia's choices.

Marcia came to me to help her sort through this very difficult decision. Here is how she framed her problem at our first meeting. "Jerry doesn't talk much, and I've finally realized it's because he doesn't analyze or reflect the way my friends and I do. He doesn't know how he feels about things, and he is not much interested in finding out. My question is, how do I live with it? And should I live with it—when I know there is so much more?"

Marcia's understanding of her dilemma was unusually far along. That made it less acutely painful, because she was beyond the day-to-day misery of trying every way she could think of to get what she expected and needed, and failing every time. In place of this daily tension or disappointment, though, was a deeper sadness. Marcia was a woman contemplating marriage without the narcotic of illusion to sweeten her picture of the man she was thinking of marrying.

We began, briefly focusing on Jerry's flaw *(Why is he like this? Is it something about me? Is there some way I could get him to change?)*, and then refocusing, with a minimum of effort, on Marcia. *What was it she needed? Why did she need it? Where else could she get it? Could she live without it? And if she could, should she?*

The first step for Marcia and me was to define the boundaries of her problem. When we are paying close attention to our own pain, it begins to loom larger and larger. Not only do we put our partners under a microscope in order to try to get them to change, but that microscope can also act as a magnifying glass.

Therefore, we needed to get a sense of the real scale of Marcia's disappointment. What hurt? Could she put it in a sentence? A paragraph? What were her most vulnerable moments? What were Jerry's? I asked her to describe various situations in which she had been unhappy or unsatisfied. What exactly was she hoping for? What had she imagined? What did Jerry offer instead? How did that make her feel?

This process took some time, because, after all, Marcia's disappointment was a part of her own inner tangle of anger and fantasy and fear, of her past experience and inherited assumptions. Before such a snarl is sorted out, the most that Marcia (or any of us) can usually clearly identify is an overall bad feeling: *You aren't giving what I need to get. That hurts. I'm mad.* To get beyond these broad emotional brush strokes, Marcia needed to take a deeper look at herself.

Eventually, Marcia was able to clarify what she meant by Jerry's being "totally emotionally disconnected." The fact was, Jerry seemed reasonably interested in what Marcia thought or felt. Actually, if the time was right—i.e., not at the end of the day—he seemed to enjoy Marcia's monologues on friends or colleagues—on most subjects, except those that might involve conflict between the two of them.

Marcia learned that by "totally emotionally disconnected" she meant that Jerry didn't offer much of himself in return. He was a fax that could only receive, not send. (Well, Marcia corrected me, it could—it just wouldn't.) The next question was: why did she need him to?

Most of us answer as Marcia did. "Why? Don't you think I should need to know what he's thinking or feeling? Don't you think I should be able to discuss my problems with him?"

We began to talk about *should*, about Marcia's mental picture of marriage and partnership. In the abstract, the question of what marriage *should* contain is compelling, because we have the sense that a well-reasoned portrait of a good marriage may make us more likely to have one. (In fact, to a point, it can, by educating us as to what works, and encouraging us along that path.)

But once a person is inside a relationship, the question of what it *should be* becomes less relevant. The most important measure is not of what should be, but of what *is*. The significant question was no longer whether Marcia should expect to be emotionally close to her husband, or whether their relationship was "sick" or "healthy" without such closeness. (My personal pet-peeve question.) What mattered now was the actual quality of emotional contact between Marcia and Jerry—why Marcia felt so frightened by it and angry about it, and was there any change *she* could make, to help herself feel more satisfied.

We started to speculate. Perhaps Marcia was uncomfortable with Jerry's absence of emotional expression because she was uncertain about his feelings for her? No. Marcia felt confident that Jerry loved her and he was happy with their relationship. That was part of the problem: Marcia felt loved. She just hadn't expected also to feel lonely.

Could it be that Marcia was socially isolated and she needed Jerry to be more of a social friend to her? That didn't seem to be the case. Marcia wanted closer contact with Jerry, but he was by no means her only option. She was in frequent communion with a network of friends, and Jerry didn't object to the time she lavished on them. In fact, he liked her friends and he was happy for Marcia to have them. Marcia's problem was that she wanted to come home to this warmth, not order out for it.

Gradually Marcia discovered that the intensity of her reaction to her uncommunicative lover had more to do with her than with him. "I think I hate his silence because it looks just like my parents' marriage. They had nothing to say to each other. Every evening, my mother was in their bedroom watching one channel and my father was in the living room watching another. That is not what I want to end up with. And here I am."

Over time, Marcia became more clear about what she needed, and why not getting it was so disturbing. "What scares me is that our lack of contact is really O.K. with him. When I push it, try to get more from him, try to get him to talk, we end up fighting. But I'm afraid that, if I don't keep pushing and pushing it, we'll just drift apart. Because, honestly, if I give up pushing—it gets worse. Then we're not talking at all."

Marcia began to see that she was caught up in an emotional cycle: She would push Jerry to communicate, because his distance made her too anxious to tolerate for long. Then she'd back away in frustration, because her pushing only made them fight. Soon the gnawing sense that she needed more would escalate and she'd make another push for Jerry to be different. And he'd get mad, and she'd eventually back off, and so it went.

Throughout this cycle, Jerry remained himself—a stolid and satisfied creature of habit who maintained an even emotional tone unless his inner rhythm was disrupted. When Marcia attempted to squeeze more out of him, or when she complained because, try as she would, there was no more to get, he reacted with an angry growl.

But when she backed away, when he felt she was "letting me be," he settled comfortably back into his pattern. He was mentally occupied with business, he enjoyed his leisure, he loved Marcia, and he wanted her to be happy. He just couldn't be a more complicated, deeper, more creative, or more communicative person *in order to make her happy.* He couldn't—because he wasn't; frankly, he resented Marcia's idea that he should be.

It was Marcia who was on the roller-coaster. She had thought of herself as reacting to Jerry. But now she could begin to see that she was reacting to the shifts in her own internal state. Careful examination of several telling incidents revealed the pattern to her.

For example, she and Jerry spent a weekend hiking with another couple, and Marcia was envious of their apparent closeness: "Those two talk more in an hour than Jerry and I do in a week." Alone again on the ride home, Marcia and Jerry had an explosive fight, because "he wouldn't tell me anything about his experience of the weekend. He keeps every thought to himself, and it's not fair to me."

Initially Marcia thought that she got upset in response to Jerry's intolerable way of shutting her out. When she looked more closely, though, she saw her own contribution.

In the beginning of the car ride, Jerry was being Jerry. He was quiet, listening to the radio, looking at the scenery, thinking Jerry thoughts about the work week ahead.

Marcia, however, was feeling anxious and disconnected. Her weekend with a couple who apparently had what she and Jerry lacked had been deeply troubling. "See?" she thought. "I'm not crazy. It does exist! He just refuses to open up to me." Her anxiety pushed Marcia to try again to get what she needed from Jerry. When he didn't give it, she got angry. She attacked, criticizing him. He countered furiously.

This assault did get an emotional rise out of Jerry, which may have been one reason Marcia attacked so readily. But it was the wrong kind of rise, so, in response to his anger, Marcia generally retreated. As she did, Jerry was able to resume his familiar rhythm. Eventually, Marcia calmed down—until her anxiety or frustration was stirred again and the cycle would resume.

The deepest source of Marcia's anger and anxiety was her resolution that her marriage would be different from her mother's, because the man she chose would be different from her dad. This was both a conscious resolution and an unconscious childhood vow.

Time did not allow Marcia and me to explore whatever mysterious combination of forces had led her to attach to a man very like her dad, in the very way she had hoped to avoid. At the moment, all she had was the bottom line: Much of what Marcia needed in a relationship, she got from Jerry. One of her critical needs was unsatisfied. She had proved that nothing she could do would change this. Marcia had to assume that this need would go unsatisfied, not because no man had it to offer, but because *this* man did not have it to offer.

Could Marcia allow herself to love him without it?

The willingness to love what *is,* instead of staying attached to what *should be,* is the heart of loving more. Note that we are talking about allowing love, and not about deciding to marry. So many of us resolve this dilemma by deciding to marry but withholding love until we get what we feel we should. We stay angry or grudging, stay in our cycle of push and retreat. Always trying to get, reluctant to give until we do.

Wrestling with these realities, alternately denying and confronting them, Marcia eventually allowed herself to realize the axiom on which all love depends: "I have to love him as he is, don't I? It comes down to acceptance. I don't know if I can do it. And I don't know if I should."

She hoped for guidance, for a rule to tell her what one may or may not, should or should not accept. I don't know such a rule, beyond those obvious extremes of abuse or addiction. Marcia needed to focus back on herself as her own guide. **It's not what we should accept, but what we can accept.** Could Marcia feel close enough, feel loved enough, and allow herself to be loving enough—even though there was something important she didn't get from the relationship? Her first answer, as you saw, was "I don't know."

Acceptance is the leap to a much higher level of love. Maybe it's the leap at which true love begins. Perhaps everything that comes before this inner struggle to accept another person—the delight of sexual chemistry, the satisfactions of companionship, the anxieties of commitment, or the pleasures and frustrations of romance, romance, romance—is actually just the necessary forerunner to love. These factors may simply set the stage for our inner stretch to accept another soul, and to insist on acceptance for our own. Yet we pay such close attention to each of these lesser factors, as if we would be spared the struggle to accept the unacceptable if only we got these others right.

Well, each of these lesser elements helps. And the struggle to accept plays more of a role in some relationships than others. But it is still there more often than not, still a factor in our anger and disappointment with a mate, still grounds for withholding love or nurturing a righteous anger.

Even when you come to appreciate the role of acceptance in love (and, truthfully, so few of us, female or male, ever get that far), acceptance is no small psychological task. Marcia took a first step by coming to see that acceptance would be necessary. She took a second step when she was able to focus on her own reluctance to accept his limits, rather than on Jerry's refusal to be less limited in what he had to give. True, she was asking herself to make more of a stretch than Jerry asked of himself. But that was Jerry's business. Why should Marcia hold herself back, simply to keep pace with Jerry's different process of emotional development?

That refocusing was a start. There was more to come. Marcia first had to rethink her ferocious fear of settling, as if loving Jerry as he is meant she deserved no better. She began to look around, paying attention to other couples and their conflicts. She spoke to women in long relationships, asked how they dealt with a mate's inadequacies. She discovered that there were women who were bitter and women who seemed happy and comfortable, but one could not predict which would be the happy woman on the basis of who seemed to choose the better man. Satisfaction had more to do with how each woman handled the consequences of her choice.

Some women married to unemotional men seemed chronically pained by it; others made jokes about it, and appeared to be undisturbed. More startling was her observation that some women could find an emotionally expressive man a burden, too. Marcia's hiking friend confided, "Earlier in our marriage, I wasn't comfortable hearing his every worry. It made me feel like he was leaning on me too much, and if he was leaning on me, who would I have to count on? I used to dodge those conversations, or cut him short when he started one. He'd get hurt and furious, and I would deny having done anything to hurt him, because how could I tell him it was distasteful to hear? Things got better when I stopped running away and asked myself why it was O.K. for me to be anxious, but wrong for him to be. Once I saw it was more my problem than his, I could handle it better."

Observing these different reactions confirmed to Marcia that it is not so much the flaw but a person's own reaction to the flaw that makes for "settling." A friend helped her to reframe "settling," saying, "Settling is what you do when you still believe in perfect love and you can't quite allow yourself to face reality. Accepting is what you do to make love real."

This new perspective did a great deal for Marcia. For one thing, it gave her a way to think about acceptance that separated it from the dreaded need to settle for less than she'd hoped for. Acceptance, in comparison, was a goal to strive for, a step forward on some internal path, rather than the step down she and all her friends had been resisting.

Yes, she still worried, as should we all, about how much was too much, about where to draw the line between acceptance and exploitation. Her very consciousness of these questions served to guard her from going over the line into passive acquiescence. Acceptance is neither taking a step down in standards nor a step down in spirit. It is a stretch forward into love.

Reframing the idea of acceptance helped. Now Marcia needed to become more concrete. She saw how it could work in theory, but in the here and now, acceptance means more than just living with someone's difficult trait. It actually means coming to see his flaw less judgmentally. In this case, Marcia had to confront her unspoken sense of superiority, the deep conviction held by many verbal and introspective people that they are somehow more advanced specimens than their less thoughtful or less open counterparts. *"Aren't we?"* she asked, when I confronted her.

Frankly, no, we aren't. At least, not necessarily. Nor are the silent ones necessarily stronger than the communicators. Sometimes introspection and self-expression reflect a deep and sensitive appreciation of life. Sometimes they only amount to contemplating your navel, just as a silent presence sometimes indicates mysterious depth and sometimes signals a person with nothing to say.

As Marcia worked her way towards viewing Jerry differently, she had to let go of a long-cherished vision of herself and her husband as soulmates, people who would understand each other without a word's being spoken. "Well," she admitted, starting to laugh now at Jerry's silences, "he definitely does the 'not a word spoken' part perfectly! But I do not always understand him. And I don't think it's fair that he won't let me in so I can."

Marcia's laughter was the first sign that this was going to be all right. She was going to move towards loving him, towards accepting him, warts and all. You see, acceptance does not mean that what once appeared to be a flaw is now somehow transformed so that it no longer bothers you. **Acceptance simply means you view the flaw with loving eyes.** You love this person, and this is how he or she is. You are not angry about it, scornful of him because of it, or frightened of what it might create in the future. You just take the risk of loving him as is, and see what happens.

But, you may be wondering, what about Marcia? What about her needs? Several factors came together to make Marcia more comfortable in her love for Jerry. First, Marcia began to respond differently (believe me, very slowly and very reluctantly) to Jerry's habit of tuning out the world. As a step forward towards feeling accepting, she decided to act accepting.

For example, she would no longer allow herself to complain about Jerry to her friends. (This was tough for both Marcia and her friends. The stories she could weave around his grunts were wonderfully funny.) She disciplined herself to resist criticizing Jerry, nudging him, or provoking him to respond. She decided just to let him be and see what it felt like.

One result of her backing off was that Jerry slowly came to trust her feelings for him again. He was more willing to discuss problems between them, now that those discussions no longer led ineluctably to the topic "What's wrong with Jerry?"

Still, Marcia had to live with less than she had hoped for. She still drove home with a man who had not much to say about the party. She still came home to a man who would rather zone out than tune in. She still felt emotionally closer to some of her girlfriends than to the man she married. She still had many of the same concerns—but they worried her less.

Marcia had learned to pay attention to the other ways Jerry showed his love, so that his verbal distance was less anxiety-provoking than it had been. She read Jerry's silence more as "This is just how Jerry is," than as "This is all Jerry has to give me." Marcia had learned that, if there was some thought or reaction of his that she absolutely had to know, she could get it out of him, as long as she acknowledged how hard it was for Jerry to give, instead of condemning him for being unable to give it freely.

Finally, Marcia was able to move closer to accepting Jerry by responding to his silence differently. She lightened up, took to teasing him about how unforthcoming he was. ("I'll pay you twenty bucks if you'll tell me what you thought of the party.") Amazingly, Jerry teased her back. ("You have already had every possible thought anyone could have had about that party.") Even more amazing, she laughed at his teasing. Marcia had learned to see herself in a more balanced way, learned that, whereas Jerry is underexpressive, maybe she herself had too much of a good thing. Looked at in this light, they made a pretty even match.

CHAPTER FOUR

How Do We Love
from Here?

"Before I became Mother Superior, I was a Geisha Girl. You'd think this would have required major renovation, but my divorce made it easy."

Bonnie was indeed a Geisha Girl—that is, a woman whose every move was automatically adjusted to woo and win a man. She prided herself on sexual abandon followed by fresh-squeezed orange juice, and woke to brush her teeth in the middle of the night to avoid the offense of morning breath. At the same time, Bonnie made every effort to disguise her hopes, for fear of defeating herself by appearing "needy." "My shrink says they can smell it," she explained.

Eventually, she married Richard, whose unusual combination of looks and sincerity made Bonnie refer to him as "the last decent man in New York." They moved to his hometown of Montreal and settled down to live happily ever after.

Two daughters and ten years later, they were enemies, locked in the cruel war of aggression and attrition that is divorce. That is when Bonnie became Mother Superior. The focus of her life narrowed to her two daughters, to their need for both love and money, and to Bonnie's realization that she was the only person her daughters could count on to provide either. Bonnie, who had been completely focused on the pursuit of love and relationships, now lived as if the world of men and romance simply did not exist.

"The man-woman part of my life is totally absent. I have no expectation of some wonderful romance. I never run into an available *man who could be my companion. And yet my youngest is just two years away from leaving for college. That means I am two years away from being all alone—just like when I was single.*

"But then I was so desperate for a relationship, and now I am actually the opposite. I dread the idea of meeting someone. My experiences have been so painful that I have no desire to try again. I've built a good life without a man, and I never had a good life with one. Even so, I don't want to be alone, living on the edges of my daughters' lives for the next thirty years. But I'd have to need a man a lot more than I do, in order to face those stresses and risks."

Certainly we do not all live out the either/or extremes that Bonnie has adopted in her life. But many of us do get caught up in an all-or-nothing view of love—that love is either passionate or platonic; that we will "know" it is real, or it is wrong; that an affair is either love or it is "just sex"; that a man either "meets my needs," or he does not. This set of extreme alternatives makes love much more difficult for us simply to experience.

An all-or-nothing view of love makes it is easy for us to fall (or be pushed) into an either/or perspective of ourselves, too. Am I a Geisha or a Mother Superior? Feminist or traditional? Desperate for love or indifferent to it? Anxiously accommodating, or angrily confrontational?

These tidy little pigeonholes are rarely a perfect fit, because most of us have a psychological foot in each camp. Straddling these poles, we tend to flip-flop. Some of us, like Bonnie, ricochet over the course of a lifetime from one pole to the other. Many of us move from extreme to extreme in a single relationship—from cautious evaluation to commitment in the space of an orgasm. And back again.

What Bonnie has not realized, what many women are beginning to discover, is that **there is a middle ground that works in favor of love without working against ourselves. That middle ground is a new point of balance between loving and need-**

ing. This chapter describes that new balancing point in detail, and begins to outline our path towards it.

To begin, we need to be able to distinguish between love and need, and that is sometimes difficult to do. As you may know from experience, loving and needing blur together when each feeling is at its most urgent extreme. If I need him this much, it must be love, right? Or, conversely, if I love him so desperately, how could I not need him? Which of us can clearly feel the difference?

But there *is* a difference. Love is all about *giving*. It is about going beyond the bounds of your own self-interest, because of the strength of your feelings for someone else. Need, on the other hand, is all about *getting*. It is about longings, fair shares, and feeling entitled, about noticing what comes our way, or registering its absence. Very few of us confuse what we give him with what we get in return.

Every relationship is an inner seesaw between what we need for ourselves and what we have to give. The balance of love and need requires constant adjustment to each other and within ourselves, like the automatic righting of your body when you are on a moving ship. The better we balance loving and needing, the closer we come to a real-life version of our vision of love.

The middle ground described in this chapter—loving more, needing less—is a midpoint that has only recently become available to us. It became possible as women developed enough sense of a powerful and separate self to make "loving more" an act of strength, rather than one of submission; and to make "needing less" a display of our increased resources, instead of an act of sacrifice.

Our goal is a new balance of love and need—to be women strong enough to maintain our voice, and loving enough sometimes to risk softening it. You don't "find" such a balance, and it is never given to you by the right man. You strike that balance within yourself, because it is in your power and in your interest to do so. And you are able to strike it because you have a vision of the middle ground. I am going to give you a map to get there.

Needing Him Less

Some years ago, I sat on the board of a community mental-health center in San Francisco. Naturally, as a community board, we were divided into dozens of democratically organized committees in which all the work was done behind the scenes, but we had to show up at meetings anyway. Of these committees, my all-time favorite assignment was the one called *"The Ad Hoc Committee for Unmet Needs."* Do I have to tell you that it was composed entirely of women?

I eventually left San Francisco, but in a way I've never stopped meeting with that committee. You've probably attended your share of meetings, too—with lovers, psychologists, girlfriends, talk-show hosts, politicians, your mother—all in an effort to answer the great female question: how can I *get him to give me* more of what I need?

As far as I can see, only one answer has ever worked long-term. Eliminate your focus on him, and then ask yourself the same question: how can *I* get more of what I need? Once you refocus the question on yourself, you will be pointed directly on the path to the only real answer. In other words, need him less.

Needing him less is, first and foremost, an inner shift of emphasis. It is a change in where you place your attention. This shift usually means a move away from one or the other of the two extremes we've just discussed. Those of us (or that piece of many of us) who look to men for too much of our happiness need to focus less on our expectations of love, and more on what we expect from ourselves. At the other extreme, those of us who deny love *(There are no happy relationships, no men worth the effort required. Why bother?)* in order to avoid pain need to risk more and avoid less.

For simplicity, I call both of these moves "needing less," because both are moves away from the emotional extreme and towards a new central balancing point. Both of these changes of emphasis will require your strength and concentration. Both stem from the same fundamental principle: in order to need less, you must do more, have more, *be* more yourself. Making more of you is at the heart of needing him less.

Doing more, having more, being more—each of these strengthens the self we bring to the relationship. Stronger selves can risk loving more, because they are less dependent on a man for other needs. And stronger selves are able to feel loved more easily, because they need fewer reassuring signs to feel secure.

The whole idea of needing men at all is a cultural hot button, easily misunderstood, as we discussed in chapter two. Remember, **needing a man less does not mean needing less in general.** Whatever you are hoping for in life, whatever you dream of, I'd never suggest you shorten that list. Needing men less means only that you look beyond men to satisfy many of those needs.

Many—but certainly not all those needs. Needing him less does not mean needing nothing from a relationship at all. This is all about balance, remember? Being too anxious, cynical, or angry to need anything from a man is not much improvement over needing a man to deliver everything.

Nor does needing less mean loving less. Sadly, women have long been advised to love a man "a little less than he loves you," because loving less was the only way we could have the upper hand in romantic relationships. Loving less encourages those of us who fear love to pride ourselves on how little we need it, while those of us overwhelmed by love practice various techniques by which to hide our feelings.

Loving less was advice based on the rock-solid belief that loving weakens both a woman herself and her appeal to a man. These twin assumptions honor neither women nor love. Worse, they reflect only a narrow sliver of truth. It is true that, when we love a man less, we often do need that man less as a result. But needing less by loving less is a lonely, unsatisfying route. There are far better ways to strengthen yourself than by denying yourself love.

Needing men less basically means only two things:

- Needing him to *be* less of a romantic ideal, in order to feel loving
- Needing him to *do* less, in order to feel loved

Needing Less of a Romantic Ideal, in Order to Feel Loving

Needing less begins with a discussion of everything we believe a man *should* be in order to deserve our love. Match any real-life, long-term lover to your mental model of the man who would be ideal to love. Chances are great that between the man you do love (or did love, or tried for a while to love) and the man you've envisioned loving there is something of a reality gap.

Much of this gap is trivial—that is, trivial because you are not troubled by it. Some missing piece, however, could feel crucial to you. This particular difference between your fantasy and his reality can disturb you deeply.

These important differences between what you need or expect, and what he actually has to give, are not necessarily immediately apparent. That's why falling in love is so blissful. When you two have merged into love, there are no gaps between what you hoped for and who he is—at least no gaps that matter at the moment. It is pure feeling.

Whether instantly ("He doesn't even remember if he read *Catcher in the Rye.* How seriously could I take him?") or eventually ("Yes, I knew he was a big party type. But I assumed marriage would change him."), the man emerges, and with him the glaring differences between who you hoped for and who you got. Most of us react predictably to this new and bleaker picture—somewhere between "Why does he . . ." and "How dare he . . ."

These feelings signal the beginning of our personal struggle with those two universal obstacles to love, anger and anxiety. This is the period when we either move on and continue to look for a closer match to our ideal, or stay and do our best to make him into one. Most painful of all, some of us never get beyond these two choices.

In this context, the meaning of "need him less" is clear. You will need to make your mental list of *should*s less important than the real man. You will probably keep the list itself—your requirements, desires, and expectations for the ideal lover. (That portrait of the prince was indelibly etched on too many of our brains before we had a chance to protest.) But needing him less means, in part, giving up all the work you've been doing to update your list, all the effort spent figuring what you *really* need, what you could *really* live without, what you should be willing to compromise on, as opposed to what you could never be satisfied without. Whether single or attached, we give these mental lists huge attention, using them both as a vehicle for self-awareness and as a guide for making better choices.

To a limited degree, they can be both. But we have focused too much attention on these templates of *should* and *must*. In order to need a man less, you must wrench your attention away from these ideals and focus on yourself and on what *is*. Needing him less means taking your list lightly.

Yes, but how? Allowing yourself to love him more fully as he is, is a change in attitude more than a change in action. It is that relaxation of your emotional restrictions, the sense of release we have discussed. This inner difference might be reflected in how you act towards him. Maybe you will criticize less, or compliment more. Maybe you will be more openly affectionate or more sexually responsive, only because you have given yourself permission to be. On the other hand, you might appear to him to be exactly as you always were. Sometimes our greatest leaps forward are known only to ourselves.

You will know you are in the process of this forward movement as you think less about what he *isn't* than you do about what he *is*, less about what you will miss out on if you love him and more about what you will gain. You are beginning to need less of a romantic ideal as you begin to measure love by what it really offers you, not by your imaginary loss. And when you stop measuring altogether, maybe you are already there.

Needing Less from Him, in Order to Feel Loved

"Finally, I want to thank my husband. He didn't help very much.
But he didn't get in my way."
 —Natalia Makarova, in her acceptance speech for the 1983 Tony Award

We began by talking about who and what we've needed a man to *be*, in order to feel comfortable loving him. The other half of needing less concerns what we need him to *do*, in order to feel loved.

For each woman, there is a unique combination of signals and behaviors that make her feel loved. One woman feels valued when a lover agrees openly with her opinion, another when he respects her enough to argue back. Some of us crave public testaments of affection, some cringe at the very thought.

Three needs, however, are so common to women, and such frequent sources of conflict, that I describe them as our killer needs. These few killer needs make us apt to be either desperately dependent on men as the sole source of our satisfaction, or conversely, so resentful of this dependency that we rid ourselves of the needs by ridding ourselves of men. With respect to these killer needs, needing him less means:

• Relying less on a man for economic security
• Getting less of your sense of emotional security through his attention and/or approval
• Having other resources to awaken your sense of passion and aliveness

Money, approval, and **passion** are three constellations of desire that can turn us towards men with the urgency of a phototropic plant. The needs themselves—a solid economic foundation, the feeling of being valued and accepted, and the need for intense emotional awakening to feel most fully alive—are natural parts of being human, created by the biological and social forces that shape our very beings. *They become killer needs only when men are our sole resource for satisfying these desires, and when our needs are so in-*

satiable that we will sacrifice huge chunks of ourselves at their altar. That is how we come to need him too much.

I've identified three separate needs, but of course they weave in and out of each other, like everything else. Money, for example, provides economic security, but it may also increase your sense of emotional security by making you more likely to win social approval. And, God knows, money can inspire passion. Making clear distinctions between these categories is not important. What matters is understanding the force with which these factors operate in your own life.

Though all three categories describe inner urges common to most women, none of us is "most women." Remember, too, your package of needs and drives will vary over the course of your life. The need for financial security, for example, typically increases as we get older, whereas our need for anyone else's approval can begin to fade. The discussion below is meant to outline the most common patterns women struggle against, as we work towards needing less.

Economic Security

Sometimes I think the flavor of our relationships with men is all about money. Other times it seems that money is the least of it. Though we hold in contempt those who marry for money, and envy those who marry for love, the money/men connection runs very deep. It plays a profound role in what we look to men for, in how we recognize the value of men, and in what we are willing to put up with from men.

Money—our very real need for it and his greater access to it; our great admiration if he is able to earn it, or our disappointment in him if he is not; our open expectation or shameful secret wish that he get it for us, so we are not forever worn by the battle to get it for ourselves; our cultural belief that beloved women, or perhaps just clever ones, get men to spend money on them, and our slight self-deprecation if our man doesn't do the same for us. No doubt about it, money exerts a major influence in our relationship with a man.

The economic imbalance created because men usually earn more of the family money and have more economic opportunity than women, becomes a dynamic mold into which a relationship is poured. This imbalance freezes into place some particular balance of loving and needing, which will remain until either you begin to make more money than your partner, or you make a major inner shift in your perspective on the men/money connection.

Even when we have enough of our own money (and few of us do—though that's changing, ever so slowly but surely), we do not instantly need a man or his money less. Money is much more than the ability to pay a bill. It is a scorecard and a message of love.

Love and money blur; emotional and financial security can meld into one another. He expresses his love by spending his money. Or, at least, that is sometimes the message we receive. It's not so much that we confuse a passion for a person with our material lust (although, frankly, that has been known to happen). It's also that money spent can make us feel so protected, so cherished and valuable, that the money becomes a vehicle for love.

Needing a man to provide less of your sense of economic security can express itself in various ways. It could mean that a man does not need to be as much of a financial success in order for you to love him. You find it easier to accept his level of ambition and competence for what it is, instead of extracting promises for improvement.

More subtly, needing him less may mean being less emotionally invested in his professional success. Of course his professional well-being is crucial to the economic well-being of your family. But some of us are so overly invested in his performance that we panic at his every career problem, or fume every time he doesn't treat the boss the way we think he should. We become back-seat professionals, nudging, criticizing, monitoring someone else's work life.

Finally and foremost, needing him less means having some money of your own. Money you earn or money you know for a fact you *could* earn—if you or your family needed the money—because you are trained in something that earns money. Money in your name. Money under your control. The need for money is a fact of life. If you have no other way to get it except through him, you need him too much.

Emotional Security

Emotional security covers that whole glorious fountain of attention and approval, affection and acceptance that we recognize as the heart of love. The secure feeling of being loved is built on an infinite number of signals of deep attachment. Some women feel well loved by a man who spares them the changing of the kitty litter. Others need to hear love openly stated before they believe it. Every couple sends its own kind of messages, and we all look in our own favorite places to find them.

Whatever the form, these signals help to assure ourselves that we are valuable, good, or important—not just in general, but to him in particular. Each sign implies, *I love you and I recognize your special worth to me. Therefore I will never leave you.* This lavish promise means escape, however momentary, from our great dread of rejection, of being inadequate, alone, or, ultimately, unlovable. Many of us will nearly kill for it.

Kill ourselves, that is—bury parts of ourselves so deep that we become only that which we think a lover desires. When we crave security, we aim to please. Period.

Sometimes those buried pieces of ourselves are resurrected when a relationship reaches certain solidity and the need for emotional security has been somewhat satisfied. We may discover a renewed interest in life beyond the confines of love, and a lover may then discover other aspects of us. (*"You've changed,"* he complains, justifiably noting that you are lately less accommodating, less devoted to his happiness. *"No,"* you think. *"I haven't changed. I'm back."*)

In a way, we make a tradeoff with men: I will trade you my self-esteem for your promise of enduring protection and love. But you'd better get my self-esteem back for me by being a hero. I'll win your love, and that will mean I'm great—but only if you're great. Work on it!

The signals of love, in one form or another, will always be important to you. Needing less refers to the frequency and intensity with which you require the reassurance they provide, and the lengths to which you will go to get it. The signals can be small, but the need to receive them is sometimes overwhelming.

There are women so driven by the need for male affirmation and protection that the possibility of independent power holds no appeal for them. Irene, for example, spends her life orbiting around the needs and whims of a powerful man. She is emotionally starved by her husband's consuming preoccupation with himself, and by her own reluctance to invest herself in anything or anyone else, for fear of displeasing him. ("This is how you spent your day?" he'll ask, looking at some sketches she'd begun for a children's book. Instantly, the book idea loses its appeal to her.)

Irene spends the time away from her husband in a state she calls "mall daze," moving through a vague procession of chores until her children come home from school. From time to time she thinks of "doing something," but, she explains, "I can't. He gets mad if I'm not available to him when he needs me. He's even jealous of our kids, though I try to never let them interfere with important plans."

By the time Irene came to see me, she already showed a sprinkling of the symptoms so common to women who are desperate to please the powerful—the occasional shoplifting, the food binges, the tantrums, self-recriminations, and depression. She had, on two occasions, grown so angry with her husband's "selfishness" that she left him. But whenever she pulled herself out of his force field, Irene bounced aimlessly, unable to respond to the "nice" men who "bored" her, and anxious about having full responsibility for finding a focus in life.

Irene is deeply uncertain of her own worth, and feels valuable only when she wins the approval of someone "worth pleasing." She does not include herself in this worthy group. Irene could learn to need approval less, but she is too frightened of the burdens of separation even to envision the possibility. Instead her fantasy of resolution is to get the courage to leave this man so she can find another, nicer one to build a life around.

We professional types like to feel smug about the Irenes we know, women whose very existence requires a man to confirm it. Sweet as smugness may feel, it is not particularly accurate. We, too, can find ourselves needing male approval far more than we care to examine. One woman, Greta, came face-to-face with her own need for approval during her first pregnancy.

"William married me because of who I was. I don't think he'll divorce me because of who I'm becoming. But I am so afraid that he won't love me anymore. I wouldn't blame him." Greta is a forty-year-old power player, senior vice-president of an aggressive investment-banking firm. It is a world of very few women and she has always prided herself on playing by all the same rules as the men—and winning. William fell in love with Greta because, as he said, she was "like looking in a mirror only with great legs."

Only Greta, at forty, is no longer his mirror image. She is seven months pregnant, often sleepy and utterly uninterested in work. William is not going through the same transformation. He misses his partner, with her eye as critical as his and her remarks as scathing. Greta forces herself to go to the office every day, grits her teeth to talk deals that once excited her. She intends to continue to do so after the baby, though she admits that she'd love to cut back.

Greta has lost her passion, or found a new one. But she cannot give herself permission to follow her heart in this unexpected direction. Greta doesn't need the money. What she needs is William's guarantee that he will still love her, even if it turns out that she's like all the other girls.

If I am not what he wants me to be, will he still love me? There is the fear, secreted in the hearts of some of the strongest amongst us. This is the fear that sometimes comes upon us unexpectedly, washing away the confidence so carefully built and nurtured.

Here is how one woman talked about her seemingly inescapable dread that she might not please the man in her life:

"I could be feeling perfectly fine about myself, actually not even thinking about myself at all. Then a man comes into my life and I am suddenly filled with self-hatred. I don't know what else to call it. I look in the mirror and I look so ugly. Whatever I do in the relationship, I say to myself, 'I shouldn't have done that.' The feelings are at their worst when I'm around him. Some mornings, I can't get out of the house and away from him fast enough, because it's the only way I know to get rid of the sickening tension. I get away from him and back into my own life, and it's better—till later."

We all need some form of approval and acknowledgment to assert the special connection that exists between ourselves and the people we love, and we usually try to avoid making those important people angry. But some of us are so driven by such needs that we cannot feel loved without constant reassurance. Others are so imprisoned by them that the only way to feel free is to avoid love. If you avoid love entirely, or need constant reassurance once you risk love, you may need approval too much.

Passion

Romantic relationships always involve a balance of opposites: Him or me? Separation or attachment? Anger or anxiety? Fantasy or reality? As you may have noticed, our killer needs reflect this same internal struggle.

On the one hand, the feeling of security, both emotional and economic, is essential to our sense of well-being. Without the feeling of a stable foundation, we just get too anxious to feel good.

Ah, but on the other hand . . . What is security with no lightning to illuminate it? Zero scrutiny may be intolerable, but total security is not much better. It implies a predictability, a sameness that is eventually emotionally numbing. To have things feel totally secure, you must have it all and want for nothing. Yet, if you strive for nothing, what is there to care about?

This thrill of excitement, this awakening of the senses and intense, exquisite emotion, is what we call "passion." We need it every bit as much as we need the security of commitment, the comforts of intimacy, or the sure knowledge that we can earn a decent living.

Passion is a zest for something. It is a heightened sense of pleasure, an edge of anticipation, a jagged excitement that magnetizes one's attention. Lust easily fits this description, as does the incomparable mixture of tension and bliss that accompanies falling in love. Sex and love, though, are only two of several things that can stir passion.

True, sexual love is the purest form of passion. Nothing else evokes driving hunger or spent satisfaction in exactly the same way. But several other experiences create their own form of physical and emotional arousal as intense in their way as sexual passion. There are people who achieve that same needle-sharp awareness from physical risk, extreme speed, dangerous climbs, astonishing dives, and so on. Some feel the thrill through the business competition, enjoying the ecstasy of the deal, the high of the winning bid, or even an acute physical gratification at the moment of extreme and extravagant purchase.

A cause, whether political, social, or personal, can be as passionate as any affair, fueled by an anger easily as sweeping as lust and an empathy as tender as in any love affair. A big-stakes political campaign, the team playoffs you get to be in, the lab's nearing its moment of breakthrough are all situations in which people experience passion. We all need to feel it, and we long to know that we will feel it, could feel it, at least once more before we go.

The problems created by our need for passion are clear. For the usual reasons of social and biological restriction, love, sex, and romance have been women's main source of the opportunity to feel that sense of being fully alive that is passion. We want a permanent attachment, preferably with a partner who moves us to passion. The thing is, even if we get it, it usually goes. That passion—for which you may have hunted a lifetime, or sacrificed a life's stability—ebbs. When sexual passion fades over time, women can be faced with a depressing choice—find it from someone or somewhere else, or live without.

Many women do not accept the prospect of fading romantic passion. Indeed, we are frequently advised not to. Instead, we make dates with our mates, brave the porn corner of our local video store, and serve up an infinite amount of candle-lit roast chicken. None of this hurts. Quite often, it helps to restore or improve our sex lives. Though more satisfying sex is not the same as the thrill of passion, it can be a very fine substitute.

Still, no matter how much wishful advice we pass on to each other regarding staying married and staying passionate, many of us stumble onto an unexpected life choice: stay in my (often perfectly tolerable, even pleasant, or at least as good as most) marriage for all the right reasons, but never feel that feeling again, or rediscover that feeling, that life spark, through another lover, but risk the pain and devastation that could ensue. This is *The Bridges of Madison County*, and none of us needed to explain why we cried.

Some of us have the affair. We rediscover the old charge of sexual hunger and emotional intensity through a relationship, just as we always did. The affair may enable us to need less from the man to whom we are married, and therefore to love him more. (That's why some women report that an affair strengthened their marriage. Women's extramarital affairs, however, still meet with such social disapproval that few are willing to believe these reports.) Other women find themselves in a roil of pain precipitated by discovery or guilt, from which they are a long time recovering.

Some women respond to the gradual quieting of romantic passion by focusing not on another man but on another source of emotional intensity. Mother love, for example, has the same emotional force as sexual love for some women. Religious fervor has been a source of passionate commitment for others. And more and more women are opening themselves to other sources of passionate intensity—success, physical risk, intellectual accomplishment, social mission.

The principle is the same: the less you rely on romance and sex as your sole source of passion, the more you can love a man, even when he provides less of that passionate spark than he once did. It is true that nothing substitutes for the divine insanity of a new sexual love. It is also true that, under certain circumstances, a new sexual love can make you sickeningly anxious, destroy your family, infect you with disease, cost you a fortune, isolate you socially, or just plain break your heart. With that in mind, there's a lot to be said for the thrill of rock climbing.

Besides, overwhelming sexual love cannot be conjured on demand, nor can we always pursue it when it drops in our laps. The bottom line is that you will need that sexual passion less keenly, yearn less frequently for a new man to deliver it, if you have developed sources of passion beyond men. Push yourself in that direction. Being alive to life is at the heart of your ability to get to love.

Yes, but How?

How do you make the emotional shift from loving the man you pictured, to loving the man he is? How do you learn to look to him for less, yet still feel loved? How do you need him less?

Emotional security comes from understanding, finally, that the vote is in on you—and you passed. You are good as you are, warts and all. You see clearly that you are not the best of the best (and that sight took a while to accept). You see equally clearly that you are not the worst of the worst (and that your sometimes dramatic self-recrimination is just another way of striving to be special). You are good enough to be loved, to be respected, to be treated decently. Though you would strongly prefer that a lover share this opinion of you at all times, you recognize that he may not. It hurts when he doesn't, but it doesn't change your attitude towards yourself.

Financial security comes from what is in your name, not from what is in his heart. Keep this in mind, no matter where you stand on the "he works, she works, we work, or, hell, just put the kids to work" spectrum.

Passion, most readily stirred by erotic love, does not need to be limited to that. If you push the edges of your own imagination, ambition, and courage, you will experience passion independent of a lover.

Beyond these general principles, there are three specific steps you can take to need a man less, in the service of loving him more. First, learn to tolerate the pain of an unmet need without panicking. Second, take more care of you and less care of him. Third, create a firmer boundary between yourself and your lover.

TOLERATING THE PAIN OF AN UNMET NEED

Isabelle, whose anger and anxiety ruled her life, describes her experience of mastering her needs:

> "I never realized what I was doing or why. I just start feeling sad, and I show it. I'll be sighing, looking upset and tired. I see now that it would come on me when I was feeling sorry for myself and I needed some attention. Here I am, a working single mom, which I never expected to be. Look how hard even my weekends are! I wanted Jimmy to notice and give me credit. I don't think I wanted him to say, 'Oh, marry me so you don't have to do all this alone.' I just wanted him to say, 'You poor thing. You really had a hard day. Here, let me rub your feet,' or 'I admire how well you handle your kids,' or anything to give me a little support.
>
> "But I tell you, I thought something was wrong with him. He never did any of those things. We'd come home. I'd put the kids to bed. Then I'd come in and look to him for some acknowledgment or sympathy. Nothing! He'd be so lost in the Sunday-night movie, he never gave a thought to my day. Never picked up on the sighing or the suffering.
>
> "That made me so mad, I would end up interrupting the movie

to confront him. I'd ask him, 'Is this a pattern in all your relationships? Don't you talk? Is it that you are just so selfish?'

"We went through this sequence so many times that we finally broke up. Initially I would think that was for the best, because I didn't want a relationship with another insensitive man, like my ex. I figured, if he wouldn't pay attention to me or what I needed, he wasn't worth the bother.

"Then, all of a sudden, it didn't matter what I thought. I'd get so freaked out being without him that I would run after him, call him, say anything, even get so out of control that I would drive by his house and wait for him to show up. Or I'd call all of my friends, always in the same frenzy, always saying, HELP—I'm hurting so much, please make me feel better.

"It was a close girlfriend who got my attention, and only because she was fed up with me. It was like she snapped. She told me off, told me I'm a person who just needs, needs, needs, with no limits in sight, and that was why my marriage broke up and why Jimmy left, too.

"I don't know why I heard it that time. Maybe because it came from her, or maybe because it sounded exactly like my ex. But when I got done with hating her, I thought about what she'd said and something went 'click.' It was like when you learn skiing and people keep telling you, 'Bend your knees, bend your knees.' And you say, 'I am, I am,' because you really think you are. Then, one day, you do something slightly different and you sail down the hill, and, click, you get it. 'Ooohh,' you say, 'bend my knees.'

"That's how this was. I thought about Jimmy and my ex, from a slightly different angle. I asked myself different questions, and suddenly the whole picture shifted and I could see myself differently.

"I started to see that the whole thing had something to do with how I automatically see myself as helpless once I'm in a relationship. Why is it that around a man I want to be Poor Miss Pathetic? When there is no man, I don't feel the least pathetic. In fact, sometimes I feel like Wonder Woman.

"Plus, I figure it's O.K. to need sympathy, but I turned it into a *test, like, if you care about me, I shouldn't have to tell you what's wrong—you should know. Meanwhile, he was pretending not to notice all my sighs and sad faces, because they usually meant a speech was coming about what was wrong with him.*

"First, I had to learn to handle things more directly. That piece was not as hard as I thought. Every time I caught myself going into my sigh routine, I just stopped to figure out what was up. Do I actually want him to turn off the movie and pay attention to me? Sometimes, that's exactly what I want, though I feel like it's pretty greedy and I don't ask unless it's an emergency.

"Mostly, though, I need a little appreciation or a hand on my head, and I've learned to let a man know what I need and observe what happens. If he doesn't respond, I say to myself, 'Maybe that's just how he is. Or how is he during a movie.' I might decide to live with it, or I might decide it's not enough. But I don't need the attention so desperately now that just not having it drives me into a frenzy."

For Isabelle, as for many of us, that last piece was the tough part. How do we stop needing so desperately that we become frantic if we are unsatisfied? Isabelle faced the fact that, no matter how few or how legitimate her needs, there could still come the time when she would need something and it just wouldn't be there.

She had to find the strength to handle that pain when it strikes. Isabelle needed to be less frightened of what life might require that she do without, and less ashamed that other people would know she was willing to love without it. She might want a husband who would call her from the office every day, just to touch base. But if she loved a man who kept his distance and his own counsel, she did not need to fear his independence, or her own. She needed to learn she could dive through whatever wave of loneliness might wash over her and come up on the other side. If other people wondered at the silences she tolerated, Isabelle needed to hear their judgments without embarrassment. Criticizing other people's choices is a great human pastime, a common and pleasant leisure activity—as long as you are not the one under scrutiny. The judgments themselves need not be taken as gospel.

Most important, Isabelle had to stop confusing need and love. A man who failed to look up from the television, who did not offer sympathy when she wanted some, panicked Isabelle—not simply because she longed for the attention or the support, but because she interpreted his response as meaning he did not love her.

Isabelle began by, as she put it, "facing the worst first." Maybe these small signals did mean that he didn't love her, at least not in any way that she recognized, as love. When she faced this deadly fear head-on, she was able to remind herself, often and emphatically, that she had experienced both the pain of loss and the pain of attachment. She knew that she could survive both. Once this was faced, she could also acknowledge that she could need something a lover would not or could not provide, without its necessarily meaning he didn't love her.

Next, Isabelle began to handle her anxiety differently:

"When I notice myself in the old crazy running-around frenzy, the first thing I do is to force myself to sit down. Just sit down. Then I deliberately try to face the pain. Whatever it is. Sometimes I write the fear in a sentence. Sometimes I say my worst thought out loud to myself. I hear it and I tell myself over and over not to be scared, just feel the pain.

"I might still get frantic for a while, but I don't give in to myself so much. I'll try to limit myself to one phone call to a friend and absolutely no calls to him until my brain is in gear again. Yes, sometimes I have to sit on my hands, or see two movies in a row, in order to distract myself. But I keep me under better control.

"Then I do whatever I can do to make myself feel better. Being around people is one thing that helps me, so I'll go down to the gym or try to find a tennis game, or cook. I see friends as long as I can resist the temptation to make my suffering the topic of conversation.

I've actually put some time into getting back to my professional meetings and skiing and stuff—things I used to enjoy that I gave up when my marriage started to unravel.

"It's weird but I find that, once I've faced my worst fear, the less attention I give it, the less devastating it seems. I feel much more in control and so much stronger. It helps me sort out my thoughts when the pain comes.

"I do still need too much reassurance from a man. If the man I see goes to see his son's ball game when he and I might otherwise have gone away for the weekend, I still sometimes freak out—just over being alone. But now I can freak out privately, and then think about whether I have a good reason to feel neglected or not. If I reflect and decide he's giving me too little, I will certainly discuss it with him and let him know what I need. But the less I howl and complain in reaction to that awful pain, somehow the less it actually hurts."

Isabelle was able to get less attention from a man and still feel loved. She doesn't need less attention, per se (*"I live to be noticed,"* she said, laughing). But she added to her life many other sources for the spotlight.

The turnaround came when Isabelle stopped asking, *"What's wrong with him? Why is he so insensitive?,"* and when she got beyond *"What's wrong with me? Why am I so needy?"* Instead of judging either men or herself, Isabelle looked deeper. She began to ask herself questions that were not easily answered. *If it's true that I am frequently hurt or disappointed, what is it that I need? Could I get it somewhere else? At another time? Or in another way? Why is it so important to me? Could I do without it?*

Isabelle's success in making these changes was partly determined by how strong and resourceful she actually is. She is an example of those very powerful women raised in a highly traditional culture who are taught automatically to look to a man if a man is around and to look to themselves only when a man is not.

When she crossed that barrier and began to look to herself even in the context of a relationship, everything opened up. As Isabelle considered the question of what *she* could do to feel better, rather than what *he* could do to make her feel better, she saw a new range of possibilities. She could see none of these when all she saw was her own frenzy.

Past the frenzy, by the way, we are left with a difficult adult truth. There are things we need from love or a lover that we may never get. The important question of where and how to draw a bottom line is discussed in chapter five, "A Map of the Middle."

TAKE MORE CARE OF YOU, AND LESS CARE OF HIM

"A few years ago, I fell down a flight of stairs. I remember I was so angry because Paul wasn't standing at the bottom to catch me. 'But, Odie,' he said, 'I didn't know you were going to fall.' 'Maybe so,' I told him. 'But I would have been there for you.'"

Too often we give to excess, and then feel righteous anger because we fail to get the same consideration in return. If you give *yourself* that tender care, at least some of the time, you won't need so much in return to balance the scales.

This is another area of enormous overlap between loving and needing. We give to him, we believe, because we love him, and love expresses itself through nurturing. Then, since we give so much as an expression of our own love, we need an equal amount in return in order to feel loved. This is the emotional cycle with no exit: *I don't want to do less for him!* we protest. *I need him to do more for me. She always wants more from me,* he complains. *Nothing is ever enough.*

Bringing this loving/needing overlap back into a reasonable balance requires two steps.

First, as we discussed in connection with Isabelle, it helps to separate love and need in your thinking. You need a cleaner house and you firmly believe your standards are reasonable. Reasonable or not, he may still never make a bed or get the yolk off the dish before he puts it away. Keep this in mind: He may never give you something you need, and that does not necessarily mean that he does not love you.

Second, if you feel you give far more than you get, you have an option other than engaging in the constant battle to get him to give more. You can give less. With the energy left over, give to yourself. Give less, so you need less back to balance the scales. In *Too Good for Her Own Good*, family therapists Claudia Bepko and Jo-Ann Krestan provide a simple guideline by which to measure your giving: *"Never do something for somebody else that they are capable of doing for themselves*

- *unless they ask you directly*
- *unless you honestly chose to*

And so long as your doing it won't result in a negative consequence for them or you."

Notice that, no matter where we begin, we end at the same central point. It's about us, not about them. It's less about whom we choose than who we are. The more we look to ourselves, the more we are able to see clearly both what we need and where to get it.

CREATE A FIRMER BOUNDARY BETWEEN "THIS IS ME" AND "THIS IS HIM"

You are not him, and his every shortcoming is not a reflection of your own inadequacy. A firm boundary means you can be separate enough to recognize a lover's flaws without immediately putting their correction on your agenda. After all, though you may enjoy a degree of reflected glory, you rarely get the credit for his strengths. If you are not the sum total of his successes, why feel so diminished by his weaknesses?

The one need that we cannot satisfy on our own is our need to give and receive love. We need to love and we need to feel loved. How do we keep this love at our core without letting it become too important? We do so by giving it the ballast of a strongly developed sense of self. This is the only way, even if it takes a lifetime to get the balance right.

Needing a man less is not something we decide to do. It's something we inch towards. This is equally true whether you are coming from the desperately needy Geisha end of the spectrum or are entrenched in the I'm-doing-fine-without-love posture of Mother Superior, or of all those wonderful women at the dinner party. Plenty of women do fine without love, and so do plenty of men. It's just so much finer with.

Loving Him More

A single woman who recently consulted me because of her painful experiences with men expressed her frustration, saying, *"I just want a man who will meet my needs and I will meet his."* Her statement, and the feelings that stoked it, were both understandable and fairly common. Yet it troubled me deeply. What she said made perfect sense. But there was something unnerving about the spirit behind it.

When did we start talking about love as if it were a trade agreement with Japan? More to the point—we know we started talking needs and thinking deals in order to take care of ourselves, but when did we lose sight of the difference between taking care of ourselves and loving someone else? The balance of power and obligation in a relationship is very important. It's just not a synonym for love. And love is very important, too.

We've been talking about equal partnership with men for two decades. But we were talking about sharing power, as if love should be a consequence of this equal balance. It is, in fact, one possible consequence. But love is also the spirit that makes this new balance possible. It is the feeling behind the fifty-fifty formula, the fuel for any change between the two of you or between men and women as groups. Loving men is not our albatross, it is our energy.

Love him, feel for him, shine on him—all this is separate and apart from whether he has what you need, or gives it generously enough. Love is an inner experience different from the experience of shared responsibility, shared access to resources, and shared decision-making. You've probably felt this difference if, for example, you've enjoyed a well-balanced working relationship with a male colleague. The sense of fairness and respect this balance generates is very satisfying. But it does not necessarily feel the same as love, right?

Of course, love is strongly affected by the giving-and-getting dynamics of a relationship. There are men we love who prove themselves to be oblivious to anyone's needs but their own. The monstrous inequities of these relationships enrage us, frighten us, or depress us. Each of these feelings may temporarily submerge or even completely suffocate whatever love we have for such men.

What we need affects our experience of love, but having our needs satisfied does not *cause* love. Nor does an unmet need necessarily kill love, either. Its effect depends on you—on whether you have other sources to satisfy that need, and on your own capacity to love.

Because we are so keenly aware of the built-in imbalance in power, obligation, and access to resources between women and men, the idea of loving men more is disconcerting on the face of it. Love him more? Never! To consider clearly what loving him more might mean in your life, remind yourself of what it does not mean.

Loving men more does not mean tolerating abuse, always giving in, or avoiding conflict. It does not mean love without boundaries. As we have been discussing, we are now able to love more because we are finally strong enough to set boundaries to protect ourselves. Chapter five, "A Map of the Middle," discusses this boundary setting at length. For now, keep in mind that **loving him more never meant loving you less.**

Loving more does not necessarily mean loving at high volume, either. It is easy to confuse love and vivid drama, partly because what we read and see depicted of love is usually presented in a dramatic context. (The impact of *Romeo and Juliet* would hardly have been as great had the two lovers slowly accustomed their families to their relationship, all the while dating other people to be sure.)

Too, we confuse love and intensity because as women we are sorely socially restricted in our sanctioned outlets for passion. When sexual passion is separate from love, we face a moral and social struggle. When passion *is* love, we are viewed and we view ourselves far more tolerantly. Naturally, a love full of urgency fits the bill better than one based in serenity. Loving more may indeed be an emotionally intense experience. But it can also be a very quiet thing.

Finally, loving more does not mean making excuses for him. Excuses suggest that you are loving the man you'd like him to be. Loving him more is about the struggle to love a man as he is.

Loving a man more basically means letting him be, and loving him anyway. Let him be who he is, instead of who he should be or could be—even if the person he should be is demonstrably superior; even when you know that he'd be happier the new way; even when you know that the only obstacle in his way is his own unnecessary fear. Stretch your love to include his less lovable self, instead of withholding love until he has the sense to change.

Can you encourage him to be his best self? Absolutely. Support him as he faces a fear? Of course. But here is the crucial difference: *loving him more means that you help him to change in the direction that he wants to go, not the one that you need him to go in.* Worse, it means supporting the changes he genuinely wants to make, not just the ones to which he pays lip service in order to get you off his back.

What if he doesn't even know what direction he wants to take? What if he isn't aware of the ways in which he holds himself back? Hey, let's be realistic. If you see an opportunity he has failed to notice, of course you'll want to point it out. If he smells funny after he jogs, picks his nose while making a speech, or is unwittingly about to insult his friend, you will find it hard to resist pointing these out, too. And why should you? We can be each other's second pair of eyes, when we care enough. That is a rich resource, even if we do sometimes see what our lover would prefer we did not.

There is, however, a huge difference between pointing out an opportunity and browbeating someone into taking advantage of it. Pointing out a problem behavior is one thing. Campaigning against it is quite another. Generally speaking, pointing out includes mentioning something once or twice, and campaigning covers everything else.

Does accepting him mean that you aren't entitled to ask him to change, just to make you happy? Well, yes and no. Yes, there will certainly be things that you cannot and should not tolerate, and many others that you would simply prefer not to have. And there are any number of other alterations you might encourage him to make, simply to satisfy your needs. Asking is fine. Encouraging is fine. Rewarding, by the way, is even finer.

Just keep a clear sense of how much tension your request is generating in either of you. Sure, ask for what you need. But need a little less, so you can get a little closer to love.

Perhaps, for example, you wish that he would sometimes be the one to bring up a problem between you, so you are not always the heavy. You explain to him what you want, and he agrees. Next week, though, you notice that he is still not taking the initiative, still pretending things are O.K. when they are not.

Do you refuse to bring up an issue because it's his turn? Do you bring it up but focus your anger on the fact that he broke his promise? Do you bring it up with a grudging shrug, indicating that once again you had to be the one to bear the heavy load? Do you think, "Oh well, maybe next time," and tease him about your role as messenger?

There is no right answer. It is perfectly reasonable to want your partner to share the burden of confronting difficult issues. But the fact that you want it or need it doesn't mean he'll do it. How much should you push for what you want?

Push most where it hurts you most. Be guided as much by the urgency of your need as by the abstract principle of fairness, unless, of course, like Isabelle, you find your every need urgent. Then you must exercise your judgment as carefully as possible. Your question should be *Is this important to me?* rather than simply focusing on the principle *Is this fair?*

For example, you might be far better than he is at confronting the problems between you. Perhaps you are more intuitive, more honest with yourself, or just braver about conflict. If you are better at it, you don't have to insist that he do his share of bringing up problems, just out of the abstract principle of fairness. Insist on it only if you feel you are staggering under your load. Loving him more means that it is in your interest to temper some principles with love.

But, you may be wondering, what if you give more than you get? Does that mean that you've given too much? Maybe. Or maybe it means that you began with so much more to give.

It is pure self-defeat to deny someone love because he doesn't "deserve it," or because you expected better. Does it punish him? Probably yes. But it punishes you far more. Go ahead, love him.

When I ask a woman what makes her feel good in her relationship, I have noted that she says something like "He brings me my morning coffee," "He lets me do the crossword puzzle first," "He never lets my mother say a mean thing about me." Men answer on the same scale: "She straightens my briefcase without throwing a thing away," "She meets me at the airport and she looks glad to see me." These small gestures *are* attention, approval, security, attachment; and if they are not passion, then they are passion's legacy. They are small loving acts with surprising power.

Of course, loving acts also include the hard sacrifices relationships may call on us to make—the long vigils kept through serious illness; the step-child we accept at great personal cost, because we love that child's parent; the fuss we make over his ungrateful aging parent, just because it makes him happy. Sometimes, though, these larger acts of self-sacrifice come more easily than the small daily gestures of love. It can be easier to rise above our self-interest or injured feeling in a state of emergency than when in a simple snit because he (once again) left the car without gas.

Loving him more, then, means initiating more of these small loving acts even when you may feel least loving. (Not only at those moments, of course. It's just that, when you are in touch with the flow of loving feeling, you are more likely to pay him a compliment or pick up the book he has been wanting to read. It's the rest of the time that is more difficult.)

Loving him more may mean giving him a real kiss hello, even though he selfishly demanded your attention the second he walked in the door; it may mean telling him where his keys are, though it drives you crazy that he never bothers to remember; or reporting to friends his recent success, even though privately you think he's claiming more credit than his contribution to the project actually merits.

Why? What's he done to deserve all this? He doesn't necessarily do the same for you. The answer is simple. **The point of loving more is not what you give to him. The point is that loving more gives something of great value to you.**

Small loving acts create space within you to feel for a partner the warmth that you have hoped to feel. These small gestures work on the same principle as deliberately responding differently. Acting angry helps you to feel angry. Acting lovingly helps you to feel more love. Making a gesture of love at a moment when you are feeling irritated may help you to feel more loving and less annoyed. Loving gestures are medicine for your own internal state. Don't deny yourself that salve simply because it makes him feel better, too.

Loving more, though, goes beyond any specific loving gesture. Loving more reflects an overall attitude of indulgence and generosity. That may mean erring in the direction of making him happy, rather than making sense. For example, my family recently moved to a house with a lawn, which inspired my husband to create something he called grass sculpture. He accomplished this by mowing random patches of the lawn to different heights, which he thought would create an interesting visual pattern from an aerial perspective. This is true, although it is also true that we so rarely enjoy our yard from the air. Still, it's a creative thought.

My mother found it a less interesting thought than I did. Actually, she found our backyard rather peculiar. Mother is from the school that says, if your husband wants to do something crazy, you love him best by explaining to him why it is crazy and helping him to do the sane thing. Applying this to lawns, she suggested to me that either she or I tactfully take my husband around to the homes of some friends he admired, whose lawns looked more like—well, like lawns. That way my husband would get the right idea.

Though I understand her point of view, I have a different philosophy. When my husband wants to do something crazy, I think he should just go do it, unless (a) It threatens our nest egg or (b) I could get a disease from it. To me, loving him more means giving a person lots of room just to be. To Mother, it means helping him be the "best person" he can be. Perhaps the truth is somewhere in the middle?

That spirit that is "loving more" goes beyond what you might do, what you might allow, or how you might indulge him. At its heart, loving more is reflected in how you think about a person. Loving more is reframing, from whatever perspective allows you to see him most kindly.

In this sense, loving him more means seeing through to his heart. It means keeping in mind the beauty you know is in that soul, on those occasions when what is showing is his gruffer, less attractive exterior. That is, after all, the lesson of "Beauty and the Beast." Once Beauty saw through to the heart of the Beast, he was in every way a prince.

In the end, loving a man more means that you have unlocked some inner door, opened some guarded chamber of your heart. It is a feeling of release, rather than one of achievement. It is a move away from your focus on his capacity to change, and towards your own capacity to accept. "Loving more" is just that simple. And just that frightening.

Allowing yourself to love a man—fully, wholeheartedly, without a plan to improve him or an illusion that exalts him—goes against everything we've been cautioned against, or everything you may have concluded from painful experience. If we have learned anything along the way, it is to WATCH OUT. Don't give away too much. Hold back. Love may be magic, but the hunt for it can kill. Wear protective clothing. We have seen hunger for love as the great female Achilles' heel: It is a part of us and we cannot exorcise it—but at least we can be ever conscious of the dangers it presents.

"Love him more" is the exact opposite of this conventional wisdom. He is your person. Love him even though he gives you a good reason not to. Love him for no better reason than how good it feels to love instead of to judge. Love him even though he's not what you pictured, not what you deserve, even though objectively there is plenty that could stand improving. Love is not objective. It has everything to do with what you will allow yourself to feel, and nothing to do with how worthy he is of those feelings. Love him.

Love is a benefit of the doubt, softening the stance, a balm to soothe the roughest edges of perception. Let yourself be biased in his direction. Let him look better to you than he does to more dispassionate observers. Give yourself the joy of cherishing another person, of indulging that person, just because it brings great happiness to do so.

I promise you—**you will not lose anything by looking at him with kinder eyes.** Yes, loving more does make you more vulnerable. But you are stronger now, stronger than you think, stronger than you've been encouraged to believe. We are always given advice about how to avoid the pain that men can inflict. You may have yet to discover that you are strong enough to stand your ground, now that you can reach a balanced middle.

Lily

When Lily's husband, Franklin, has a business setback, he blames everyone but himself. In their early days together, Lily blamed them too. She sees things more clearly now, and she has a pretty good idea of what Franklin does to create problems for himself at work—probably the same things that he does at home. There, he retreats into his own world, doesn't hear what other people need, just goes off and does what he wants. Franklin doesn't absorb criticism; it seems to bounce off his shell. If his boss or his customers get as frustrated with him as Lily does, she figures, no wonder he has setbacks at work.

Franklin's trouble at work has made problems at home for Lily. Franklin wants her sympathy and support, wants her to be a sounding board for his problems with his "nitpicky" boss and his "suck-up" colleague, the one the boss prefers to Franklin himself. Knowing perfectly well what Frank wants to hear, and knowing that it's not what she really thinks, Lily might feel:

Anxious. Lily could feel stuck. If she doesn't agree with Frank, he'll be hurt and furious, complaining, "You never take my side." If she does agree, she's a phony. Lily has a battery of evasion techniques, perfected in the early years, for just such dilemmas. She may try to avoid the whole question, changing the subject or leaving the room. Or she may vaguely agree, strewing "Yes, dear"s around in a general way, reassuring herself that she has no other choice.

Still, that will not entirely erase her concerns. Beyond the immediate situation, Lily is worried about what Frank's problems could mean for her. If he doesn't get over them, Lily is afraid he's never going to get ahead. Does this mean she's going to have to take up the slack? Or settle for going only as far as he can go? Frank begins to appear weaker and weaker in her eyes. How do you love a man you lose respect for? Of course she's anxious.

Angry. After all, Lily has pointed these shortcomings out to Frank, but he refuses to hear her. She might frame her anger gently, thinking of it as tactful criticism. ("You know, Frank, you tend to follow your own agenda instead of tuning in to what your boss wants done. That's happened with us, when you plan what you think I ought to like, instead of what I really do like. It makes me mad, so it's probably irritating for your boss, too") or she might explode ("This is nobody's fault but your own"). Either way, she is saying, "I told you so," and she feels perfectly justified in saying it.

An angry Lily tells Frank exactly what she thinks, regardless of what she knows he wants to hear. She is true to herself—to her own thoughts and to her honest feelings. Frank may be angry with her in return, but she is not cowed by that. She is proud of her ability to stand up for herself and say what she thinks.

But there is a problem. Not only is Frank likely to be angry. So is Lily. Lily took care of herself at the price of love. Her reaction to Frank's story increases her frustration with him. She sees him as a man who keeps making the same mistakes and refuses to recognize his pattern. In her eyes, he is a man so fragile, or so dictatorial, that he has a tantrum if she dares to disagree. There is very little to inspire love in these versions of Frank. She may respect herself for refusing to be bullied, but she does not feel more loving.

There is a third choice, one that does not force an anxious Lily to sell herself short out of fear of conflict, or to sell Frank short out of contempt for a weakness. Lily could see Frank as he is, and be at peace with what she sees.

Lily could be at peace with it. Being at peace with Frank's problem—his "flaw," as it were—means several different things. It means that Lily feels less need to confront Frank with her own version of the truth, feels less need to say, "I told you so," or "That's what I've been trying to tell you," because, in fact, she has told him so. She knows he'll hear it when he's able. She doesn't need to take every opportunity to make her point about "What's wrong with Frank?"

At the same time, being at peace does not mean going along, or pretending to believe what you do not. How peaceful could that be? Instead, Lily is at peace in a balanced middle. She sympathizes with what Franklin needs to hear, rather than indicting him for it. But she does not say what he wants to hear, because she doesn't have that to give.

When Franklin vents his frustration with those he blames, Lily sympathizes with the fact that he has a problem. But she does not endorse his perspective on who's to blame for that problem.

Lily might state her perspective of the problem, but with empathy, instead of accusation: "It's so tough for you to do what someone else thinks should be done, when you are closer to the job than your boss is." She doesn't need to add that he really should do what the boss wants. Frank already knows that, much as he fights against it.

How did Lily get here? What has made it possible for her to be at peace though she is faced with the part of Frank that has hurt and disappointed her? Why is it that Lily can choose to be at peace, whereas the rest of us are caught in the grip of bad feeling—of anger, anxiety, or both?

Lily can make the third choice because she has developed a different perspective. She felt all the same frustration or worry that the rest of us feel when confronted by the darker side of the person we love. She felt it, and she responded differently to those feelings.

She let go of the idea that she should work to help Frank see his problem, or to help him fix it. Naturally Lily hopes, for his sake and hers, that Frank will develop the self-confidence to take direction from others without feeling diminished himself. But she has accepted the fact that she can't push him to develop this.

Instead, she focused on herself and her own troubled emotional reaction. She said, in effect, "Frank may have this problem forever, but I can get beyond my frustration and anxiety. I can respond to this differently." She accepts that, though Frank may or may not continue to irritate his boss, or overlook her, she doesn't have to continue to suffer when he does it.

How does Lily help herself to suffer less? First, she takes another look at what hurts her. Like Frank's boss, Lily has been hurt and angry when Frank ignores what she wants and follows his own agenda. To Lily, if Frank ignored her, it meant he did not love her or respect her. Naturally that interpretation makes her both angry and anxious.

But closer examination has helped her to reframe Frank's behavior. She took a step back and saw that Frank follows his own agenda because of his own issues with independence and authority. They have nothing to do with Lily, except insofar as she is yet another important person who tells him what to do. Lily is still left with the problem, but it feels less personal, less of a reflection on his feelings for her, and therefore less infuriating.

It's also easier for Lily to be at peace, because Frank's weaknesses don't frighten her as much as they once did. She does not need Frank to be the fantasy Frank she conjured when she first married him. She has faced his flaws, held them against him, and, finally, forgiven him for them. This process was not an immediate epiphany. It was a gradual and grueling process of maturation in Lily.

Lily has grown in the years of her marriage. In part, Frank's single-mindedness was helpful to her. She had to learn to stand firm about what she needed, because when she did not insist she found her needs ignored. Lily had to develop a clearer sense of herself.

Over what should she struggle with Frank? What was worth it to her? What could she simply go and do for herself? What could she let go of?

Through this process she discovered she is more competent than she once thought, and more creative as well. Frank helped her to enhance her view of herself, because he has great respect for her shrewd assessment of people in his business. At one time Lily resented the fact that Frank listened to her opinion on everyone but himself. Now they are able to laugh about that irony.

As Lily grew stronger, she needed Frank to be less of a paragon. Yet, because she appreciated that so much of her growth was spurred by his support, she was able to view his shortcomings more lovingly. She can now say to herself, "There's Frank butting heads with a boss again," without reacting more intensely. This is not catastrophe, this is just a personality obstacle with which he struggles. Frank's done fine, even with this obstacle. No one else in his office is perfect, either.

Since Frank's problem doesn't scare her or infuriate her anymore, she can recognize it and still see him through loving eyes. In fact, when Frank feels her sympathy, he is more receptive to her different point of view. Aren't we all?

As Frank's problem began to scare her less and to infuriate her less, Lily was able to recognize his soft spot and still see him through loving eyes. **Ultimately, it is the genuineness of Lily's sympathy that allows her to be at peace with the situation, yet still be true to herself in her response.** Lily really is able to sympathize with Frank's struggle over taking orders from someone when he feels he knows better—*even when the someone is herself.*

Sympathizing with Frank's problem is not technique; it reflects the inner shift Lily has accomplished. She is able to view Frank lovingly, and to sympathize genuinely, because she does not require him to be everything she needs in order to love him or to feel loved. She is at peace because she has accepted the part of Frank that once troubled her. To Lily, that's just . . . Frank. You know how he is.

CHAPTER FIVE

A Map of the Middle

Ask a woman why she returns to a man who lies to her or demeans her, and often she will say, "Because I love him."

Ask a woman why she remains available to a man who is constantly looking for someone better, and she may say, "What else can I do? I love him."

Ask a teenage girl why she is sleeping with her boyfriend, though she says the sex is kind of awful, and she will explain, "He said that if I didn't I must not really love him. And I do, I do."

Why would a woman dump an old friend, distance herself from her family, or even disregard the best interests of her kids? "Because I love him, and he doesn't love them."

Why starve off ten pounds that never bothered you, color the hair that you used to be fond of, or sneak cigarettes so he'll think that you've quit? "Because I love him and he loves thin, blond nonsmokers."

Each of these women has made the same error. She has confused love with sacrifice. It's easy enough to do, because, after all, love requires sacrifice all too frequently. You might eat Chinese when you wanted Italian, live where you would never have chosen, even make love when you'd rather make almost anything else— simply because you judge it to be a fair or reasonable or loving thing to do at the moment.

At that moment. Sometimes. Even frequently. But not always, not most of the time, not on something important, not if the something you sacrificed was *you*. Love certainly requires weighing your own interests against his, for the good of us. But love and self-sacrifice are not synonymous.

You do not have to limit love in order to be strong. The secret is to limit what you will do in the name of love.

In the Name of Love

Most of us suffer under a self-destructive misconception: we fear that loving makes us weak. Loving more, therefore, could only make us weaker: "I can't love him more! He'll take total advantage."

But love itself is not a weakness. True, many weaknesses have been explained away in the name of love. But that is love's bad reputation, not necessarily love's reality. Yes, love does make us vulnerable, in that it softens us, helps us lower our first-line defenses. But we are stronger now, and have less need for brittle, suspicious self-protection. When the core is strong, the outer layers can afford to be soft and receptive.

Consider Anna, who loved the king of Siam, and catered to his every vanity, though she saw through them all. Yet she stood her ground when her principles were challenged. Love did not make her back away from herself.

Think of Rhett Butler. He loved Scarlett for most of his life. But he saw her as she was, and he refused to be victimized by her selfishness or her scheming. His love was strong, and so was he.

Recall Eleanor of Aquitaine or Golda Meir when you think of Richard Lovelace's lines, "I could not love thee, dear, so much, Lov'd I not honor more." The true risk of love is not, and never was, in the strength of what we feel. We are vulnerable not because we love but because of what we have allowed or tolerated in the name of love.

The fact is, you can love a boy as much as you will love ever again, and still be fifteen and not ready for a sexual relationship. The fifteen-year-old who is able to say, *"I love you, but zip up your pants. The answer is 'No,'* " is not the one who loves her boyfriend less. She is the one who needs his approval less.

The woman who drinks or eats in plain sight of her disapproving man is more likely to be a woman who can control what she puts in her mouth, because she takes sole responsibility for it.

We know, all of us who have been there and back, why we stayed with the man who cheated or lied or scorned us or hoped to do better. It was never because we loved him so much that our love was a joy in itself. It was because we needed him so much that we could not bring ourselves to let go.

The woman who drops a close friend when her boyfriend is jealous of that friend, or who neglects her family because they remind her husband too much of his own, does not do these things as an expression of her love. They are an expression of how she deals with conflict. Conflict avoidance says, *If it makes you this mad, it must not be worth it.* Love says, *I care about how you feel. How can I maintain these relationships so that they will cause you less distress?*

The woman who loves and sets limits might see her friend alone, but she does not make a secret of it. She might agree that her husband does not have to attend most family events (even knowing that her decision will throw her own mom into a disapproving tizzy), but she also insists that her husband act decently at the few he attends out of courtesy.

Loving a man more means sympathizing with what he wants or needs, if that is at all possible. But it does not mean you have to give it to him. Nor do you have to be angry in order to set the limit.

Limit setting does not require your rage. It requires only a strong sense of yourself and what is important to you. Remember the three husbands standing at their bureau drawers? You don't have to provide clean underwear, but you don't have to be angry just because he wishes you would.

Far from requiring anger, limit setting can make it easier for you to let go of anger. Consider again the woman whose possessive partner gave her a hard time about seeing her friend. That woman was probably angry, whether she gave in to her lover or not. If she gave in, chances are she's still angry, though she might have buried it deep or taken it out on him in some other way.

But the woman who is able to love and still set a limit can allow herself to overcome her own anger. She might begin to think of his possessiveness as a wound on his spirit, rather than as a weakness in his character. That reframing might make her less contemptuous of his angry insecurity. She reframes his jealousy and responds differently to his outbursts, in order to feel more loving in response to his less lovable side.

Loving more without losing an intolerable amount of her own freedom makes it easier for that woman to help a man with his jealousy—by going out of her way to reassure him, by paying him special attention on occasions that are tough for him, by publicly acknowledging his importance to her in front of her friend, and so on. This woman is able to sympathize with her lover's painful jealousy, because she is not controlled by it.

These three points summarize the path by which you can finally love a man more, without being either so loving that you are totally vulnerable to exploitation, or so angry that you cannot feel love:

• Sympathize with what your partner wants and needs—if you can find a way to view those needs sympathetically

• Without having to give it to him

• Without having to be angry, in order to say "No"

Use this three-step process to maintain the balance between what you give to him and what you need for yourself. Love as fully as you can, love with abandon—but limit what you do and what you will endure in the name of love. Love is a feeling; limits are judgments, decisions, and, ultimately, deeds. You won't have trouble telling them apart.

You are, however, likely to have another kind of difficulty. We all do. It is one thing to endorse the principle of limit setting, even in the context of love. It's another to know where and when to set those limits.

The Boundaries of Love

Learn to love him more—but to what extreme? Need him less—but how little should one require? Isn't there a point where compromise really *is* a lowering of standards and acceptance costs integrity? Absolutely.

At the behavioral extremes, of course, the line is clear. Physical abuse, verbal abuse, substance abuse, and sociopathy are outside the boundaries of what may be tolerated in the name of love.

Physical abuse, including sexual abuse, means the use of physical force, no matter how small the gesture, or how slight the injury, by either your partner or yourself. If you have heard yourself explaining away a mate's behavior or your own by saying, "It didn't really hurt," "Underneath he really loves me," or "He wouldn't have done it if I hadn't . . ." *you have crossed the limit.* Calling it loving him too much, needing him too much, being addicted to him. Call it anything you like. Just call from a shelter.

Verbal abuse is a less obvious but equally definable limit. Occasional temper tantrums do not necessarily constitute verbal abuse. Nor does criticism, however stinging or unjust. Verbal abuse is a pattern of verbal bashing. If either of you is regularly demeaning or belittling, name-calling or ridiculing, *you have crossed the limit.* Don't love more. Don't need less. Just get out.

If either you or your lover is an unrecovered substance abuser, a compulsive gambler, or a pathological liar, con man, or sociopath, don't bother trying for love. These behavior problems and character traits so dominate a life that the capacity for loving attachment is lost in an ocean of impulses. You can support a recovery, but you simply cannot get to love inside these problems.

These three extreme situations require that you limit your involvement, no matter how you feel. You should, *you must,* limit love when judgment tells you that the person you love is poison.

There are softer signs that also signal poison. You dread going home, not just through a tense patch of time, but most of the time.

You hate to admit it, but you are frightened of him, though you have no specific reason why you should be. Or perhaps you aren't frightened so much as overburdened by his presence. It's not just that he is always negative. It's that he resents your joy. You've learned to tone down happiness, so your mood matches his.

You will recognize a soft sign of emotional poison if you find yourself automatically tiptoeing through your marriage on eggshells. Always, you rush around trying to make things right. Shhh, quiet the baby, hide the scratch you got on the car, hang up on the friend, if your lover's body language starts to signal impatience. Sometimes, for a while, you succeed in pleasing him, and you are rewarded with a sweet affection. Inexplicably, other times, nothing you do is right.

If you redouble your efforts to please and live with a chronic tension over your inevitable failure, you are breathing poison. Or, over time, you might begin behaving in a way that feels unlike yourself. You are sneaking, whereas you have always been forthright; lying about where you were, whereas you have habitually told the truth. You omit a lot that you would normally share, like whom you have lunch with, or even what you ate. It's just easier than facing the battle you know will ensue if you tell the truth.

It could be that you find yourself growing more isolated. You've lost touch with friends you used to value. You miss them, but they put him in a bad mood and it's not worth it. He doesn't like the open-door policy, so, however reluctantly, you set limits that pull you away from your family. Still, you reason, it's his house, too.

The clearest signal of danger is a new, bad feeling about yourself. He is critical (only in your best interests, of course). You thought it was rolling off your back, but lately you find yourself looking in the mirror and disliking what you see. Or you sit silently where once you would have participated, because you are more conscious of what he might think.

These soft signs, and others you may have experienced, all revolve around the same issue. Attachments are not just about the way we feel about other people. They call up feelings about ourselves. If you find yourself losing your sense of confidence, your feeling of worth, or your autonomy, take a careful look at your central relationships. The chances are great that you are taking poison.

These are the limits we must place on love that are easy to define—though, as you may know, they can be frighteningly difficult to live by. **Beyond these extremes, there are no rules. There is no person we should not love. There are only people we cannot easily love,** because we have come to the limit of our own current ability to give, to take emotional risks, to be vulnerable or tolerant or compassionate. We have reached the current inner limit to our capacity to love and feel loved.

The pain is that we rarely reach this limit in the abstract. Instead, we reach it in a relationship. Or on the way to a relationship. Or, over and over again, as a signal of the end of a relationship. We hope for love and crash into our own limits, or his, or both. The question is—then what?

Whether you are single and seldom meet a person who stirs your interest, or twenty years married and ignoring a creeping disenchantment, you are facing the same fundamental barrier—a limit in your capacity to love and feel loved. The question you will struggle with as you face this barrier is: *Should I try to push myself past this? Or should I respect my own hesitation as wisdom, or intuition, or just the truth about me and what I need for love?*

A part of us resists love, because we are afraid of the pain it can cause us. A part of us withholds love, because it disappoints us and frustrates us. And we are always wondering, consulting: *When do I listen to this part of me? When do I push it aside? How much love is too much?*

"*I love being good to him, being generous to him. But I don't want to be a complete fool. How do I know when I'm going overboard? How do I get him to give back?*"

. . . .

"He had an affair with a friend of mine! And left the phone bill around to prove it. Now he regrets it, wants to stay married. But what kind of woman forgives a betrayal? A weak one? A coward? An idiot? Or a smart woman, who looks at reality and knows how to cut a deal?"

"He lied about his salary, and about how he left his last job. But he finally told me the truth, and explained that he was embarrassed. Am I ever supposed to trust him again?"

"The problem for my friends and me is that we can't get started. All the men we meet are looking for that perfect '10.' I'm attractive, the women I know are attractive, and these men discount us totally. They want perfection. We represent settling. And you wonder why we might be too angry to try anymore?"

"My husband is a wonderful man, but he is not the most wonderful lover I've ever had. I've always enjoyed sex, and I want to spice things up, to make sex more fun for both of us. I've told him in every possible way, from books to videos to specific suggestions. I'm happy to take the lead or try out a fantasy of his, but he won't participate. No matter how I put it, he won't even try it. When I stop being angry about it, I realize that he's not being spiteful—he's just never going to be that sexually free. Does that mean I have to do without it forever? Is this it?"

This is the universal dilemma of love: we dream of deep certainty and find ourselves hesitating. *He doesn't love me in the way I deserve. He isn't who I hoped he'd be. Aren't I entitled to . . . ? How can I trust a man who . . . ? How could I love a man who . . . ?*

Somehow, we believe we must be able to determine what few things we really do need, in order for it to be wise to love more or need less. Perhaps more careful self-analysis? More clear-eyed assessment of a lover? We would prefer, but do not all agree on, a universal standard—a formula for "good" relationships, for example, or for "happy" or "healthy" ones. But we cherish the idea that there must, at least, be some individual measure by which we could be guided in our own choices.

So we seek standards. What *should* I hesitate over? What *should* I put up with? *Should* betrays our hope that someone, somehow, has devised a set of rules about love that we could learn to follow with some degree of confidence.

Actually, there are many relationship rules, rules of the traditional "look away when he looks at you," "keep him guessing," "he won't buy the cow if it's already been milked" Traditional variety; and of the "men don't change," "get it in writing," "don't sign your tax return unless you've read it," Women's Revision type. Some of these rules are smart, some are unspeakable, but all have one thing in common. They are rules about courtship, about romance, about relationships, about marriage. They are not rules about love.

"Could I really feel something like love for a man who has failed so often that I can't bring myself to think well of him?"

Yes, when you see him differently by focusing on your own fears and failures.

"Yes, but should I?"

I don't know. Should you?

"But don't you think sometimes people have just made a mistake? They were simply too young, or they just married the wrong person?"

Yes, I do. The personal qualities required to stretch to love come later in life to many of us. Even if those qualities are developed, the bitter history between two people can leave a residue of mistrust or rage too daunting to overcome. It can be better, easier, to begin fresh, bringing what you've learned, but without the wounds you got from learning it.

I agree, too, that we sometimes marry the "wrong" person, by which I mean someone who poses too great a challenge to our capacity to love. Some people are so much easier for us to love than others. Sometimes the reasons for a compelling attraction or a chronic conflict are mysterious, reflecting needs and patterns outside our conscious awareness. Often a person is easier to love because he overlaps with us in more places, shares common life principles, enjoys similar pastimes, envisions a similar family. The more we overlap, the less likely we are to struggle with our differences.

There is nothing inherently wrong with differences between two people. In fact, they are inevitable. But if the gap is wide, the battle to close it will be more fierce than it will for couples with more overlap. When the battle to accommodate is savage, so are that battle's emotional side effects, which threaten to drown love.

The more important question is, *what do you do when you recognize the problems that make you think of a relationship as a mistake?* You have three choices:

• Leave, and begin to get to love again, drawing a straighter course because of what you've learned from this experience.

• Stay, because you must, or because you decide to, or because it's not perfect but you believe it beats the alternatives. Whatever the reason, you might choose to stay and do everything possible to awaken your loving spirit. "Love him more" is not easy for you, but it is a real emotional goal.

• Stay, and stay mad. Stay, and stay hurt. Stay, but love him less and less, as you are overwhelmed with all these easier, more powerful feelings. Stay, and resign both of you to a buffet of unhappiness.

Too many of us take this third alternative. We choose it in part because it is often, ironically, the easiest road. It requires no effort, no inner push, no outer move. We wake up angry, pained, or frightened, and we go to bed the same way. We believe that he is the cause of our pain, and we stay helpless in its grip because every other option lives outside the picture we have of ourselves.

We stay, believing in family, devoted to our children, trapped in our financial limitations, overwhelmed by the thought of being single in a world so patently unkind to single women, so we stay. Often while we stay we still believe in love, still hope to get him to love us, to listen, to pay a compliment, or pay a bill. We stay, enduring, feeling that we give more than we get and trying to make peace with it, focused not so much on loving him as on enduring him.

We stay and we think about other men, or we stay and we make love to another man and feel torn and sexually alive again, anxious about how calm we are and in love and upheaval, too. Still, very likely, we stay and bear and then maybe he leaves first, for the bitterest of reasons—for another woman, who sees him in a way we have not or will not, because we stayed.

Again, knowing the answer is easy and living the answer is not. If you are going to stay, do so with a loving spirit. Find it within yourself. Rock the boat. Push your limits. Push his, too. Challenge yourself. Stay without cheating yourself of love. If you cannot dredge up even a shadow of that spirit, leave. The third alternative—stay, and stay absent love—is a path to a sad, empty place. Don't call that place home.

"I don't want to give him up. But he did this thing that I've always thought of as unforgivable. Doesn't this mean I should let go?" Like our fantasies of love, our rules of conduct are so clear in the abstract. Observe a friend and you know that you would never allow a man to order you around the way her husband does. Recall your parents' marriage and vow never to accept the passive withdrawal your dad got away with.

We all hold these rules with devout certainty, unless one day we find ourselves in the precise situation we knew how to handle until we were in it. From this vantage point, *should* is very little help.

Unless you are in one of the extreme situations already described, define your limits according to what is within your capacity to love or tolerate. It doesn't matter whether you *should* forgive selfishness or infidelity, put up with a possessive lover, or lavish love on a cold one. It only matters whether you *can* do these things, and what it will cost you to love him more, with these burdens.

Remember, you do not have to limit the love you feel in order to even things out; nor do you have to restrict your own capacity to love in order to avoid exploitation. By loving more but setting firm limits on what you will ignore or endure in the name of that love, you will find your way to the middle. It is a middle we achieve with someone else by finding it first within ourselves.

As you venture to find your own middle ground, think of my friend Marta. Marta is—well—maybe not seriously obese, but definitely not thin. She loved a man who returned her feelings but worried that he might shut down sexually, because Marta's body was so far from his romantic ideal. Marta could have easily assumed a take-it-or-leave-it, who-the-hell-are-you attitude. Many of us would. Or she might have gone the other way, acknowledging that she, too, thought she was too fat or too floppy and vowing to improve. Many of us choose this route also.

Marta chose neither option. She did not take offense. She did not promise to diet. Instead, she sympathized with his dilemma. "Adam," she'd say, "I know how hard it must be to envision a lifetime of making love to a body that doesn't match what you were jerking off to as a kid. But here you are, and you love me. Sex will be incredible once you get over the shock of my not being what you were taught to turn on to. Believe me, I understand. After all, I didn't dream I'd love a picky little bald guy, either. Think of it as a surprise ending." Marta has found her way to the middle of love.

The Middle of Love

We are closing in on the fulcrum of the seesaw. What will it look like if you are able to make this shift towards loving more and needing less? How will you be different? What will you actually do, and how will you do it? Most important, how will it feel?

Loving more is, first and foremost, an inner difference. The actions you might take as a result of this difference are quite varied. There are no special rules for your behavior, no musts or nevers to which you always adhere, in order to proceed properly along the path.

In one situation, loving more may mean that you give in where before you wouldn't have. In another, you might stand your ground more firmly, but less harshly. And, like needing less, sometimes loving more is something of which only *you* are aware. You do exactly what you've always done, but your actions come from a different place within you.

Sometimes that can be as simple as not rising to the old familiar bait.

He says: "What do you mean, you'll just throw on a pair of pants? How could you go to dinner without a shower?"

Usually when she hears one of his critical digs, she snaps back in kind. "The same way you can go without hair," she might say. Or, less inspired, "Don't tell me what to do." At the very least, his remarks receive a furious look and fifteen minutes of daggered silence.

When she needs his approval less, she can step back a bit and hear his criticism as an expression of his own cranky tension, rather than as a reflection on her. He can invite her into their dance, but she doesn't have to RSVP.

"How could you go to dinner without taking a shower?" he says.

"Don't worry, darling," she says, laughing, "smelly is sexy."

Remember, change how you take it. You have the power to respond differently.

Still, you may be thinking, his remark was obnoxious. No, she shouldn't have to put up with that constantly. Sometimes loving him more means clear, firm, angry confrontation:

"How could you go to dinner without taking a shower?"

"Michael, ordinarily I love your criticism, but I don't have room on my plate today. Save it for me, O.K.?" Or even, "Michael, STOP." She may even make this clear statement in public, if that is the frequent site of his attacks.

But that's it. Make the remark and move on. No long discussion of the problem, no lingering sulks or grudges. Just a simple statement of terms. He will probably have to make at least one more remark, an under-the-breath grumble or an open complaint. When you have moved to the middle of love, you can ignore that one. You know that, when you give anyone a direct rebuff, he or she needs to yell "ouch," in one form or another. The middle leaves room for his last "ouch," just as it left room for her firm limit.

Sometimes loving men more means keeping your sense of humor when it is so much easier to take offense. I thought Rebecca presented a fine example of this:

"I was wearing a tank top, sitting in an armchair with my arm stretched out across the back. He walked over and gave the flattened underpart of my arm a little squeeze. 'Looks like you're getting the beginning of Hadassah arm,' he said. 'Better keep an eye on it.' How dare he! I had an instant impulse to sock him, when suddenly I heard the whole thing inside out and it struck me funny. Poor Cal—he was having perfection panic. So I tortured him with his secret fear. 'Cal, that is all a part of my plot to trap you into marriage. Do not trust this great body I am walking around in. The instant I have you hooked, I will gain forty pounds, just so you can spend the rest of your life stuck with a fat wife. How did you see through me so fast?' "

Consider Phyllis and Susan: Phyllis is two hours late and does not call to offer any reassurance, though she knows that Susan can't help envisioning car crashes and other catastrophes if Phyllis is even twenty minutes overdue. By the time Phyllis gets home, Susan is furious, because she has been made to suffer so much unnecessary anxiety.

The two sit down for a long talk. Phyllis apologizes to Susan and gives her a fair chance to vent her anger. Phyllis then goes on to explain that, though she doesn't want to cause Susan to suffer, neither does she want to be a prisoner to Susan's anxiety. She doesn't want to be on such a tight rein, or have to report her every move. Phyllis resents feeling that if she goes to a movie with a friend (as was the case this evening) she must walk out in the middle of the picture and hunt up a phone—or else. Isn't there some way they could work things out so that Phyllis felt freer, without Susan's feeling so anxious? They discuss possible solutions until bedtime.

The talk is very satisfying to Phyllis. She has finally been able to present her point of view without feeling as if she has run smack to Susan's defenses. ("All I want is one phone call. What is such a big deal about that?") Happy with the idea that they might actually make progress on this old familiar fight, Phyllis reaches up to turn out the light, saying softly, "Good night. I love you."

To which Susan responds in the long-suffering tone Phyllis knows and detests, "Whatever 'I love you' is supposed to mean."

Ordinarily, this would be Phyllis' signal to explode with frustration. "Whatever that's supposed to mean," she would mimic, understanding that Susan was implying her old "What good is 'I love you' if you still do things that hurt me?" An hourlong talk about their relationship, and in the end Susan goes right back to her "If you don't do what I want, you must not love me" theme song! What is the point? Typically, Phyllis would respond furiously, and the fight they had both been trying to avoid would be upon them.

But Phyllis has been struggling to stay in the middle of love, to stay loving instead of giving up in frustration. She sees that they are both oversensitive on issues of time and control and freedom, each for reasons of her own. This perspective allows Phyllis to respond differently. Instead of hearing "Whatever 'I love you' is supposed to mean" as a frustrating complaint, Phyllis takes it as a real question.

"I guess 'I love you' means that you stay with me, even though I sometimes do things that make you angry," she said, "and it's what keeps me with you, even though, when you're angry, you say things that hurt me."

. . . .

The middle of love can also mean seeing a problem or having a concern and doing nothing at all. Loving more may help you to understand that you are not necessarily losing ground if you choose not to fight. Needing less can give you the emotional strength and the maturity necessary *not* to confront what bothers you. Naomi was able to do that recently, with an interesting result:

"I went away for a five-day conference, and Andrew didn't call once. He seemed fine about the idea of my going, and when I called him in the middle of the week as we planned, he sounded the same as always. But still—we've been together six months. I thought this was a little early to be able to let me go so easily. It gnawed at me the whole time I was gone.

"Normally, I'd be telling him how I'd felt on the ride home from the airport, because I would just be too anxious to hold it in. This time, though, I decided to handle it myself. It wasn't like the old 'ooh, don't let him know it bothered you or else he'll think you care' stuff. I care and he knows it. I thought he cared, too.

"It was just that I thought that my anxiety was my business, and I didn't necessarily have to dump it on him. I'd be better off trying to think about it a little. I wanted to give myself a chance to figure out if this was a simple insecurity hot flash, or if I was intuiting something important.

"By the time we were back together a day, I had decided that it was my own anxiety that had caused me to suffer. I was feeling much better, and then a funny thing happened. A few days after the trip, Andrew asked, kind of casually, about the conference. He brought up the director a lot, and finally asked me straight out, 'So . . . I heard he was pretty attractive. What did you think?'

"Naturally, it had not occurred to me that he might have been feeling anxious, just like me. I never would have known, either, if I had had my usual emotional purge the moment I saw him. It made me wonder how many times I've gushed out my own fears and saved a man from risking his."

. . . .

Each of these is an example of how one might act differently in the new middle of love, depending upon the circumstances, one's own style and sensitivities, and the moment in the relationship. The common thread to these and all the other new options for responding is this: **Whatever you do outwardly, inside yourself you stay closer to a feeling of love.**

Loving eyes might help you hear a remark differently. Or, however you understand the remark, you might respond differently because you are looking with love. Whatever you do, you won't have to feel as hurt or angry when you do it. When you need less, you can step back a little.

That step back makes you less of a target and more of a decision-maker. Instead of being instantly reactive, you are a person with power, responding to a problem. Loving more means that, whatever you choose to do, you do it in the direction of love—not necessarily to cut him some kind of break, but because love is where you have decided *you* want to be.

Whatever your specific changes of behavior, the middle of love has an underlying unity. You have new options in what you might do, because you have made a fundamental change in what you are able to feel. That change is akin to the shifting of the great plates of the earth. They may only move inches, but those inches are an earthquake. That small, powerful change in what you usually feel was made possible by pushing yourself to see from a fresh perspective—even though you may be looking at the same old thing.

Taken as a whole, the result of loving more and needing less is love at a higher level. It cannot be measured, but it certainly can and has been experienced. Women describe themselves as feeling calmer—"more rooted to myself," as one woman put it. Some talk about a feeling of freedom, others about a sense of relaxation. Some find it easier to love more or need less through a period of crisis. Others regress then. The changes are subtle and not necessarily uniform. Listen for yourself:

"Something feels different to me. It's like I see a light flickering inside. My outside life is not perfect—actually, it's not all that different. But I feel so different about it, because I take things differently. If my umbrella breaks in the rain and the phone man doesn't show up, I don't get hooked into thinking, 'Why is this happening to me?'

"Even better, when my boyfriend shows up and then spends an hour on the phone with his office, I don't feel like that has to do with me, either. If I think he's being rude, I tell him. If I'm busy doing something else, that's fine, too. But his preoccupation with work no longer hurts me the way it did, because I see it so differently. It's not about how he feels about me. It's about how he feels about work or himself. I couldn't see that before."

"The first two years we were married, I was hurt so often, angry so much. Gary was not mean, never mean—just not . . . not romantic, I guess. Not sweet, you know? No little notes under my pillow, no surprise treats if I had a bad week, none of that 'Here, dear, I picked up the movie you wanted to rent.' No . . . well . . . no nothing like that at all. I would tell him and tell him, and I swear he had no idea what I was talking about. The transformation I had to do was on me. I had to accept, and thank God I could accept, this one thing no one told me about: He doesn't love me the way I want to be loved. But he loves me the best way he knows how. What else is there?"

"The ugly fights stopped, they just stopped, when I stopped having to fight back. Not fighting back didn't mean that I started to give in much. That's still hard for me. But I stopped needing to prove that whatever I was doing was the right thing or the best thing. Now I can pick a restaurant, and if he doesn't like it I don't get my feelings hurt, or start complaining about how it's a great place and he's impossible to please. I just pick a restaurant if it's my turn to pick, and we eat. Whether he likes it or approves of my choice or even of me is his own business. One day I saw the whole thing flat out. He is *difficult to please. I don't think he wants to be, but that's how he is. But that's his problem. The point is, where is it written that I have to try to please him? That's the problem I've been working on. I started to see that I could love him, even if he's hard to get a stamp of approval from. And he loves me, totally apart from the fact that he is picky about most of life."*

"When someone is fixing me up—say, with a guy who's divorced and has custody of his kids—I now actually like the idea that I'm going to meet someone who is not perfect. Always before, I was trying so hard to be perfect myself that I thought I was at least entitled to a man at the same level. Now I'm more relaxed about just presenting who I am, instead of forcing myself to be the best thing ever. I'm open to more of a man, less of an image. You have no idea how many phone calls I used to not even bother to return, because, once I spotted the flaw, I moved on."

"Something's changed for me. I believe in myself more. I'm not so quick to think I'm bad. It's not all about me. When he starts yelling at me, because I got another parking ticket, or I forgot to write down two checks I cashed, it doesn't hurt me so much. I don't like it, but mentally I . . . I go to another spot. I remove myself. Then I think about what I might do to help him ease up inside."

"I think I was always frightened of men, although I didn't realize it for a long time. Not frightened of violence or that kind of thing. I was frightened of the power a man had over my happiness. I never went for the men everybody else would want. I was safer with the oddballs.

"Gradually, that huge shadow lifted. I wish I could tell you how, but I know it's not that the men changed. So I guess I did. The more I worked, the safer and happier I felt in my life, the more willing I

*became to see the person behind the man. I guess I started to feel
stronger, too, less anxious for each new man to decide on me and
more like I knew I was O.K and he was probably O.K., too, and we
could take it from there.*

*"One night, as my then boyfriend and I were drifting off to
sleep, my little dog jumped up and threw up on the covers. We both
heard him, we both rolled towards each other and exchanged a
glance. Then we both rolled back over and continued on to sleep. It's
six years later and we are still together and, I think, still happy together too. The King is dead, long live the King."*

These women have experienced men, love, and themselves in a very
different light. Whatever they may say about how or why or what
occurred, I can assure you of one thing—none of them would say
they expected the change to be easy.

In fact, though they are very different women, worlds apart in
situation, each in her own way said the same thing when she first
considered the possibility of a new path to love: Love him more?
Need him less? *I can't!*

Joan

In the seven months after Mark lost his job, Joan tumbled from perfect wife to perfect bitch at an Olympic pace. She held Mark responsible for this ugly transformation.

True, it wasn't her husband's fault that he was laid off. But he'd had months of corporate hinting that layoffs were coming. Had Joan been in a similar position, she would have prepared for the possibility of disaster. Mark, on the other hand, was someone who hoped for the best and faced the worst when it was upon him. Usually, Joan appreciated Mark's relaxed optimism. This time, however, his reluctance to face the possibility of a problem left him suddenly without a job, or even a career path.

Joan's anger grew in exact proportion to the difference between how Mark handled his job problem and how Joan thought it should be handled. Suspending her own fears because there didn't seem a tactful way to mention them, Joan tried to point Mark in a productive direction. She hunted up career-development programs and résumé guides. Mark would thank her profusely and let them pile up by the bed. She suggested contacts that he failed to follow up on, vocational manuals he never read. Joan kept mentioning that finding work was a full-time job, and Mark kept agreeing, while working out new chords on his old guitar.

As the wedding money ran out and they were relying more and more on Joan's earnings, the tensions between them grew. Joan became a nagging mother, alternately reminding him of phone calls he had yet to return, and scolding him about leads he had not yet pursued. Mark responded by either defending himself ("I did call once, you know. How many hundreds of times do you want me to call back?") or diminishing himself ("I hate myself for taking money from you," he said repeatedly, which made Joan feel worse, because she hated him for it, too, though she tried not to show it).

Their sex life slowly evaporated, replaced by Joan's agitation and Mark's vague depression. The more Mark withdrew, the more Joan pursued, trying every tactic to assist, mobilize, or otherwise motivate the frog she'd been sleeping with to transform himself back into the man she had married.

Joan was prepared to be financially responsible for her own life. But in no way was she comfortable with the idea of supporting a husband. She felt her anger and her concern were perfectly justified. ("Wouldn't you hate it, too?" she inquired of her friends. They agreed that, yes, they'd hate it.)

At the same time, Joan knew that months of critical carping were not exactly a great foundation for a new marriage. She loved her husband, was baffled by his sudden unraveling, and very much wished her marriage to succeed.

So Joan came to see me, seeking advice. She wanted a professional opinion as to what might be wrong with Mark. Was he just lazy or spoiled? Just too scared to go out there and face a hard job market? Or was it something more serious, some kind of depression or deep insecurity?

Joan also wanted to know if there was something wrong with her. Was she secretly drawn to weak men? Was she somehow making Mark worse? If he loved her more, would he try harder? How could she determine where to draw the line? When do you give up on a man? When are you a fool for sticking by him?

Finally, Joan loved Mark, but she could not live like this. She believed that what she needed was reasonable, and Mark agreed. Yet he had done nothing. HELP! What could she do to get Mark to change?

Nothing.

Nothing? Nothing at all? The most important issue in her life, and she should do nothing?

Well, not exactly, I said. It just seemed to me that Joan had already tried every known strategy, from support to confrontation and back again. Frankly, I couldn't think of a thing she'd missed. There was nothing more to do for Mark.

"Well, what am I supposed to do now?" she asked. "I don't know," I responded. "Do you have to do anything?"

Joan explained to me that she did, in fact, have to do something. The situation was intolerable, because it was both frustrating and scary. She didn't think her expectations of having an employed husband were out of line. Did I?

No, not particularly. I think most of us expect our husbands to remain employed for most of their lives. Still, the fact that it's reasonable to expect something doesn't always mean that it will occur, or that you can make it happen. *And it doesn't mean there is only one way to react to that disappointment.*

Then I made a suggestion to her. Instead of focusing on Mark, on whether he was too insecure to look for work or simply too lazy, I suggested we refocus on Joan.

The very suggestion made her protest. She'd married a man with a serious problem; that was no reason for her to have to review her own toilet training. I quite agreed with the toilet-training part, but I thought that she'd come to see me because she had a problem. She'd done everything she could to help Mark with his problem. Why didn't we discuss how Joan could help herself?

Joan began to cry. Just under her anger and frustration was Joan's own self-doubt. Wouldn't a sharper woman have seen this absence of ambition in Mark? Had she just been desperate to marry and therefore overlooked the obvious? It was so unfair. She had never imagined herself divorced, a failure, starting all over again. But she didn't see a lifetime supporting The Blob, either.

She went deeper. If he ever did get a job, how could he love her again? She'd been so mean. She'd tried to be supportive, but these nasty remarks came out of her mouth before she could bite them back. She wanted to be sympathetic, but what she actually felt was resentment. "Like, I bought him a gym membership, because I thought exercise would help him feel better about himself. Every morning, when I know he's enjoying the gym and I'm at my office, I just hate him."

In our first meeting together, Joan had spun out the questions on which we all overfocus when a man we love fails to give us what we need: What's wrong with him? What's wrong with me? What can I do to get him to change?

This brings us exactly to the point Joan and I had reached in our conversation. The answers to the these three questions are usually pretty straightforward.

What's wrong with him? I don't know. I've never even met him. ("I'll bring him in. You can tell me then," Joan said.) He may not even know what's wrong himself. Frequently, though probably not in Joan and Mark's case, the man under this microscopic female examination does not consider that he has a problem at all.

Joan's own speculations as to the cause of Mark's paralysis ("He has no confidence. He's waiting for someone to rescue him, as usual") were probably pretty accurate, if only because she'd put in so much time and careful observation. The problem was that, however accurate Joan's analysis, the answer didn't necessarily change Mark. Analysis of a problem could help Joan to reframe Mark's problem, and that could help her be less angry with him and with herself. Without these emotional clouds, Joan would be able to see her options more clearly and to proceed more deliberately. But no analysis of Mark could change him. Only Mark could do that.

What's wrong with me? Probably nothing. At least nothing outside the ordinary maturation process. Joan had a very clear vision of how things should be. Now she was dealing with how things were. It can be quite a shock.

She was angry because her new husband had let her down in a way she hadn't expected, wasn't prepared for, and didn't think she deserved. Perhaps she wasn't handling that anger in the best of all possible ways, and that might be making bad things worse. On the other hand, who amongst us does handle anger well? Sometimes I think there are only varying degrees of handling it poorly.

Joan was frightened because she'd done what she could to make the situation better and it hadn't worked. That's scary. She didn't want to leave a man she loved, she didn't want to live with a man she didn't respect, and she was just discovering that these could be, and often are, the very same men.

In the past when a man had deeply disappointed Joan, she had taken it as evidence that he wasn't "the right one" and moved on. That wasn't always easy, but when he wouldn't change, she didn't know what else to do. Moving on was a tougher solution now that she was married.

Yet Joan had no clear picture of how love and serious personality problems could coexist; no clear standards of what it was O.K. for her to "put up with" and what was too much. After all, she had known herself to turn down a date with a man just because he talked through his nose. How could that same woman stay married to a man who was unemployed?

What can I do to get him to change? "Wouldn't seeing a therapist help? I'd even be willing to come with him if it makes it easier for him," Joan asked. (Translation: "I've done my best and I can't seem to fix him. I don't want to live with him as he is. It's time to call in a professional.")

I was very sympathetic to Joan's plight, so I hated to deliver the bad news: yes, seeing a therapist might help him to mobilize, but not if he went just to get Joan off his back.

Psychotherapy is a process of self-examination. No one could force Mark on that journey—no one. But all kinds of lovers and mothers and judges and bosses can pressure a man (or woman) to show up in a therapist's office. When I meet the person who has dutifully appeared under those circumstances, I am not a psychotherapist. I am the junior-high-school principal and he is the bad boy sent to my office for breaking Rule Number 1 (Good Men Work). None of us goes to see the principal for self-examination. We go because we have to.

Joan's dilemma—each of our dilemmas, when we are suffering because we need him to change so that we can be happy—is this: No matter what she does, not matter how right or justified she is, she can't make Mark different. Now what?

First, respond differently.

Joan needed to drop her struggle with Mark. Having tried everything she could think of to help Mark find work, Joan now must let his problem go completely. No more asking him who called or what he did today. No more passing on articles of interest or generating lists of things he should do. If there was something Mark chose to discuss with her, of course she would be available to talk with him. Otherwise, the problem of finding Mark a job was entirely on Mark.

This was so much easier said than done that Joan began referring to the part of herself that could not be restrained from nagging as "the rottweiler": "The rottweiler got off her leash this week," she would report, explaining how she had found herself restructuring Mark's résumé to suit a job she thought was a possibility, though Mark had shown little interest.

Responding differently requires a constant self-monitoring. Otherwise, habit and anxiety drive us back into the cycle of suggesting, nudging, and nagging in an effort to get a partner to do what we need him to do. It was pure inner battle for Joan to see something Mark should do, yet not allow herself to remind him to do it or ask if he'd done it. The battle, she discovered, was waged against her own anxiety. She felt driven to tell him, to remind him, to check on him, though she knew this was self-defeating.

Eventually, Joan discovered that the only way she could resist her own anxious need to take charge of Mark's bad situation was to distance herself from it entirely. She forced herself to know as little as possible about what was going on. If a business letter was lying on the kitchen counter, she did not read it. If Mark asked her for advice, she tried to be helpful without taking charge of whatever he needed done.

Joan turned her attention to other things she and Mark had in common ("Hey," she reminded herself, "we must have talked about something else before he lost his job.") By deliberately distancing herself, by connecting with Mark in other ways, and by resisting Mark's conscious or unconscious invitations to rejoin him in the nag dance, Joan was able slowly to learn to respond to Mark differently. As she began to act differently, Joan began to be able to think and feel differently.

Second, reframe.

Reframing was difficult for Joan. Initially it was impossible for her to think of Mark's repeated failure to act in any way that would soften her anger or make his behavior more tolerable to her. Slowly, though, as she developed a more thorough understanding of herself and her own underlying emotional issues, Joan began to build new ground from which she could regard Mark more calmly.

"We really are two separate people," she said one day, suddenly aware of something that she had known all along, but now knew in a deeper way. "He isn't doing this to me. He is in his own struggle. It affects me, but it's not about me." This new vantage point freed Joan from the great bulk of her outrage. She was still very sad— bitterly disappointed to find that Mark had an emotional burden for which she had been unprepared, and pained for Mark himself, because his inner battle was so hard, and because it seemed that it might defeat him.

Joan's new point of view allowed her to begin to forgive Mark for all the ways in which his difficulties had hurt her. Forgiving did not mean that whatever Mark did was O.K. It was not O.K., and for Joan it never would be. Forgiving simply meant that Joan had been angry long enough. She found a greater strength by looking at Mark in a way that allowed her to let go of the heavy weight of her anger and go on with her life.

Third, refocus.

"What is it about Mark's apathy and unemployment that is a problem for you?" I asked Joan. The answer to this question seemed so obvious to Joan that she hardly knew where to begin. We got stuck for a while on "Wouldn't this bother you?" or "Everyone else says it would bother them, too." That might well be so, I pointed out, but each of us would be troubled for her own individual reasons. Joan began to struggle with the question, trying to understand the roots of her own tremendous discomfort with Mark's behavior.

She was angry for all the obvious reasons—resentment at being forced to carry an unfair share of the economic load; frustration because Mark could find a job if he looked hard enough; embarrassment because her family and all her friends knew Mark was out of work. (Just last year, she had been the star bride. Now she was the woman married to the loser.)

Finally, Joan was angry because she was afraid. Mark's inability to mobilize was posing a real threat to her. She might have to face the choice between supporting him and leaving him. Though it was easy to threaten to leave, it was far more wrenching to carry it out. The more afraid Joan was, the more she pushed on Mark. The harder Joan pushed, the more resistance she encountered from Mark and the angrier she got.

I suggested to Joan that she interrupt this cycle by focusing on the fears that fueled her anger. Not that her own fear was the sole source of Joan's anger. Mark's behavior was a major source of that anger. Joan needed to focus on her own fears, simply because they were the only source of her anger that she could control.

We focused on Joan's fears of failure, shame, and loneliness. Joan clarified her hazy but powerful vision of the life she had believed she would live—an image of home and family, and a set of expectations for the husband in that picture. She spoke about how uncomfortable she was when she could not fit Mark into this image. We spoke of Joan's financial opportunities and about her fears of supporting a family on her own. Joan identified the people in her life who would most disapprove of such an arrangement and examined her fear of disappointing them.

She took a look at what it would cost her emotionally if she supported Mark, and what it would cost her if she left him. Each of these questions had the same aim: *to help Joan realize that, whichever direction she chose, she was strong enough to absorb the cost.*

To be able to appreciate this strength, Joan had first to grieve for the loss of her fantasy that love and happiness would come to her with no cost at all. She had to wrestle with the injustice that other women she knew, women who were, perhaps, less deserving than she, seemed to have far easier choices.

In the end, Joan had to come to terms with the loss of a piece of herself—the protected, grandiose, invulnerable piece that believed nothing really bad could happen because she was a good person. Either way, stay or go, Joan had to mourn the loss of her image of a special life, an unscarred, storybook life. Now she would have only a life.

Just like the rest of us.

We went over that same ground repeatedly, until Joan found these revelations less of a shock and more of a reality. Gradually, as this way of thinking became more familiar, Joan turned a corner. She could see that, even without these sustaining illusions, she could have good days, great laughs, and a feeling of possibility. She saw that just a life could be more than enough.

Joan's renewed feelings of possibility came largely from her work. As part of refocusing, she faced her own fears of risk and achievement, which she'd been able to ignore as long as she focused on Mark's. Joan saw that, though she considered herself a professional success, she had avoided being economically ambitious. She realized that there were ways in which she, too, resisted doing what needed to be done to advance her career, which took an edge off her anger at Mark. Mark felt the difference, and he relaxed more around Joan. Some of Joan's good moments were with him.

I'd like to tell you that they lived happily ever after, that Mark became more and more active in his job hunt as Joan became less and less involved. I can tell you that I have seen that outcome a hundred times: a woman stops smoking only after her girlfriend utterly abandons the campaign to get her to quit; the extravagant husband becomes more responsible only when his conservative wife gives over full control of the bills and the checkbook and allows him to struggle with the consequences; the uncommitted lover steps forward with a ring just as his would-be mate begins to feel she is better off without him.

Things did not unfold this way for Joan and Mark. Joan did back away from Mark's problem and become more focused on her own issues. Yet, though the tension between them slowly receded, making day-to-day life more tolerable, Mark did not take any steps towards a professional recovery. In fact, he did less and less, abandoning the gym, the telephone, and any pretense of looking for work. As far as Joan could determine, he seemed to spend his days watching television. Their time together was not unpleasant, but she sensed it was increasingly temporary.

Eventually, Mark's parents grew concerned and suggested he come home for a visit. He did, and over time it became clear that he was not coming back. Joan grieved, of course, and felt frustrated, angry, relieved, and confused, as anyone would. But because of all the time she had invested in strengthening herself, none of these feelings was at a devastating pitch.

Even if Joan was not happy about being single again, she was not as frightened of it as she had been. She was very disappointed in Mark, and shaken by the fact that, if *he'd* changed in such an unexpected way, so could anyone. But she could balance this newly harsh view of love with a more realistic appreciation of her own strengths. She didn't have to be intimidated by strong men, because she was strong, too. And she no longer required a perfect man, because she'd reckoned with her own weaknesses.

What Joan did want, still, was a man to love and to be loved by. Many women would have seen their experience with Mark as evidence that men are damaged, or untrustworthy. A woman as angry at the end of the relationship as Joan was when we first met would have been stuck with that anger for a long time, carrying it forward into every encounter with a new man. A woman as frightened as Joan had been might have retreated into the super-safe world of friends and family, avoiding for a long time any other relationship and its potential for loss; or fear might have driven her in the opposite direction, hunting for a new man so hungrily that only the neediest men would make themselves available to her.

Joan was saddled with none of these emotional burdens. She was able to find men to love, and men interested in loving her. To her rather surprised delight, she found them frequently, and regularly. Eventually, she came to know one of them intimately.

Would you call that a happy ending?

....

CHAPTER SIX

To Eros Human, To Forgive Divine

"It's four o'clock on Sunday, and he's been in bed all day because he's not feeling well. That means he's now about six years old and he wants me by his side, making clucking sounds and waiting on him. I'm not great at mothery stuff, but I've been doing my best, because he really has had a god-awful week, and he does have some fever and what the hell, why not?

"By four o'clock, though, I've had it. So I tell him I have to run an errand. He says fine. Then he tells me, 'You know, I just have a taste for a little bowl of ice cream—say, a small scoop of strawberry, a small scoop of rum raisin, and maybe sprinkled with a little bran?' That's fine, I say. Does he want it now, or later? 'Later,' he says. 'I need to nap now.'

I go off for about an hour to restore my sanity. Then I come home, get the strawberry, the rum raisin, the bran, the tray, and the napkin together, put a smile on my face, and deliver it to him. He takes one look at it and actually slams his fist onto the bed. He starts to scream, 'I said a little bit! I wanted a little! That's not a little! You never listen to me! I always tell you, you never listen to a thing I say.'

"And you really think that I should learn to love him more?"

T̲he theory is to move further down the path to love without sacrificing yourself in the process. The reality is that it is sometimes all you can do to keep yourself from killing him.

This little irony results from the fact that our path is seeded with land mines.

At any time, your progress towards love with be blocked by:
- **Anger,** and the pleasure we take in holding on to it
- **Anxiety,** and our powerful desire to avoid it
- **Fantasy** in its every form, which makes both anger and anxiety thrive

Each of these elements acts as an internal barrier both to loving more and needing less. If you think of getting to love as going through a gate, then anger and anxiety are the dragons guarding that gate, while fantasy shrinks the gate itself to the size of the eye of a needle. Each element makes passage through that gate as difficult as possible. But the good news is that each of these barriers can potentially be controlled by you.

The distinctions between these three elements are arbitrary. Every disappointed fantasy, every unmet social standard stirs both a degree of angry rejection and a shrinking embarrassment. *If he loved me, wouldn't he . . . ? Shouldn't he . . . ? Why can't he . . . ? How could he . . . ?* For the sake of clarity, I have separated the elements of fantasy, anger, and anxiety. In real life, however, they are the clot that blocks our passage.

This chapter focuses specifically on those two internal dragons— anger and anxiety—which warn us away from love. We have referred to both of these internal states repeatedly in previous chapters, and discussed various techniques by which they might be overcome. Here our focus is on women's most common angry/ anxious objections to loving more or needing less, *and on our unconscious resistance to overcoming these objections.*

Anger and anxiety are not simply powerful feelings that drown out love, or fearful punishments that must be endured in order to get to love. The experience of anger and the avoidance of anxiety each has its own rewards, which must be sacrificed in order to get to love. Very often that sacrifice does not feel worth the trade.

In a way, anger and anxiety are the conscious experience of those subterranean gods of separation and attachment. Anger and anxiety are, in effect, tantrums thrown by each of these inner urges when it is thwarted.

Anger is largely the fury of your urge to be separate—whole, satisfied, and uncompromising. It stamps around in your mind, shouting things like, "Why should I have to put up with this?," and "Love him more! He doesn't deserve what he gets now."

Anxiety, on the other hand, is the awful fear whispered by your urge to be connected. "Don't make him mad," it cautions, "he'll leave." "Don't show your feelings. You'll frighten him away." "Don't be too strong. But don't be too needy. In fact, don't be anything you think he may not want." Anxiety squeezes us from both ends, restricting us to a very narrow path.

Our own anxiety enrages us, just as our own anger makes us fearful. We try to escape them both in the world of fantasy—where true love magically ensures harmony and eliminates both risk and the fear that rides in with it. The cotton candy of romantic fantasy is a wonderful temporary retreat. But in reality, the dragons of anger and anxiety are always guarding the gate. You have to go past them to move into the world of real-life love.

You may think, at first, "I can't! They are feelings too overwhelming to face down, too fierce to ignore." You may even tell yourself that you shouldn't try to bypass those dragons, preferring to believe that your fear and anger protect you rather than stand in your way.

Some of us cherish our anger and defer to our own anxiety, as if each is signaling some important warning. We believe them when they say, "Danger! Do not love here!" or "Danger! Do not risk here!" Pay close attention to your reaction to these signals. The more you heed the warnings signaled by your anger and your fear, the more angry and fearful you'll remain.

Instead, "Keep your eyes on the prize." You are on the path to love. Of course you can slay the dragons in your path. They are you—a part of you, at least. They are your fears and wounds, but they do not have to be the boundaries of your emotional life. As we've mentioned, it will feel as if your anger and anxiety come and go of their own accord, provoked by something outside yourself. Very often, though, you've unwittingly or self-protectively invited them—by where you choose to focus your attention, by whom you seek to please, by what you deliberately allow yourself to avoid or to seek out.

We remind ourselves of our emotional sore spots in the same way that a tongue keeps returning to a sore tooth—by habit, rewarded by the strangely pleasing presence of a familiar pain. We could, just as deliberately, remind ourselves to focus elsewhere or to look through kinder lenses. We could allow ourselves more room to act out of love, and restrict our freedom to act out of anger. We could choose to face up to our fears, instead of allowing those fears to limit our actions.

The prize is love. Claim it, don't wait for it. You may think you can't, but you can—if you will.

I Can't!

My husband and I have a chunk-light versus chunk-white tuna disagreement, which has caused me to sabotage his shopping cart for years. I would like to tell you that this was all in the spirit of marital playfulness. And sometimes it is. Sometimes, though, I view his attachment to what is obviously the lesser tuna as evidence of his lack of taste and sensitivity—two flaws that make him unworthy of me. On those occasions, a can of his tuna in the cabinet can trigger my complete contempt. The love we envision is grand. It is always a shock to realize how easily a small annoyance can dam the flow.

You may have larger wounds to overcome, too: the deep gulf since his affair, where you punish him by staying, though it punishes you as well; the way he bullies you until he gets his way, then refuses to admit he's a bully; the demeaning remarks about the size of your diaphragm or your breasts, remarks for which he refuses to apologize because they were "jokes"; or the way your image of him was forever altered when he cheated his business partner, or turned his back on his sister.

In essence, we fall in love by merging into each other, sliding electrically through each other's boundaries into a harmony that can only be love. This blissful merger doesn't last, nor was it intended to last. Falling in love was meant to be an inspiration, not an end point. Think of it as God's way of giving you a taste of what the reward could be for stretching yourself to love him more, even though it's easier to be angry, or for steeling yourself to need him less, even though you are afraid.

Falling in love is a much-sought first step on the path to love. Part passion, part symbiosis, it is the too-brief instant fusion that puts you both temporarily beyond the abrasions of conflict or the disappointment of a failed expectation. That merger is bliss. Then we come to the next step, the natural pulling apart, the re-establishment of our separate selves. We go about the business of finding a way to make room for both of us inside this love.

This sounds reasonable enough, although in fact it can be anything but reasonable in real life. Finding room can provoke strain and worry and confusion. It sometimes requires pure aggression and sometimes extraordinary self-sacrifice. Living through the accommodations of love means constantly envisioning how love will be and then, over and over, revising your vision.

This next step past merger, the step after falling in love and towards loving, is unavoidable and difficult. Once inside a relationship, we chafe against each other, rubbing away the presentable façade, leaving us face-to-face and, often, unhappy with what we see. Still seeking love, but feeling surprisingly angry. Or fearful. Or frustrated, disappointed, suspicious, manipulated, or depressed. And angry, always, in one form or another—angry.

Anger includes the whole range of negative emotion—from your disapproval when he butters his steak, through your surge of impatience as he methodically explains every step of a problem you have long since solved, to your outrage when you learn he emptied the bank account before he told you he was leaving.

The provocation may not be easily identified, yet it feels as if your noxious inner state was provoked by something he said, or did, or just some basic way he is. ("He breathes all the time," said one woman, trying to define exactly what it was about her boyfriend that was so irritating.)

As you consider your own experience with anger, keep three points in mind:

Your anger is probably justified.

I know you usually have good reason to be angry, you know you do, and, though he may be unable to acknowledge it, on some level he may know it also. When I speak of getting beyond your anger, that does not imply that you were somehow wrong to feel it.

Don't let go of anger because you are not entitled to it. Let go of anger because you are entitled, you've felt it, and now it's getting in your way.

Getting beyond anger does not mean keeping it a secret.

Burying anger is not the same as getting beyond it. In fact, most often a buried bitterness is more difficult to overcome. If you've hidden your anger from him, frequently that means you've hidden it from yourself as well. It is much more difficult to forgive, when you pretend to yourself that you were never hurt.

There are better and worse ways to make anger known, but that question is not our focus. The point is that most often (no, not always) the step before overcoming anger is acknowledging it.

Anger and anxiety are a package deal.

Anger towards a lover usually arouses some thread of uncertainty. *If I'm this angry, what does it mean? What will I have to do about it? How will he react if I let him know I'm mad?* Easing yourself beyond anger requires that you address these fears, acknowledge the risks involved, and reassure yourself of your own strength and the strength of the bond between the two of you.

. . . .

The rest of this chapter is a discussion of the most common conscious objections to the idea of loving more and needing less. There are, of course, an infinite variety of individual objections that could be made to this philosophy, just as there are an infinite variety of ways that someone you might prefer to love could enrage, threaten, irk, aggravate, abandon, frustrate, or inflame you instead. It adds up to the contradictory feeling that *I can't love him more because I'm too angry to care at all,* **and** *I can't love him more because I'm too anxious that he won't love me back.*

I can't need him less affects us in this same paradoxical sense—*it makes me mad to have to need him less,* **and** *it scares me, too. I'm scared because I'm afraid I can't take care of myself as well as he could,* **and** *I'm scared that if I'm strong enough to take care of myself, I'll be too threatening to be lovable.*

I've teased out these psychological twists and turns into six emotional themes, so that we could examine each of them in turn. You will note, though, that each overlaps a bit with the others. Each theme is driven to some degree by both anger and anxiety, though usually one of the two is dominant.

The six themes are as follows:
- **I can't love him more! If I do, he'll never change.**
- **I can't love him more! He won't even see what he did.**
- **I can't love him more! He doesn't deserve it.**
- **I can't love him more! He'll run away.**
- **I don't want to need him less! I want a strong man.**
- **I don't want to need him less! He can't handle a strong woman.**

I Can't—If I Do, He'll Never Change

"I know this is crazy thinking, but it's like I'm frightened to be happy with the good things about him. It makes me feel like I'm say-

*ing to him, 'That's good enough. You can stop right there.' And I
don't want him to stop. I want him to change."*

I want him to change. He promised he'd change. I thought he
would change. This is just not acceptable. It has got to change!

   Most of us have a mental list headed Things I Should Not Have
to Put Up With. This list seems to self-generate, composed as it is
of all our experiences, both bitter and beautiful, with men. Our lists
tend to include his **intolerable habits** (he smokes, drinks, eats over
the sink; he is a spendthrift or a cheapskate; so impulsive that you
are the only grown-up in the house, or as rigid as the Great Santini;
addicted to model building, golf, computer games, or some other
compulsively absorbing activity that you do not happen to share—
because if you did it would be one of the things you liked about
him); his **obnoxious behavior** (he screams at you if the luggage is
lost, or at the waiter if the service is slow; he treats his mother
rudely or teases a child too harshly—fill in your own blank); or his
offensive beliefs (these may involve things that he believes about
women, things he believes about the world at large, and, often most
unpleasant, things he believes about himself). Of course the varia-
tion within these categories is infinite.

   Your list could include character traits, habits, or attitudes to
which you might respond with absolute and unswerving outrage.
These may reveal deep and disturbing fissures in the nature of the
man himself, which lead you to question both the wisdom and the
value of your attachment. They are flaws you want repaired, behaviors you want changed, things you should not or will not tolerate.

   In a way, the fury or embarrassment we suffer over his failings is
the bill presented for the all-positive, all-wondrous fantasies of love
we have enjoyed so much. When our image of love is all good, and
the actual experience feels bad—even a little—we have no model of
how to reconcile the two. We automatically react by withholding, by
thinking, *I love you, but* . . .

   I love you, but . . . rests on two bone-deep, though unexamined
assumptions: First, that if you want someone to change you must

withhold approval. The bedrock of this thinking is that criticism motivates a person to change, whereas praise somehow lulls that person into a smug self-satisfaction. And second, that a criticized person will change *if he loves you.*

These two misconceptions are the source of some of our most hopeless expectations and unpleasant dialogues. They are the reason your mother asked how your B in English could become an A, and why she always has to mention that you look better with your hair out of your eyes. That very same assumption moves your lover to be frank about your haircut, the speech you gave, or the sad state of your car. See—they love you and they don't want you to settle for being less than the best you can be. Don't you find their criticisms inspirational?

Well, frankly, neither does a lover, a boyfriend, or a husband. When you remind him repeatedly of his failings, he does what we all do—he tunes you out, tells you what you want to hear, or retaliates in kind. ("I'm selfish? Ha! What about your sacred painting time, your hours on the phone every night?") He does not say, "Gee, thanks for pointing that out again."

For one thing, it is simply wrong to think that behavior is most effectively changed through negative reinforcement. Praise is far more likely to change behavior, whether you are retraining a dog, a child, or a date. Beyond science is spirit. When you resist relaxing into love, in order to keep his need for improvement on your agenda, the reward for your vigilance is your own righteous anger. That may not be such a bad feeling, but it is far from the love you were looking for.

The second assumption—"He will change if he loves me"—is equally wrong, and far more painful to be wrong about. We have caused ourselves untold anguish with this misguided belief. It leaves us saddled not only with whatever irritant we were hoping he'd change, but with the unnecessary pain of doubting his love.

The argument goes like this: "If he loves me, won't he want to make me happy?" Why, yes, he will—right up to the point where that change makes him unhappy. Just like you. You love him and you'd be glad to change to make him happy—when you can, if it doesn't cost too much energy, too much anxiety, too much pleasure, too much of *you*.

Ideally, we would each change a bit to make a partner happy. But mostly we change from some place inside ourselves, out of the press of our own development, because each of us, female or male, is on her or his own path.

If you are still hurt, angry, or disappointed much of the time, and he is still pretty much the same, anger doesn't seem to be getting you anywhere. Even so, you may stay angry, because, after all, this irritant is probably something you shouldn't have to put up with. The thing is, though, your anger doubles your own load. You have to put up with him and endure the tension of your own anger.

Your choice, other than leaving, is to be less angry, even though he stays the same. How? Well, in all the ways we've discussed. Stop trying to change him. Instead, change the eyes through which you see him; change the way that you react to him; put a firmer psychological boundary between you; shift the focus of your problem; and, most of all, at the heart of it all—stretch yourself to forgive.

How very easy for me to offer you this neat little paragraph of how-to tips. Very simple and very far from real-life experience. This stretch to forgive, to move yourself from resentment to loving acceptance, is as easy as carrying a piano across a desert on your back, only to discover that you have yet to cross the Rockies.

It is the spirit and strength underneath the application of these techniques that make the difference—the hard self-awareness that makes refocusing something deeper than a mere shift of attention; the intelligence and courage of the woman who struggles to empathize, even though she has been hurt by the person with whom she is trying to identify; the perseverance required to press inch by inch towards forgiveness, fending off the warnings of those who view your tolerance as a measure of your weakness. Loving men more as you work to need men less, trusting the wisdom you've gained from this process, and summoning the strength to apply it at difficult moments asks the most of us. Keep in mind—it pays in kind.

I have observed many women through this process, and listened to dozens more describe their efforts and frustrations. Each woman's experience is surprisingly individual, though the themes of relinquishing anger, facing anxiety, and struggling against fantasy are common to all.

Frances' story captures the flavor of the process by which you might face down the dragons, in order to love a man more and need him less. Frances, thirty-six, has been married to Joe for nine years. It is a second marriage for Frances, which she believes may account for the sustained effort she has been willing to invest in her relationship with Joe. That effort is reflected both in her campaign to change Joe, and in her efforts to find love and accept Joe when he stayed the same.

"My husband tends towards the artistic side of things, while I tend more to the science of life. At the beginning, this was an exhilarating combination, because he is brilliant and quirky and brings fresh eyes to subjects that I and my all-too-similar friends have ground into sameness. Plus, he loves me and lets me know it, supports anything I want to do, in any way he can, and he's still the person in whose company I most prefer to be. With a man like that, what could one wish to change?

"Plenty.

"My main irritation had to do with his work habits. This is an area where we efficient scientist types have it all over those creatively chaotic souls. I am organized, productive, scheduled, and efficient. I keep date books, tickler files, financial records, and phone logs. I am obviously a saint.

"Joe is well intentioned, forgetful, easily distracted, undisciplined. He keeps scraps of paper, old beer caps, and sketches of ideas that he finds inspiring, although he cannot always remember why. He might make two opposite plans for the same evening, because it is, after all, two days from now, and he hasn't focused that far ahead. I have a five-year plan.

"This all sounds too cute in the retelling. The fact is, he drove me

up a wall. I woke up angry every morning, because I instantly remembered something he hadn't done, should have done, or was not
going to do. I would buy him appointment books and still people
would call, angry, asking what happened to him. I would mentally
record all his obligations and keep score. Was he doing what he
should be doing? Sometimes he was. Then I could relax. Many times
he wasn't. Then I either watched and brooded, stewing in outrage
("How could he suggest we picnic today! When does he plan to start
the bills?"), or I popped out a tight-lipped reminder.

"You know what? He hardly ever thanked me for helping him
onto the straight and narrow. Yes, he sometimes admitted that my
way was better, more adult, more productive, and so on. But, no
matter what he said, he kept being—himself. And he was often mad
at me in return, receiving my gentle reminders snippily, or walking
away when I began to nag.

"My campaign was worse than a failure to improve him. It began to fill our marriage with conflict. To reduce the tension level, I
had to focus away from what he was doing wrong, and ask myself
why it was so important to me that he change. Why did he have to
do what I thought best? Why did he even have to do what was best,
if he didn't want to? Why am I angry when he isn't like me? He is
not me.

"I found, in the beginning, I had to remind myself about forty
times a day: he is not me. Just because we're married does not make
me responsible for every aspect of his life, nor does he have to live
according to my rules. Instantly, I would argue back with myself.
'Yes, but he affects me. If he doesn't pay the bills, I get in trouble. If
he messes up at work, I could be hurt by the consequences.'

"That was true, to some degree. The fact is, though, I was way
past that point. I was not just monitoring behavior that had a direct
impact on me. I was monitoring his life, as though everything he did
reflected on me, and he should therefore do things the right way—
that is, my way.

"Besides, if everything he does affects me, it would follow that
everything I did must affect him. Yet he didn't seem so troubled. At

least, I didn't often hear him telling me what to do. ('Because I do things the right way,' came the whisper of the saint. 'Oh, shut up,' is what I said to it in return. 'Sainthood is very lonely.')

"I had to stop feeling responsible for the way he led his life. I began by mentally creating an objective, though admittedly artificial boundary between him and me. Defining separate boundaries was my way to 'need him less.' Beyond this boundary, I decided, I would not allow myself to need him to do things my way. I would not need him to fit my picture. He is entitled to his own picture.

"I made his work the boundary. My work was my business, so his work should be his business. Rationally, I knew that his work habits, while not ideal, were obviously quite functional. He'd been supporting himself since long before he met me. He wasn't getting fired. What made me and my schedules and reminders suddenly necessary to him?

"Putting this new boundary into effect did not come easily to me. I found I could only successfully maintain it if I knew very little about his work life. The minute I knew he was forgetting something or overlooking something, that something would burn in me until I was able to expel it. I am the kind of woman that, should he suddenly wrap his arms around me and pull me close, might choose that very moment to look him in the eye and ask, 'Did you remember to give the dog his heartworm medication?'

"So I gritted my teeth and did what I needed to, in order to feel and act differently. I left the room when he was making an appointment, so that I wouldn't know if he was scheduling properly or not. I still gathered his paper scraps into a pile, but I no longer allowed myself to read through them, because I would only get upset when I discovered something he had forgotten to do. I deliberately stopped following up on previous conversations, stopped asking whatever happened with such-and-such, or why he had never pursued something.

"Yes, it killed me not to ask, not to read, not to listen and monitor and control. Yes, the whole thing made me a nervous wreck. When I focused away from him and back on myself, I was able to recog-

nize that I was propelled by some awful fear that my husband would fail, a fear quite unrelated to what I knew about him, and all out of proportion to the actual risk. Somehow, without me to nip at his heels, I felt that something catastrophic would happen to him, and that I had to protect him from that consequence.

"I was wrong. When I stepped back, I couldn't help but notice that things were pretty much the same as when I was watching his every move. He was still brilliant, still an original thinker, and still an organizational disaster. He still offended people when he forgot them or misscheduled them. But, to my amazement, nothing much worse happened than that. He still failed to meet a deadline occasionally, but it didn't get him fired, flunked, or any of the other things that I vaguely thought would happen if a person ever missed a deadline.

"It's been years since I took on this battle—first to change him and finally to love him as he is. His work habits don't make me as mad anymore. If anything, once I called the cease-fire, we grew a bit closer to each other in style. He grew up some on his own, took on more professional responsibility without my urging. I had truly stopped needing him to do what I thought best. In fact, I relaxed a bit myself. I was no longer quite so hyper, no longer driven to make every small task into a model of thoroughness.

"Once I withdrew my energy from his success or failure, I had so much more to devote to my own. I needed to face my own dilemmas of how to invest time wisely, how to push myself to face my anxiety when I am avoiding something important, how to push against myself when I am too perfectionistic. Somehow it had been so much easier to know exactly what he should do, than to decide exactly what I should do."

This is not meant to be a happily ever after. Frances is still the saintly worker, the employee any boss would rather hire; Joe is still the creative artist, the person with whom many colleagues would prefer to work. His procrastination and forgetfulness can still drive

Frances mad with frustration. (She told me she was actually temporarily homicidal when Joe put off calling the air-conditioner guy for seven months, until a two-week record heat wave helped him to remember.) And Frances' list-with-a-life-of-its-own, which details everything that should be done but never includes anything that would be fun to do, still chokes Joe some days.

The point is not that things get perfect. It is that love can coexist with a great deal of imperfection, if you are willing to make room for it. Frances was willing to make room. Joe, for his part, loves her far more for the room she made to let him be himself, than he ever loved her for caring enough to improve him. He sees the difference when he checks out his friends' marriages. He notices that his is the wife the other men talk with, his is the one they don't mind having along. At the end of a social evening, Joe notes to himself and quite often to Frances as well, "Honey, you are the only woman at that party I would ever want to be married to." This is not Joe's attempt at romance. It's just his simple truth.

Frances herself is proud of what she has built with Joe. Their home is relaxed, and their lives are full, and she's a happy woman. She gets a private chuckle out of one completely unexpected result of all her efforts. As she has come to love Joe as he is, the rest of their world has begun to see Joe through those eyes, too. "You don't know what it's like," her girlfriends will tell her, when they begin to discuss men. "You got a perfect guy."

I Can't—He Won't Even See What He Did

You two have a movie date, but at the last minute he gives in and brings along his whiny nine-year-old son. You know Jason only insisted on going because he wants all of Dad's attention. What makes you furious is not that this child wants to stake his claim on Daddy. It is that Daddy always lets him. You can't believe he put you second—again. It's insulting. And it hurts.

When you finally have an opportunity to be alone, Dad wants to make love. You comment that you are apparently scheduled for servicing somewhere between his son's bedtime and his son's nightly bad dream, the one that will once again require Daddy's comfort at your expense.

In psychology texts, the ones that show models of "healthy" couple communication, the man who receives this sarcastic remark responds with both feeling and sincerity. "I did do it again. I understand why you're mad. I really have a problem saying 'No' to Jason, even when I know it would be better for him if I did."

Actually, you wouldn't even need him to go this far. He could disagree with you, as long as he seems to have some shade of appreciation for your feelings. He could say, "Look, I know it hurts you if I put Jason first. But I believe that I'm doing the right thing where he is concerned. I don't want to hurt you, though. Is there some way I could make this easier for you?"

Those were the ideal responses. Here is what is more likely to happen in real life: You've leaked your anger through your sarcastic comment. You feel his body go rigid, and he remarks with ferocious calm that it sounds as if you dislike Jason. Three seconds later, you find yourself in a testy interchange that will end in a blowup unless you back-pedal immediately and hate yourself later.

Now you are finessing, arguing that of course you like Jason (ha!), it's just that you don't like how you are treated when Jason is around. You start giving examples to prove your point, each of which he undercuts by explaining why your precise memory is inaccurate, or why that was an exceptional situation, or why *anything*, in order to prove that you are wrong to feel what you feel, or to think what you think.

So often, we stay angry not because a partner disagrees, but because he stubbornly refuses to acknowledge our point of view at all. (Empathy—remember? Probably should be a high-school graduation requirement.) It feels as if you can't stop being angry until, at the very least, he recognizes *why* you feel as you do. Agreeing would be nice, apologizing even better. But at a bare minimum, you need him to acknowledge that you are neither crazy nor overly emotional. You are angry or anxious, with good reason.

This very understandable need to be acknowledged urges you on. You elaborate your argument, proving your point, until he makes one of those dead-end remarks, such as, "Well, I don't know why you put up with me if I'm so awful." End of discussion, but not of the feelings behind it. Without a sense of being understood, it is easy for anger to fester.

You are left with the difficult chore of overcoming that anger without the comfort of feeling that your anger got your message across. Everything in you says, *I can't stop being mad. He'll think that means he was right, that I had no reason to be angry in the first place!* That's a challenging little mental cul-de-sac from which to extricate yourself. Because, of course, it doesn't pay to sit there marinating in your own poison.

You may find it easier to relinquish your anger when you see that it has helped you all it can. Anger was a signal from your separate self, tugging on your psyche yelling, *Hey, what about me? I need a little attention, too.* That feeling was true enough, and reasonable to boot. Your anger helped both of you to recognize it.

Your anger has a down side, however. **Anger is a good way to signal a problem, but a bad stance from which to solve a problem.** When you come at anyone in anger—confronting, criticizing, accusing—he or she is most likely to react exactly as you would under the same conditions, namely, to defend himself as vigorously as possible. I attack, you defend. You attack, I defend. It's almost a law of nature.

True, when one of you attacks, the other is sometimes strong enough to acknowledge the merit of the criticism. "You know, you're right," one person might say, "I hadn't realized that would hurt you." But not often—at least, not often enough to justify a strategy of staying angry until such an admission occurs. Instead, once you've expressed your anger, try some of the following to help your anger cool: Take the time you need to put the provocation in perspective. Make sure you have been willing to acknowledge a point or two in your partner's behalf. ("It is tough to be a single dad. I understand that, when you've left a child through divorce, you never want to turn him away again.") Tack something positive on to the end of every mental complaint. ("He spoils his kid at my expense, *and* he's always interested in every aspect of my life.") Say something loving, though you don't really feel it at the moment. ("Jason and I agree. You are good company.") Any of these techniques might cool your anger enough to help you take a step towards solving your problem.

When your hurt feelings and/or your righteous indignation ease up a bit, you have a better chance to resolve the conflict. That's when you can choose an optimal time to discuss the issue with him. Try to state the overall problem (of which last weekend was just one example), rather than beginning with a review of last weekend's events. Too often, we stick with the concrete example in order to prove our point. But that has the effect of reawakening the anger and bad feeling connected with that specific example, leaving you both bogged down in the awful who-said-what-when conversation we've all come to know and loathe.

Instead, simply state your problem. You may be able to tolerate many less-than-perfect outcomes in terms of sharing time with Jason, but they would all be infinitely less painful if Tom would at least acknowledge your feelings and your point of view. Say so, clearly. "I understand that, if Jason needs your attention, you want him to have it, no matter what. I can live with that." (Assuming you've decided you can.) "But I would find it much easier if you would at least tell me that you know you've disappointed me and you're sorry about it."

He might still be defensive, responding with something like, "Well, of course I'm sorry about it. What do you think? I like having a kid along on our dates?"

You will need to avoid reopening the argument, resist telling Tom again that he doesn't always have to say yes to his son, that he is spoiling the boy. His decision is made. Now only he can change it. You will even have to be firm with the part of you that wants to say,

"Well, you sure didn't act like you were sorry about it." All of that leads you down into the anger you came from.

Keep your focus on your problem, not Tom's. You are trying to reach up to love. "I don't know what I thought. I just know it would be easier for me if you said you understood why I was disappointed, and you wish we could be together more, too."

If what you need most is to feel that he understands, don't hang back. Tell him what you need to hear, in order to feel understood. There's no guarantee that he'll say it, but it improves the odds. Part of needing him less is not needing him to know things without your having to tell him. Just tell him.

Then take yourself one step further down the path: loving him more means that, when he says what you told him you needed to hear, *you don't discount it just because you asked.* Love means granting the benefit of the doubt. If you asked, and you received, err on the side of presuming the gift was sincere.

I Can't—He Doesn't Deserve It

You might be asking why, for God's sake, should you go to that kind of trouble for a man who is unable to say "No" to a child but too easily able to say "No" to you? Are we that desperate for love, or for a man, that we need to turn ourselves upside down to find a way to love him anyway—no matter how selfish he might be? Do you think you would ever see this guy looking into a woman's heart so he could figure out what would make her happier, so he could struggle to love her more, even while she is acting badly and treating him worse?

Well, I have seen it, and probably so have you. We've all known men to agonize over women, puzzle over women—a man frantic to figure out a woman, so that he can make her happy to be with him. Love is a human phenomenon, not a female one.

It is true, though, that this father, at least at this point in his life, is unlikely to be that man. Perhaps, male or female, your lover is also unlikely give back equal energy or consideration. *Why should I struggle to love him more? He doesn't do the same for me* is one of the greatest barriers to love.

There is only one reason you would want to aim yourself towards a higher level of love, anyway. Love is not a commodity, and loving has nothing to do with a fair exchange. It is an experience. It does not belong to the object of the feeling. Loving belongs to the person who feels it. You stretch to love a man more, not because he merits it, but because you want to feel it.

You are with a romantic partner in the hopes of getting to love. Whatever he may do to get in the way of that feeling (and he may do plenty), you can either stretch yourself past those obstacles, wait for him to stop creating them, or leave in the hopes of starting again with a man for whom love is easier to feel. Excepting the extremes of behavior, which we've discussed, the question is not whether a partner deserves to be loved. It is whether you deserve to experience loving.

There is something else, too. When the two of you get together, you are far from equal in every respect. You are stronger in some areas, he is better at others. In most instances, people accept, sometimes even welcome these differences. In our capacity for love, however, we do not tolerate differences well. Both partners look for a tit-for-tat exchange, worried that we are fools if we give more than we get.

Yet how likely is it that our capacities for love would be equal, when in many other ways our strengths and weaknesses are very different? In any romantic connection, one partner is apt to be further along the path to love, more comfortable with loving, easier at expressing love, and more receptive to it than the other. As we've discussed in chapter four, if you are better at loving, why hold back simply for the sake of an even exchange?

Will you allow yourself to be as loving as you can be, take your relationship to the highest level, even though this means you will, of necessity, give more love than you get? Or will you limit yourself to giving just what you can expect to get in return? Will you hold your love back, keep your relationship at the lowest common denominator, just to ensure emotional parity?

The person with the greater capacity to love has the power to choose. I believe that we should always choose the highest level of interaction of which we are capable. At best, you may well take your partner along with you to that higher plane. At the very least, don't hold yourself back because of someone else's limitations. **Love as fully as you can, rather than as fully as *he* can—not to win him, not to please him, but to make yourself happy.**

I Can't—He'll Run Away

"He's not crazy enough about me. He's probably as crazy as he can be—but it's not enough. He doesn't really need me. Loving him more would make me look pathetic."

Faye is speaking of her boyfriend of two years, Jackson. Jackson is everything Faye wished for after her two marriages. By "everything" she means, of course, the conventional list of desirable male assets, plus one trait of particular importance to Faye. Jackson is completely without the usual male assumptions to which Faye is accustomed. He is not possessive, not controlling, not domineering, not even the least bit demanding.

Jack is scrupulously careful to foist no obligations on Faye simply because she and he are a couple. If he decides to spend a holiday with his children, for example, he will usually invite Faye to share the day with them. But Jack exerts not even the subtlest pressure that she go along with his plan, should she choose not to.

They spend many nights together, though he feels free to return to or remain in his own bed, if and when the spirit moves him. He would absolutely accord the same freedom to Faye, no questions asked. Both are free to spend time with whom they wish, when they wish.

Neither Faye nor Jackson is seeking marriage, both having

sworn off it long before they met. They live four blocks apart, in homes each has fitted exactly to one person's idiosyncratic taste. Neither dreams of the day they could move in together and fight over whose couch gets the long wall. But they are very much a couple, publicly open about their attachment, privately warm, loving, and compatible.

Yet there is some link missing, something Faye cannot put into words, which ruffles the edges of her peace of mind. She doesn't see telling Jack about this feeling. It sounds, as she plays it in her mind, like a . . . complaint. He has never done anything she feels entitled to complain about, not unless she were one of those very needy, very hungry women, which she most definitely is not.

Faye tries, though, to explain it to me, because she is trying to explain the feeling to herself:

"It's like, if he goes away for business, he always calls when he says he will, he always bring me the perfect gift. But I'm not, not . . . on his mind, if you know what I mean. I'm not essential to him. Sometimes I think I am the current occupant of the slot in his life labeled 'woman here.' He is the perfect boyfriend, but it's like he was trained by others and he is turning in his usual excellent piece of work.

"How do I get him to be more intimate? How can I feel loved, when he feels so distant—so attentive, but essentially so distant? How can I feel safe with a man who is completely sufficient within himself?"

Faye gives me a telling example.

"When we go to a party, we are each free to go off and talk with whom we wish, when we wish. We both know an awful lot of people, which means we spend most of our party time apart. You know what? I realize that I don't want to spend the evening with all those other people. I want to enjoy the party with him."

"What's stopping you?" I ask.

"Well, he's off in a corner, socializing."

"So? If you'd rather be off in the same corner with him, what's in the way?"

Faye said flatly, "I just can't. I'd feel like a clinging vine. It's the last thing I'd ever be. And it's the last thing he would tolerate."

Faye is the woman at the other edge of the loving/needing spectrum, the woman who is most comfortable loving and needing men very little. She has had plenty of men in her life—colleagues, dinner dates, tennis buddies, financial advisers, and, before Jackson, men for companionable sex and romantic interludes. But no men she needed. And no men she loved.

That's the problem. Faye loves him. She didn't mean to, but she does. Jack sneaked past her defenses, partly because he held himself at such a distance that it didn't set off her usual he-wants-to-own-me alarm. It was not so much that Jackson was more lovable or more of a soulmate than other men, from whom Faye had automatically backed away. It was more that Faye forgot to guard against him.

Now she feels stuck, anxious. Faye has tried to remind herself that this romance, too, will pass, that surely she will have to let him go, that sooner or later he will reveal himself to be as fatally limited as the rest. All her language assumes that she will be in control, she will be the one to decide. But none of her fears do.

What is wrong between them is so obvious that Faye's inability to put her finger on it is the best measure of that fear. What is wrong is that she loves him, and she's afraid to love him more. She loves him and she wants that elusive sense of permanence, of unbreakable connection, of public declaration and ceremonial bonding. She wants to be his girl, his person, and not just her own. She doesn't believe in it, she's ashamed of herself for feeling it, but she wants it anyway. She wants it, and she believes deep within her that if he knows she wants it he will leave her.

Something as simple as walking over to the corner and spending the rest of the evening at his side is an admission of her need. It feels awful to Faye. Vulnerable. Suddenly, unaccountably, she isn't sure whether Jackson would want her there for the whole evening. "I mean, he's not coming over to stand by me for the evening, is he?" She hears herself and winces. "My God, I sound like I did when I was in high school."

There is only one way for Faye to get more of what she wants. She could let Jackson know she wants it, and she could offer to Jackson what she is hoping to receive in return. She could take a step towards him, and find out whether he takes a step back or not.

That step forward comes in many forms. They all have the same underlying principle: Faye needs to give what she has to give, rather than focus so tensely on what she might get in return. How can she get him to be more intimate? Only by opening up herself, by saying more of what she thinks and feels, less of what is safely packaged.

How can she ever feel loved by someone who seems so emotionally distant? By taking the risk of being loved, so that he can feel safe, too. How can you tell if someone so self-possessed will ever give you what you need? Only by taking the step forward to ask for it.

But won't he back off if he knows that he has her, if the challenge is gone, the pursuit accomplished? He might, if pursuit is his only pleasure. He might even be likely to, if it were still the earliest months of their courtship, when pursuit is appropriate and a person who pushes past it may trigger every anxious alarm. But Jack and Faye are far beyond that point. Pursuit is complete. They are attached. It's just that neither knows how to deepen an attachment without being strangled under the restrictions that usually implies. Each has learned to keep the rules to a minimum by keeping love to a minimum. It is possible to go beyond that point, possible to discover that you can love a lot but restrict only a little.

The problem is, someone has to go first. Yes, it's a risk. But as I reminded Faye, it is a risk you can break into small pieces. To begin with, she need only stand next to him at a party, hold his hand, tell him she loves him. And, of course, be brave enough to let him know she means it.

I Don't Want to Need Him Less

"Other women get taken care of. Other women get financial support and the opportunity to stay home, raise their children, to do whatever they want. Why shouldn't I?"

Who is to say you shouldn't? To twist the old saying, "I may not believe in what you dream, but I will defend to the death your right to dream it." Some of us proudly carry the banner of the traditional model of love (brave prince rampant over a grateful princess). If you have looked realistically and self-protectively at the deal, and you like the terms, so be it. God bless you for knowing what you want and for having the strength to stand up to the social winds that blow against you.

But even women who reject the traditional model hear these sentiments echoed within them, at least in part, because they are inextricably linked with our long-cherished rescue fantasy: someday, the prince will come and carry me off to a land where I am shielded from life's burdens but indulged in all its pleasures. It's not that we believe in this outcome exactly. Even those of us who aspire to it are certainly no longer oblivious to its great cost.

Still, the enormous power of the fantasy—to be taken care of by someone stronger, wiser, someone powerful and infinitely loving—cannot be ignored. Even those of us who believe we have long since buried this vision have shards of rescue fantasy unexpectedly poking through our surface. Listen to these women, talking over lunch:

"I hate it when he says, 'I don't care—you decide.' I didn't get married in order to make all the decisions on my own. And I'm tired of it," said the first.

The second was confessing, more or less, "I really emasculated him yesterday," she said. "We met with the mortgage guy and I just took over. But what should I have done? He wasn't asking the right questions, and there were things we needed to know!"

"Did your husband mind?"

"No. And that bothered me even more."

A third woman noted she felt similarly scornful when she found herself unexpectedly more competent than her boyfriend. She explained, "When I do something that I hadn't really known I could do, like fix a broken lock—well, that's nice. But when I do something that he can't, that gives me some kind of boost. I'll put him down in my mind. I'll start thinking, 'What a jerk. He's wrapping a broken suitcase with a string. Sure, that'll make it from here to Vermont.' The thing is, when I see I can do one of those boy things and he can't, I start not to like him. It's like, 'What do I need him for?' "

At the heart of our reluctance to need a man less is the loss of our rescue fantasy. It is no easy thing for us to give up our permission to be dependent, whether or not we decide to be. Yes, we've fought to have the opportunity to care for ourselves, and we meant it. But that didn't mean we wouldn't have mixed feelings about it. We do, because it is simply not possible to assume the responsibilities of an adult without experiencing an occasional pang for the loss of the privileges of the dependent children we were.

It may help to remember that what you are giving up is largely illusion. It was wonderful to feel that someone else would take care of you forever financially, should you choose not to be financially self-sufficient. Losing that illusion of safety is threatening. But it is, after all, only an illusion. The divorce courts, the economy, the whole social climate will prove to you that the safest person to bet on today is yourself.

It was a great freedom to believe that there were huge areas of life that you simply had no need to know about, because he knew enough for both of you. There is still great freedom in such an arrangement, but, as always, freedom comes with a price. The price for freedom from adult responsibility is loss of power and control over your life. Unless you are prepared to pay that price, you would be better off needing a man less.

Many women enjoy the comforting illusion of protection and safety. Ripping off that Band-Aid and exposing the untried self underneath hurts. (I always squint a little at the women who say they never felt a thing, or at those who deny the Band-Aid was ever in place. Could some of us skip from childhood to a separate, strong self with no pangs at all for what we left behind? Even if what was left was more childhood wish than childhood reality? I wonder.)

There is a flip side to this coin. *I don't want to need him less. I want a strong man* is shadowed by an associate fear: *I'm afraid to need him less. He wants a dependent woman. Men are intimidated by strong women. Their egos can't take it. If I'm independent, I'll seem too aggressive. I'll scare him away. What's the point of being so strong if you get to be alone your whole life?*

I hear this fear and resentment often. It is the Catch-22 of women's progress. We sense so much anger in men, so much resistance, aversion, and even outright rejection of a woman who is not willing to be somehow less than her man (or at least not willing to pretend she is). We've been encouraged to express our resentment of this restriction, to assume the attitude *To hell with him if he can't take it*. This worked well as an outlet for our understandable anger. But we've been left alone to handle our fear.

That fear, conscious or unconscious, acts as a barrier to our willingness to need men less. Is the fear based in reality? Is it true that many men are intimidated by strong women, are too frightened to get close to them, much less to love them?

Yes.

But does this mean that a woman must choose between being strong and being loved? No.

The problem is real enough, but it does not have to become a permanent truth, if women take a few steps to make this choice less likely. None of those steps demeans us or disguises our strength.

First, take a closer look at male intimidation and resistance. We have just discussed the strength required for a woman to rip through the illusion of security and protection expressed by our rescue fantasy. If it is that hard for the princess to let that fantasy go, why should it be any easier for the prince?

He is just as invested in the illusion of his bravery and omnipotence as we are in our dream of total security at no cost. Part of what we hear, when we experience a man who is intimidated or angry, is his loud shout of pain as his own illusion is stripped away. I don't know about you, but I kicked and screamed for years over losing mine. Why shouldn't he?

All fantasy aside, strong people of either gender are generally pretty scary, at least at first. When a powerful man intimidates a woman, we rarely look at that woman with scorn and say, "Hey, what's the matter? Your ego can't handle it?" Instead, we are apt to sympathize with that woman, reassure her, and perhaps even call that man a bully, merely because he is strong and she is scared.

But when a powerful woman intimidates a man, scorn is our first response. We think of him as weak; we hold him in contempt. Just as men may be uncomfortable with female strength, many women are equally uncomfortable with male weakness. We overreact to male shakiness, and hold our discomfort with male anxiety against men. A woman who is anxious about marriage has a girlfriend to sympathize with her. A man who is anxious about marriage has a diagnosis.

Perhaps a piece of us always wants to perceive men as powerful, so we can cling to some shred of our rescue fantasy, like the corner of our baby blankie, tucked inside our bras. We have buried this damaging fantasy deep, but every time we make a man nervous the fantasy surfaces, and makes us mad.

The three women talking over lunch earlier were reacting negatively to small signs of male inadequacy, just as they might have reacted ferociously had these same men asserted complete dominance. Both reactions are perfectly normal, even inevitable. As we strain towards a new balance, we react to missteps in each direction.

Moving to the middle of love is a complicated maneuver. Achieving a balanced perspective, one that accounts for life's paradoxes as much as for its consistencies, is a difficult social and individual endeavor. We may be trained to think in sound bites and simple answers, but that does not mean that we will have nothing but easy questions.

As women create a new vision of ourselves and work towards a new willingness to love men as they are, there will be plenty of anger, uncertainty, cynicism, and scorn that we will need to wade through. Some will be directed towards us, some will come straight from us. We can't force ourselves or our partners to feel what "should" be felt. We can, however, be conscious of the source of all those disruptive feelings, so that we respond as painlessly and productively as possible.

I point this out because I think it's time we give ourselves a break. Of course we can come into our fullest powers and have love, too. We have only to be sensitive to the fact that our fullest powers can be a little overwhelming to other people.

Will a man be intimidated by a powerful woman? Probably yes, at least initially. But you have a choice. You can turn your back on him. Or you can help him get over it. If you make someone anxious, don't hold it against him—reassure him. Help him feel more comfortable. You'll only have to do for him what you would want someone to do for you.

Think of a pool. If you had a friend who was frightened of the deep end, you wouldn't call him weak and walk away, right? Of course not. You'd tell him that it was going to be fine. You'd encourage him to test the waters. You might even offer to hold his hand and jump in with him. Keep in mind, women have become very deep ends. Don't call him chicken if he hesitates to jump.

Will he always resent you because you aren't there to have his dinner on the table and run his suits to the cleaners the way his mom did for Dad? Probably—at least to some degree. Don't you sometimes resent him for not being an incredibly successful, ambitious, and driven man who would never miss a Little League game or disapprove of anything you do. Hey—this is America. We can't have it all, but we can sure want it all.

What you can have is a man who appreciates your willingness to love him more, as he gets comfortable with the fact that you need him less. As Frank Conroy points out: "Men are too fragile and too involved to see women clearly without a woman's help. There is more than one way for the scales to fall from a man's eyes, but the spontaneous, honest, generous, passionate love of a strong woman is perhaps the fastest."

You can love more than you do right now, once you take the risk of being more loving. You can need less than you once thought love required, as you learn to go to yourself before you go through someone else. You can love more and need less, not magically, but with effort. You can—if you will.

The problem is, we have good reason to decide that we won't. Though we know with a deep and certain sense that love is our highest level, we also know that the climb requires huge effort. In order to recapture our vision of love, there will be other treasures we must decide to leave behind. These are the limits imposed by love—the price we must pay for the prize.

Barbara

F our days. Trapped in the house for four days with three
children, one ear infection, one strep throat, and only one
rickety air conditioner to fend off the heat wave that further
imprisoned her. Four days of breathing air poisoned by twenty-hour
doses of televised babysitting, of restraining her four-year-old son in
his attempts to assassinate his sister, and convincing that same little
sister that, yes, small babies do feel pain. Four days of ignoring her
own work to spoon gummy pink antibiotics into sick mouths, only to
have it snorted back at her through equally gummy nostrils.

And four days of a husband announcing regretfully that he
would be late (as usual, so how can he really call it late?), thereby
making him unavailable for feeding, cleaning, or forcing medication
on anyone from his gene pool.

Barbara entertained herself throughout with her own fantasies
of violence ("Isn't that nice," she thought, "mother and child share
the same dreams")—hers directed entirely at her selfish pig of a
husband, who wouldn't even think to pick up takeout to give her a
break. She reviewed each of the injustices he'd committed against
her in the years of their marriage, culminating in his talking her into
buying this house without central air, this house that he was free to
leave in the morning while she was in motherhood jail with no time
off for good behavior.

Barbara punctuated these internal rants with sudden stabs of
anxiety. Not that he was any help when he was around, but, oh my

God, maybe one day he wouldn't be around. Maybe, in his shoes, she wouldn't want to come home, either, given what home was like these days, given what she looked like lately, and how angry she always seemed to be with him.

Between anger, anxiety, and amoxycillin, Barbara was ripe for a major marital breakdown, the kind in which she and Peter say memorably mean things to each other, and then each retreats into silence for days. His was the defiant silence of a man who feels unappreciated and unjustly accused. But hers was the silence of a rage too intense to expose any further.

It was Barbara's long expanse of silent tundra that finally convinced Peter to agree to her suggestion that they see a therapist. I met them as a couple, though Peter did little more than show up, declare himself sane, and turn Barbara over to me, so that she could be restored to her former sexy self—the one he had married, who had mysteriously disappeared.

Barbara had first to wrestle with the irony of being the one in therapy when, in her very firm opinion, Peter was the one with the problem. Eventually, she got beyond her annoyance at Peter's told-you-so smile, and began to focus on what was troubling her.

Peter.

Well, not just Peter, but in the end it boiled down to Peter, and the ways he had hurt her, disappointed her, and exploited her.

True, Barbara was uncomfortable with her own habit of angry silence, and remembered that as a child she'd hated her own mother for treating her father with such cold contempt. She could see that her children paid a price for her periods of stiff fury, escalating their own warfare in an effort to force Mom out of hiding. But she was frozen inside her own rage and could not seem to break through it, even for the sake of her children.

Barbara felt she was silent because Peter couldn't seem to hear her, no matter what she said. Every concrete request she made met with either reluctance ("I'd be happy to help when I can, but you know I can never predict how late I'll have to stay at the office, so please don't count on me"), resistance ("Sure, I'll do that," he'd say, and then promptly forgot unless she turned herself into a needling shrew), or infuriating incompetence (which, if she dared comment on something he'd overlooked, allowed him to say, "If you are going to criticize everything I do, do it yourself").

Peter had proved to be unwilling to change anything about himself, his schedule, or his attitude for the sake of her happiness. Barbara spent long hours debating what made him so self-involved. Were all men incapable of giving? Or had she chosen a brat? Was the failure hers? Was she, as her mother-in-law hinted, spoiled and demanding? Or, as a friend hinted, was she a fool whose husband used her deep love for her kids to get out of carrying his share of the load?

Mostly Barbara thought about whether there was some plan, some technique by which she could get through, get noticed, and get him to change.

The three classic questions:

• **What's wrong with him?** Why won't he give me what I need, what I want, what I'm entitled to? What happened to the Peter who could always make me laugh? The one who jollied me out of feeling bad instead of ignoring me altogether?

• **What's wrong with me?** Do I expect too much? Did I ever love him? Why didn't I see this coming? And finally, frustratingly:

• **What can I do to get him to change?** I want to love him, I want to be happy. But in order to love him, I need him to be like the old Peter! I need him to change. Wouldn't you?

Barbara had stopped discussing these questions with Peter, because Peter never seemed interested in any of her answers, and he never provided any answers of his own. In fact, Peter did not really know that there was a question.

Though Barbara found this astonishing and hugely infuriating, she was forced to admit that Peter did not even know that they had a problem. Had she told him? She certainly thought so, recounting several recent shouting matches, plus the increasingly frigid climate at home, which even her friends commented upon. Peter, however, seemed unfazed.

The centerpiece of Peter's life was his work, where he was buoyant, skillful, and intensely absorbed. As he explained at the first therapy session, he thought he had a "great" marriage, though he was aware of Barbara's recent bad moods and, as always, found them a trial to bear. Actually, she'd always been moody—that was just Barbara.

Peter was happy with the idea that Barbara might go talk to someone who could help "even her out a little." Since the last baby, she'd been more down than usual, harder to live with. He'd even tried to help her more, though the demands his work made on his time were enormous.

Yes, he agreed, they had had a few louder-than-usual battles recently. But he thought that was pretty normal. All couples fight, right? Peter knew he could be a "hothead," especially when their sex life wasn't so satisfying. But these phases of marriage come and go, and he had a great family going, and Barbara took things too much to heart, and analyzed them too much, and "It's been great meeting you, Doc. Anytime I can help you help Barbara, just let me know."

It was easy to understand why Barbara has given up trying to break through to Peter. He had a version of their personal life that was simply not available for revision. She went silent, as her mother did.

But keeping silent did not mean letting go of her anger. Hence her growing inability to kiss him when he walked in, to smile over the phone when he bothered to call, or to turn her body towards him at night. Hence Peter's automatic retreat, his need to stay later at work, the growing infrequency of his phone calls. He hated to be around her when one of her moods, as he thought of them, was coming on.

It was now day five of the Siege—though only in Barbara's mind. Peter, who was neither trapped by virus nor stockpiling grievances, had no reason to keep count. Barbara fed the baby while Peter poured cereal for the older kids and spent a few happy minutes making them laugh. (*Isn't Daddy fun? So much more fun than that grumpy Mommy.*)

Peter drifted back to the bathroom to examine his hair, his tie, and the complete contents of yesterday's pockets, in order to get himself ready for work. Barbara called in to him, "Pete, could you watch the kids for ten minutes so I could grab a shower?" Back came the answer: "Oh, hon, I can't. I've got to leave this minute. I'm late for work already."

Barbara received his pronouncement standing naked in the bedroom, having anticipated her shower. She felt the predictable rage begin, that rumble of fury and frustration she was suddenly unable to contain. Her explosion would offer only temporary relief, at great cost. But that relief was an improvement on her only other alternative—a chronic, choking martyrdom.

Barbara saw all this in a nanosecond, and suddenly, unthinking, she surprised herself by seeing a third option. She could give herself a break. She didn't need Peter's agreement.

For ten months, I had been pressing Barbara's attention away from Peter and towards herself. Over and over, I asked Barbara the same questions:

Why are you waiting for his permission? ("I'm not. I'm not! It's just that I'm stuck. He's the only one who could dig me out, and he refuses to.")

Why does he have to be the one to give you what you need? Isn't there somewhere else you could get it? ("Because I want it from him, that's why! Aren't I entitled to a little time, a little attention? What's wrong with him? Doesn't he care at all?")

Why can't you love him, but make yourself happy? ("Because I can't! Because I'm not asking for much! Because I try all the time to make him happy. Don't I deserve something back?")

Make yourself happy? With no more thought than this sudden vision of a new alternative, Barbara walked straight to her closet, picked out a slinky sun dress she'd been waiting to wear, and stepped into it without a pause for underwear. After slipping on sandals and grabbing her purse, she popped the baby safely into his crib and walked straight out the front door into the nice air-conditioned car that Peter was intending to drive to work.

She hesitated, assessing potential damage. The absence of the car would ensure that Peter would notice the absence of the wife. She knew he'd never leave the kids alone, any more than she would. And suddenly she was free—not because he said so, but because she said so.

Barbara was free, and she waited for guilty lightning to crash in on her pleasure. It didn't. She began to conjure the hundred best things she should do with this freedom—see a neglected friend, look for full-time work, get a pedicure. She quickly eliminated some possibilities on account of no underwear, and was on her way to constructing a complete list of options when she caught herself up short.

Whoa . . . all or nothing, right? Wrong. Stop. Reframe. She was not running away from home. She was a woman taking a well-deserved break. No more, no less.

Barbara and I had been working for months on her tendency to envision only extremes. She would allow herself either total silence or complete fury. Where was the middle ground for discussion, conflict, negotiation? In Barbara's fantasy solutions, either she ran away from home with her children and a new lover who appreciated them all, or some horrible accident caused Peter to appreciate her when it was almost (or already—version two) too late.

Taking small, real-life steps to get more of what she needed (without going through Peter to get it) had been very tough for Barbara to consider. She was trying it now. Barbara drove idly to Dunkin' Donuts, took a minute to fix her lipstick and fluff her hair, and went in. She flirted pleasantly with the cops at the counter and bought two perfect chocolate-glazed beauties.

Reflecting that the flirting and the donuts, taken in the extreme, were the traditional sins of married women, Barbara suddenly realized that a teeny bit of each sin, taken from time to time, could be medicinal. Chocolate donuts were not a food binge, catching the smile of an attractive man was not infidelity, and a pleasure break was not child abandonment.

Barbara bought the newspaper and read it at her leisure in her nice, quiet, air-conditioned car. When she was done, she drove home. On the drive, she noticed that her morning's fury with Peter had been considerably reduced. Ridiculous. How could four days of frustration be soothed by glazed chocolate? But there you have it.

In place of her anger, however, there was a rising clutch of dread. Surely she would have to face Peter's anger at the door. After all, she'd made him late for work, she'd gone without warning, she hadn't left one single instruction about the children. She began to remind herself of our many conversations on this subject:

Yes, she might have to face Peter's anger. She must resist the easy, defensive "You made me do it" route. ("Peter, you have no right to be mad at me. You haven't given me a break for days, you couldn't even spare me a shower. . . .")

Instead, she would just acknowledge his right to be angry: "Of course you're mad. It was a mean, thoughtless thing I did, leaving you stuck, just because there was something I needed to do."

He would likely confront her. "What was so important that you had to make me late for work?"

"I needed a break, so I took one," she would explain. "I realize I've been waiting for you to give me one, and that just makes me whiny and mad. I don't think that leaving each other stuck is the greatest way to treat each other. We could probably work out these time conflicts better next time."

Naturally, the conversation would not end there, nor was the issue likely to be resolved in one incident. There would probably be many skirmishes, and neither partner would win them all. Something crucial between them, however, would have shifted for the better. Instead of struggling to get Peter to give her more, Barbara had begun to focus on strengthening her ability to get what she needed for herself.

Needing less from Peter was not as easy as staying mad about what he hadn't given. It meant Barbara was going to have to risk facing Peter's anger, instead of being safely angry herself. It also meant she was going to have to figure out a better way to be satisfied with her life at home, instead of waiting for Peter to help her become more satisfied. But needing less from him was the only way Barbara could love him at the end of the day. Once Barbara understood that was her choice, she began to gather the strength to act.

On her way home, Barbara reviewed what we'd practiced about facing someone else's anger. She reassured herself that it was only his anger she'd have to face, not divorce or assault. She reminded herself that although she was furious with Peter she still loved him. Why shouldn't he love her behind his tantrum, too?

Still, she dreaded the prospect. Suddenly she had a flash of Peter coming home, and wondered if he ever felt this wave of dread because he was anticipating her angry face. Even knowing how selfish he really was (in comparison with, in her firm opinion, her more generous nature), she felt a moment of sympathy for him.

In the meantime, Peter had been in a towering rage. He knew instantly what she had done and, frankly, he was shocked. How dare she? How could she? He stomped through a series of phone calls, attempting to hunt her down—if not to get to work on time, then at least to have a target for his feelings.

Peter's calls were interrupted by screams from his daughter, signaling the onset of new sibling skirmishes. Peter ignored these for as long as possible, feeling that his wife always intervened too early and that his kids would be far better off if they toughened up and worked things out on their own. (Nervous mother, crappy wife, piece of cold bacon in bed . . . Jeez, Barbara was a hell of choice. What had he been thinking?)

The screams continued, amplified by the baby's sudden howling participation. Peter reluctantly investigated. He retrieved the baby, sobbing and smelly, and carried him into the living room, where the other children were now loudly quiet. He discovered his son one inch from the television, absorbed in the murder of a cartoon villain. His daughter was feverish in the corner, making stabbing gestures at her dolls. Peter could only imagine what his son might have done to force silence on his sister. The living room itself was a sea of destruction. The baby still smelled. God. Would he be trapped in this all day? He couldn't take it.

Click. A flash of unwelcome sympathy for Barbara. Four days of this? (Barbara would have reminded him that it had actually been four years of this, in one way or another.) He would have walked out much sooner. The thought made him unaccountably anxious. She would never walk out, never leave the kids, never leave him, he was sure. But what if she did?

He loved his family, loved her. It was just that she had become such a drag, complaining all the time. Now it occurred to him that maybe she had something to complain about. He heard the car drive up and felt a vast relief from a fear he had not admitted to.

Barbara heard the usual sounds from her house as soon as she walked up the steps—the TV, of course, and crying—although not, she quickly noted, in any particular distress. She used her key to get in and, as she opened the door, she saw Peter walking down the stairs towards her. She braced, and, seeing her, so did he.

They each waited a beat. Then Peter flung himself to his knees in front of her, and moaned in his most piteous voice, "Please. Torture me. Maim me. But do not leave me alone with these creatures again, I beg you."

Barbara teetered on the edge of righteous indignation, but her half-hour of self-indulgence had restored her sense of the ridiculous. She burst out laughing, tossed him the bag with the chocolate donut she'd bought for him despite herself, and sat down on the floor next to him. "Honey," she began, "here's what I've decided I need to do."

CHAPTER SEVEN

The Limits of Love

Love does not conquer all. It doesn't even conquer most. Chapter six described how easily love can be swamped by fear and fury. We talked about how overpowering both these feelings can be, and how comforting to sink beneath them, allowing anger and anxiety to determine the limits of our love. These are two limits that we can, with effort, sweep aside.

In this chapter, we will discuss a third element that limits love, which we must also largely set aside: fantasy. Fantasy, as you will see, is built of all those details in our visions of love that ultimately get in the way of love itself. Fantasy limits whom we allow ourselves to love, because it focuses instead on whom we *should* love.

Yet surely that focus is not unreasonable. If we know what we need, we can then know what to settle for, what we should or should not compromise with. We will know how to choose between men, or how to recognize the better man for us. We can keep ourselves on course.

Follow the thread of that small reasonable assumption and it will lead you to the greatest factor that limits love. That limit is our vision itself, our inner portrait of love. Although our vision is both motivation and inspiration, the fleshing out of the vision has become a profound inner barrier. It leaves us crying, *I can't love him more. He's not who I pictured.*

Visions of Love

We honor love when we let go of all our ideas of how he *should be* **and focus instead on who he** *is***, and on how this relationship actually feels.** Yet that requires a loss we are not easily able to bear. Before we learn to love our person, we grow deeply attached to a mental image of our prince. Sadly, in order truly to love the person, we have to break up with the prince—forever.

True, the foundation of our image of love is pure emotion. But most of us build a leaning tower of romantic minutiae on that foundation. This is a case where God is most definitely not in the details.

Think of love's pure emotional foundation as a forest. Like every forest, this one is composed of a legion of separate trees, each detailing some small romantic expectation or some essential element of your romantic icon. When we envision love, these trees are the details that elaborate our hazy vision, adding texture, depth, and substance to that overall forest of feeling. Here is how he will act, what he will look like, how he will speak, how he will joke, touch me, defend me, support me. This is how I will feel, what I will say, and how I will know him when I've found him.

The problem with these details, of course, is that we become so focused on each one, we are apt to lose sight of our overall purpose. We can't see the forest for the trees. On the one hand, we believe our feeling for one another is of primary importance. On the other hand, each quality of his that does not match our detailed fantasy begins to loom larger than that whole forest of feeling.

These details gain importance partly because romantic fantasy includes our *expectations* of love. I prefer the word "fantasy," since "expectations" conveys a sense of standards and norms and other highly valued ideas, which we tend to believe we should hold on to at any cost. "Fantasy," on the other hand, conjures an image of daydreams, wishes, and hopes, which, though certainly equally cherished, we often have greater permission to relinquish, if we need to.

It is all too easy for fantasy and expectation to merge. What we imagine of love blurs into what we expect of love. It's a short hop from what we expect of love to what we *need* from love in order to be happy with it and with our partners.

Therein lies the danger. If you have merely imagined a lover one way and he turns out to be another, well, that's interesting. But if you need him to be one way and he turns out to be another—that, God forbid, is settling.

Settling makes us more than angry. It makes us anxious. *If I love him, what does it mean about me? Is he the best I could do?* Settling means loss.

Take Kate and Robert, who have known each other since Sunday school. Although they have been dating only six months, both families have their fingers crossed. Kate, however, holds back, explaining, "If I let myself really love Robert, I mean if I could, then I'd marry him. But it would mean letting go of the dream I've had all my life of finding a perfect love. I am Juliet and Guinevere and Isolde, and I cannot envision happiness as Kate and Robert, known around the club as the Montgomerys."

Of course, we are all "settling," since romantic fantasy is invariably positive, whereas reality is always a mixed bag. In *How to Stop Looking for Someone Perfect and Find Someone to Love*, I refer to this principle of romantic attachment as "The Blue Plate Special": Love is a blue-plate special. You want the roast beef? It comes with the peas. You want the chicken? It comes with the spinach. No substitutions!

A great anxiety over "settling" may signal that you have become more attached to your expectations of love than to the man himself. Some of this unwillingness to love is nothing more than simple snobbery ("I couldn't take him seriously—he's an optometrist"). Some reflects the stubbornly persistent fantasies of our adolescence ("I know I'm ridiculous, but I can't help it: if he can't dance or he's a bad driver, I'm just turned off"). And some are that same adolescence recently updated ("He doesn't know a thing about contemporary art"). Some flaws are current cultural sins that you may use as indicators of People Who Are Wrong to Love. (He smokes or drinks, he's fat or flabby, he still gets high, often gets low, or he's unemployed, sexually undecided, and undisturbed by either.)

Some of these failures to fit the picture appear trivial in and of themselves, but they touch a deeper nerve that vibrates in disdain. ("It's his table manners. I imagine bringing him home to the family. Then I imagine my mother watching him chew, with the little pieces of food slipping out of the sides of his mouth. Then I lose the picture.")

However minor a lover's flaw, it can nonetheless require a huge stretch to overcome your own resistance to love. Sometimes we cling to fantasy as a smoke screen for our own reluctance to be permanently attached—and therefore to be a grown-up, or threatened with male control, or sexually monogamous, or sexual at all, or forced to leave Daddy, or doomed to become Mother, or any of the other deeper fears and longings that make some of us back away from the man who is obviously coming towards us. We back away automatically, not understanding why, but confident of the reliability of our own reactions. ("I couldn't. I mean, he has a bumper sticker reading 'I've Been to Carlsbad Caverns.' ")

Finally, most painfully, many details central to our picture are connected to expectations so deeply etched in our psyche that we are able to allow ourselves to love a real man only by incurring great loss. Marcia, you'll remember, struggled with this loss, realizing that to commit herself to Jerry would be to abandon forever her quest for an emotional soulmate. I have seen women in equal agony because they love men who do not work as hard or earn as much as they, and are therefore unable to flesh out the provider fantasy most of us still, despite everything, cherish. I have seen women utterly immobilized because they must somehow choose between the worthy man who inspires trust and respect, and the impossible man who unaccountably makes them feel alive and in love.

How do we choose between these? What is expendable? Which of us is strong enough to make the Sophie's choices of our lives? Who are the clear-eyed few, able to face loss and deliberately invoke it for some greater good? The rest of us falter, trying to weigh and measure, making long, useless lists of pros and cons, consulting friends and experts, as if someone, somewhere knows the proper formula for this particular choice. We seek crystal balls and psychic predictions, signs from heaven or from the man himself.

Love, lovers, life itself for that matter, does not necessarily fulfill our expectations, just because what we envision is right or reasonable. Those obsessive discussions—trying to decide whether we are entitled to be mad or disappointed, whether he *ought* to be different, or whether we are being too demanding—are so often beside the point. Whether you are being fair or excessive, entitled or demanding, there is something you expected that you are not getting. You've done whatever you could think of (plus a few things you would never have believed) to get him to change. He's the same. Now what?

In the end, what you expected is not anywhere as important as what you've really got. The important question is not how to get closer to your romantic fantasy of love. It is how can you get closer to the reality of love. How can you experience your vision in the real world—*not* how can you change that real world to be closer to your vision? Remember, the heart of your vision is the feeling of love, not the fantasy of romance.

Even if you accept this logic, you are left with a problem. Reasonable or absurd, what you fantasized isn't there. Can you allow yourself to love him? Should you? Will you?

I don't know the right answer for you. I know that it is possible to stay stuck in resentment forever, and I also know it is possible to get past it. I have known women who never forgave their husbands' harsh judgments or excessive ambition, and women who were once deeply troubled by one of these painful experiences and no longer even pause over it. "That's him," they say. "That's how he is. I love him."

I know women who grow lonelier every year they are married to a silent man, women whose homes become emotional graves the instant they hear his car in the driveway. I know others who grow so in tune with a silent spouse that they discover through him a new tranquillity. But I don't know which of these you'd be, and *neither does anyone else,* because your capacity to love is neither preordained nor fixed.

You are somewhere on the path to love at this moment. If your progress is blocked by some part of a man that does not suit your fantasy, remember: **You are unlikely to have the power to change him to fit your picture. Your power is in your ability to change the picture itself.** I can tell you that you *can*—if you allow yourself to love him more and to need the picture less.

Wendy Wasserstein portrayed the steps necessary to make the shift from prince to person in *The Sisters Rosensweig.* In the last scene, the eldest sister capitulates to her feelings for a man who represents the nice Jewish boys of her childhood, the warm and anxious Portnoys of the neighborhood she fled. Sara has looked all her life for a hero who would take her beyond her neighborhood, beyond the limits of her family, her ethnicity, her inherited past. In the end, she is forced to admit to love where she finds it, instead of love where she'd hoped it would take her.

Sara finds love at the cost of her fantasy of transformation, and she is angry about it for most of two acts. Just before the final kiss, she looks up at her man and bleats, "Jesus Christ, why did your name have to be Mervyn? And you're a furrier!" Every woman in the audience who has ever made the leap from the fantasy to the reality of love, who imagined herself a Rothschild and ended up a Mrs. Goldberg, knows just what she means.

How was Sara able to let go of her romantic fantasy in order to make room for love? First, she paused in her ongoing judgments of Merv to take a clear look at herself. She reframed her perspective on male emotionality. Maybe she had been wrong to code it as a sign of weakness, and to label cooler, more distant men as icons of strength.

Sara began to see that what she had thought of as strength might actually be indifference; what she had always labeled weak might actually be evidence of a capacity to love. With a clearer look at herself and at her own distortions of men, Sara finally chose to respond differently. Instead of fleeing from the threat of Merv, she opened herself to him. She did it reluctantly, even angrily, but she did it. Just past the edge of her fantasy, Sara found love. That is where most of us find it.

You *can* love him more, even though he's not what you pictured. You *can* need him to be less of a match with your picture than you ever imagined. Yes, like Sara, you will probably be angry initially. Yes, it will probably make you anxious at first. My God, how could Sara feel different, special, if she married a man just like all the men all her childhood friends married? Did she go this far, hold out this long, only to end up married to a *Mervyn*?

Yes, Sara admitted finally, she had. Yes, she needed to prove she was special and different, and she needed to escape her family, and she needed so many other markers of distinction. But she needed love more, so the other needs had to become less important. Sara kept the man and changed her picture instead. Why was that choice so hard for Sara? Why is it so hard for the rest of us to do the same? Because, like Sara, we get the guy—but lose the prince.

What We Lose When We Find Love

"I listened to you last week and tried to be more loving towards my husband. I kept myself from pointing out the stuff he was doing wrong. I forced myself to notice what he did right and tell him I appreciated it. I guess it worked, because I found myself less angry with him. But how I felt was very, very sad."

Loving more and needing less is the path that will lead you from smart about men to wise about love. Anger, anxiety, and romantic fantasy are obstacles in that path. Much as we cherish love, there is still a part of each of us that clings to our obstacles.

We can confront and even overcome the dragons of anger and anxiety that bar our gate to love. Like Sara, we can allow the grip of fantasy to loosen and make more room for real-life love. We can—

but that does not necessarily mean we will wholeheartedly want to. It is so much easier to struggle with a lover than to struggle with ourselves.

To discover what stands between you and loving him more, or between you and needing him less, always ask two questions:

• What is blocking my path?
• Why would I want to keep it there?

Treasuring fantasy, avoiding anxiety, and nursing anger obviously interfere with our ability to love. Yet few of us are single-mindedly determined to overcome them, because each is rewarding in its own way. Each obstacle we overcome moves us forward, but each forward step incurs a loss. It is to prevent those losses that we hold back, even though what is being lost may not be clear even to ourselves.

The loss involved when we face anxiety is obvious. The instant we duck anxiety's bullet, we feel a wonderful relief. To stand straight up and face a fear is to trade that soft, safe feeling for a twisted stomach knot.

But anger is a heart-skipping, shoulder-clenching state of uncomfortable disruption. Why would a part of us cherish this feeling? Yet we do—automatically and sometimes even deliberately. We feed and foster our outrage. Why?

Because anger has rewards of its own, and forgiveness has a great cost.

Anger is a heady rush of power and an inflated righteousness, which are highs that can certainly rival love. It is also an efficient shield against having anger directed towards you. As the young wife of an older, traditional husband explained, "When he sits there, just assuming I'll serve him, I want to shove his face in the cereal bowl,"

"But you still serve the cereal?" I asked.

"Yes," she said. "If I didn't, it would start a war."

Some women find that war intolerable. Whether from our fears of rejection, from the fear of actual physical or verbal assault, or simply from those old "nice-girl" constraints, many of us are sickened when we are the object of any hostility at all. We guard ourselves against it in the most straightforward way—by retreating to the security of being the angry ones ourselves. It can be easier to give in and be the sulker than to insist on your own way and endure someone else's sulk.

Say he wants to join friends for a bite to eat after a party. You are tired, and eager to go home. You could insist on going home and risk his displeasure, go along and be displeased yourself, or, of course, comfortably go your separate ways. Half an hour later, you are waiting for a table at a popular restaurant, explaining to the two other couples that you didn't really want to be here, but "Hal always has to have his way."

One woman who discovered the hidden rewards of this mini-martyrdom describes them as "The Pleasures of Being Mad." She says, "He gets his way and I get to complain about him. When I do, I'm saying, 'See what I have to put up with. My life is so tough.' It seems to me that people feel sorry for me. I like that, I feel like they care. And it gets a lot more attention than when you tell people the good side of things.

"Besides, when I am convinced that my life is hard, and my husband is unfair, sometimes people step in to help me. Like my dad will send me a hundred dollars to cheer me up, or my girlfriend won't ask me to work on the mailing because she knows I'm feeling overwhelmed." She paused. "My husband doesn't rescue me, though, not anymore. That makes me even madder. The madder I get, the more I complain. I don't know how to get myself out of it."

"When I'm mad at him, it gives me permission to treat myself," explains another woman, who soothes her anger with shopping sprees. Plus, when she's angry with him and he knows it, he feels less free to object to her spending. Permission to treat ourselves can run all the way from a food binge to the pure satisfaction of being mean. Our anger grants us permission.

Anger carries with it the rewarding elevation of moral superiority. There is the self-esteem boost of the injured, the feeling that I am generous, while he is selfish. When I'm sick, he still expects dinner and I'm still throwing in the wash. When he is sick, he absents himself from all earthly duties. That's because I have to be a responsible woman and he is still a boy. Aah, aren't all men?

Plus, anger might be the ticket of admission to a community of smart, supportive, and entertaining women who share with each other their war stories as well as their happy endings. This is the club called girlfriends, whose companionship can make life more palatable, and sometimes even possible. Since anger may be a piece of the tie that binds, it's something of a loss to give yours up.

Probably the most important reason that we are so loath to let go of our anger, even for the sake of love, is the high price of forgiveness. Forgiveness feels as if you are letting him off the hook. When you are hurt, angry, or disappointed, you'd rather he wriggled on that hook forever.

In some not necessarily logical way, *your* anger becomes *his* punishment, often his only punishment, for his having hurt or wronged you. Whether the injury was small or large, the fact that you are still angry creates the sense that you have power back, that you are not permitting him to "get away with it." Offering escape from this punishment, by way of forgiveness, is just too generous, too difficult.

Up to some reasonable point, this makes sense. Your anger is a neon billboard flashing "Whoa! That hurt. Cut it out, you are wrong! You owe me!" It may even signal "Hey, here's what I need," or "You can make it up to me," and therefore serve a positive end. Past that reasonable point, anger—or, more specifically, your inability to let go of anger—can be your major obstacle to love.

Where is that reasonable point? I don't know. Some of us are blessed with the gift of rarely staying mad; others are cursed with the tendency to hold a grudge at the slightest insult. Obviously the nature of the injury should play a role. Betrayal would seem to merit a longer simmer than a spoiled party, real injury would logically provoke more anger than a near miss. Yet logic does not always prevail over personality, and we sometimes measure the size of the wrongdoing by how angry we are, rather than vice versa.

In *Excess Baggage,* I included a chapter describing the step-by-step road to forgiveness. I refer you to that discussion, and to the bibliography in that book, if forgiving is a particular problem of yours. The point here is just this: Anger gives the illusion of retaliation, and forgiveness can feel like an admission of weakness. In actual fact, forgiveness is a reflection of your personal strength, and the person whom anger punishes the most is the person who is angry. Anger's greatest punishment is that it keeps you from getting to love.

Anger can make you feel safe, whereas love makes you vulnerable. It can make you feel strong, whereas love forces you to admit to needs you may hate yourself for having. Anger gives at least the illusion and often the fact of control, whereas love forces us to be two interdependent equals who can only control ourselves. It's no surprise that a part of us treasures our anger as much as another part suffers under it.

None of us needs to eliminate that anger in order to experience love. We just need a way to melt anger down enough to see past it. We don't need love that guarantees no pain. We just need to be strong enough to risk the hurt, because we know we will be strong enough to heal.

Confronting anxiety and relinquishing anger both entail losses we are reluctant to face, even for the sake of love. But the heart of our resistance to love—to allowing love, to loving more, to being willing to love—is the *loss* that realism brings. If you give up the fantasy of the perfect love, you give up the brief ecstasy of thinking you've found him. The whole ride evens out, and, though none of us misses the horrifying crash, many of us mourn the absence of the high. In fact, some women worry that, if they are this sane, this clear-eyed, how could it be love at all? Still worse, needing him less threatens that we will never be Cinderella-swept-away, a fantasy that gets us through so many bad days.

Let me reassure you (and my own secret Cinderella) that you don't have to give these up entirely. We are talking balance here, not perfection. A little fantasy on the seesaw is not such a bad thing on a Monday morning. A mild measure of moral superiority may be enjoyed from time to time. The occasional helpless whine can be your way of allowing him to enjoy the pleasures of superiority, too. Responsibility for oneself is a necessary evil, but taking advantage of the opportunity to blame someone else can be one of the great benefits of marriage. It's all right to indulge every so often.

Truly, there is some loss when you go from romantic fantasy to romantic realism, but it only hurts for a little while. O.K., it does come back every so often—romantic fantasy is the acid flashback of our gender, and just as disorienting. But by and large, the gains in real-life experience make these fantasy losses smaller than we fear they might be.

If you lose the dream of being rescued, you face the complicated reality of responsibility for yourself. Most of us creep up on the adult burden of personal responsibility, grudgingly relinquishing cherished fantasies of who will pay our bills, or make things better, or know the answers. Who, that is, besides ourselves? Bit by bit, whether forced by life or self-propelled, we do move towards accepting and even appreciating these harsher realities.

Letting go of the love fantasy *does not mean* letting go of love itself. Love is as much a fact of the real world as shoes and taxes. **Letting go of the fantasy means letting go of the idea of perfect, effortless love, and that is the wrench.**

In the universal love fantasy, love simply arrives in your heart. There is no accounting for how or why. In the fantasy, you cannot will love away, nor can you create the feeling when it would be suitable or convenient to feel it. In romantic fantasy, love is something that happens independent of our will. And it allows no doubt, thereby sparing you even the exertion of your judgment.

We want the comfort of the fantasy that love is not action but reaction, that love is a gift someone has planted on our path. Like a jewel purchased on the day of our birth, unknown to us but waiting to be revealed at some special future moment, love, too, is planned for us. We have only to recognize it when it comes. We resist the lowering idea that love could be a result of action we take, an attitude we assume, a choice we make to interpret an event one way rather than another, or a self-conscious push in an emotional direction that serves us.

Best of all, romantic fantasy eases our concerns about our own limitations. Whatever emotional issues we might have—like our own anxiety, competitiveness, ambivalence, or tendency to harsh judgment, for example—we don't have to worry about them. If he's "the right one," our own issues will be overcome. That is a most appealing idea. You don't have to change a thing about your inner self (a notoriously awkward and effortful process) in order to make love work. After all, by very definition, love is not work. That's how you know it's love.

Loving him more and needing him less is at the exact opposite pole from this very delightful fantasy of effortless love. As I said earlier, we cannot wholly create love simply because it is a great way to liven up a vacation or to avoid a divorce. But there is a great deal we can do to clear our path, so that love has room to take solid root. Unfortunately, everything you can do to clear this path requires effort.

It's worth it. Not only *can* we exercise some control over what we feel, but we *must*. Love is too important to allow it to be in charge of us. We need to put forth the effort to be in charge of it. Otherwise, our most cherished relationships are vulnerable to every passing fury, every flash of heat for a stranger, every irritant of daily life. Love gets us through these narrow passages. It is folly to do without it just because of the soothing belief that if love is real, it will overcome our barricades for us.

There is one final reason we cling to fantasy in the face of all logic. It's not a very good reason, but it is very powerful, and I would be less than honest if I failed to point it out. In *The Right Stuff,* Tom Wolfe gives an example of it.

He tells the story of John Glenn's response to his wife, Annie, in the face of her reluctance to entertain Vice-President Lyndon Johnson while Glenn was awaiting his rocket launch into space. Annie was shy and had some speech difficulties, and the idea of appearing on television hostessing the vice-president appalled her. Johnson, on the other hand, was not only vice-president of the United States, he was also the guiding political force of the entire space program. He wanted what he wanted, and right now he wanted to be shown on television with Annie Glenn.

Finally, the dilemma of Johnson fuming in a limousine outside Glenn's home while Annie sat inside refusing to open the door reached the NASA bosses. They approached Glenn during a countdown hold. "John," Wolfe describes, ". . . we're having a problem with your wife. . . . She won't cooperate, John. Perhaps you can give her a call." So he did, and once he understood that she had refused to spend even a few minutes with Lyndon Johnson, the man whom President Kennedy had appointed special overseer for the space program, here is what he said to her: "Look, if you don't want the Vice-President or the TV networks or anybody else to come into the house, then that's it as far as I'm concerned, they are not coming in—and I will back you up all the way, one hundred percent, and you tell them that. I don't want Johnson or any of the rest of them to put so much as one toe inside our house!"

It's hard to let go of fantasy because sometimes, some place, it comes true.

A Piece of the Action

"We misunderstand love because we have chosen to worship power; we fail in compassion because we have become obsessed with control; . . . we do not adore because we insist that everything and every person be of use; . . . we do not care because we have come to believe that it profits a man or woman well above prime rate to trade the soul for a piece of the action."

—Sam Keen

There is one last obstacle in your path. You may resist loving him more and needing him less because, ultimately, our whole society is built in the opposite direction. If you loosely translate loving and needing as the emotional equivalents of giving and getting, you'll see the barrier immediately.

Loving more and needing less suggests we'd be better off, emotionally and spiritually, if we gave a little more and took a little less. Yet we live in a world that has built the opposite tilt into the heart of its values and its wisdom: Get a little more, give a little less. That's how you end up at the top of the pyramid.

To be smart, rich, successful, happy, we are taught one essential rule: Cut the deal in your own favor. Let him love you a little bit more than you love him. Give yourself an edge.

The tilt in one's own favor makes perfect sense, as long as you are thinking in terms of commodities, deals, value, and profit. As it happens, that is precisely how we have come to think of love.

We don't admit to this, of course. On the surface, we still hold love in a special category, venerating its power, "believing" in it, and holding doggedly to the magic of chemistry as its only real explanation. For all our romantic protest, it is easy to read our cultural passion for a great buy between the lines of our fears and expectations of love. We struggle with the idea of "settling," clearly accepting the idea that some deals are better than others and worrying over whether we got the biggest bang for our buck. We comfort each other with the reminder, "He isn't worth it."

And, most telling of all, we cringe over a beloved's failings. A fat lover, a financial failure, a husband who brags, eats with his fingers, uses poor grammar, a lover who makes ignorant remarks in intelligent company—these are not merely flaws that will briefly or permanently offend us, but flaws that fill us with shame, as if they were a measure of our own inadequacies, or public announcements of some private failing. If I love you, you—a television-junkie middle manager, an unemployed depressive, a cultural pissant—*what does that mean about me?*

Buried within this thinking is a deep-seated view of love as both a measure of and a reward for a person's worth. We are bred to the bone to be consumers. It is natural for us to express our reverence for love by seeing it as the most valuable commodity on the shelf. It follows, then, that those of us with the greatest resources to offer would get the most desirable lovers in exchange. You know, the richer get the Lexus, the regular get the Toyota, in exactly the same way that the quarterback and the cheerleader expect to end up with each other. There is a logic to this progression, and it does reflect an economic and social fact of life. The point is, none of this has anything to do with love.

Nor do those long, sad lists so many of us end up making—lists of his positives and negatives, lists of our own; lists of reasons why we should risk, lists of reasons why we won't; lists of all the things we want in the men we love; and then the agonizing arithmetic as we try to weigh each item to determine which we could, or should, or would live without.

Love, though, is a feeling quite apart from these calculations, a feeling less easy to identify, to quantify, even to justify. Think of it as a state of grace, an inner ease, a steady emotional stream to which we bring ourselves. Love is not evoked by someone else's match with your carefully thought-out list; nor is love a measure of how smart, how kind, how funny, how sexy, supportive, or successful you are, even if it always feels like that when you are being rejected.

It's very different to think of love as having more to do with our own willingness to give than with the other person's worthiness to receive. We have become confused about the difference between worth and love, and that confusion has set love almost beyond our grasp.

It's not about whether he is worth it or whether you are, or about which of you is entitled, or who got the better deal. Love is that thing between us, that thing that we built together, that bond we sometimes cherish, sometimes chafe under. Love is that inner state whose existence we've known since Eve. It was never a measure of the value of Adam.

Self-Propulsion

When we attempt a conscious push to the next developmental level, we don't just march along in our thinking, ever forward, ever forward. It's more like progress in fits and starts. We take two steps forward towards self-reliance, and then somebody beautiful comes along and we are instantly undone, leaping one giant footstep backwards into a longing to please. Two steps forward by learning to describe his irritating impatience as chronic anxiety, so you can tolerate it more easily. Then he stops the car to let you out and drives off before you've gotten your second leg out of the door. Love him more? *Please* . . .

Besides, even when you know what to do, even when you've done it all before and it worked, it can still be so hard to make the effort to turn towards love. Some days it's just not in you. Some days, if you wait an hour, your strength returns and you are able to be more reasonable, more generous. Remember, everybody regresses for a while, all of us go through a bad patch.

Sometimes loving more by needing less is just too hard to do. Most of us ask whether we *should* let go of some inner barrier, but the important question is really whether we *could* or *would*. The fact is, there are times when we just can't. This has very little to do with your lover's provocation and a great deal to do with your own capacity for love.

A person may simply be beyond your stretch, at this point in your life. Ten years from now, a lover who is unsentimental about birthdays, anniversaries, and other romantic markers may leave you unruffled, but today the man who ignores these occasions hurts you deeply. On the other hand, the man who has more ideals than ambitions may inspire you in your twenties and appall you in your forties.

So much more is relative than we allow ourselves to admit. So much that we experience as right and wrong, as universal truth, as should and must, turns out to be the narrow perspective of a momentary point of view. It is unnerving to lose this sense of the absolute. It is far more comfortable to believe that the view of life from your inner window is a relatively objective one. If that were so, then the outside world would have to change for it to look different to you. Turns out that you had only to move your chair a bit.

But that small move opens up surprising possibilities, and, frankly, a huge sense of power. You may have had an experience similar to this: For years I could not sit through an evening with a man or woman whose politics were different from mine. I never once thought I might be overreacting. I just thought I knew a fool when I met one. I have since learned to think as well as feel. Maybe this enemy has something to say? Maybe I don't have to be so angry, so uncomfortable? Maybe I could even learn something?

I suspected that this exercise in emotional discipline would result mainly in the chance to spend a lot more time with fools. Actually, the more I allowed myself to relax and to take in, the fewer fools I met. It was rare that someone made any substantial impact on my political thinking. But I enjoyed myself so much more, found so many people more intelligent, more informed than I had previously noticed. Once I wasn't so busy *reacting* to what these men and women thought, I could actually hear them.

As long as we are physically well and emotionally alive, we will always look out of our inner window and react to what we see out there. The great leap forward in our inner development is the one we make when we take conscious control of what it is we see.

It's a funny thing. On the one hand, there is no how-to kit for making that move. That shift to a higher level of awareness is related to our gradually increasing capacity to love and to revere our attachments as we respect ourselves. Your own progress on this path is a matter of individual unfolding. There is no formula to get you there. On the other hand, it seems clear that people further along this inner path have developed certain common tools that work to increase their capacity to love. *Loving Men More, Needing Men*

Less has been aimed at helping you to understand and to acquire these tools for your own use. Using them, of course, is a private matter.

Look, I know that most of us do not make the self-directed changes we so often say we should make. At least, I know I often don't. And I know that many of you who have read this book may not be ready to change either the way in which you love someone, or the ways in which you understand love itself—at least, not yet.

But I am thinking of that smaller group of women who will. You are the ones who will make this leap. I know that, because I've seen it. You are the ones who can and will get to this next level. You are the women who will clear the cloud of anger and pain that fogs each of our visions of love. You are the women who will break through and be there to show the rest of us where to go, when we can, too. I wrote this book for you.

CHAPTER EIGHT

Lassoing the Moon

"What is it you want? The moon? Just say the word and I'll throw a lasso around it and pull it down for you."

—George Bailey in *It's a Wonderful Life*

The dream is love; the reality is marriage. The dream is of a hero; the reality is a man. The dream is happiness ever after; the reality is that some of us come closer to the dream than others.

The person you are, and the path you choose, wholly determines whether the spirit of your dream infuses the reality of your life. Life with none of that spirit is simple endurance. The dream disconnected from life is only mirage. We are each the measure of our capacity to combine the two.

Yes, but it reads too much easier than it lives. The path to this ideal combination of vision and realism, the path that may be so clear on paper, is a shadowy construct in daily life. Direction signs towards our path can be so subtle. Billboards loom with false advertising for love, while serious warnings can be signaled in the merest telling hesitation—telling, that is, if you know what to listen for. And who can listen for a heartbeat's hesitation in the din of life today?

Sometimes it seems that we are running towards the millennium with frantic acceleration, driven by a primitive wish to throw ourselves off the civilized edge and so return to the caves and the quiet

215

where we began. The path was probably clearer then, if only because it was less clogged with irresistible distraction.

Yet, even today, we still sense that path. However it is that we know it—there is an emotional and spiritual direction in which to head, which gives meaning to the ebb and flow of daily events. I believe that direction is called *love*. And we've known about it since our first bite of the apple.

There are, however, two problems: **We don't always know which of our choices heads us towards love. And we've lost sight of the importance of getting there.**

The direction of love is far less obvious than any of us feels safe in admitting. And the idea that there is no *it* to get to, but that we get to love by somehow creating it along the way, is even more unsettling. Love is elusive enough. It can feel as if it has disappeared altogether if you accept the idea that your own interpretation of events, your own spin on life, has a great deal to do with whether or not you experience it.

We are comfortable within the framework of *he loves me* or *he does not love me,* or, more precisely, *he loves me a lot or a little; he loves me more or less than I love him, more than I ever imagined* or *not as much as he used to.* All this feels real, as if we could measure it or earn it or win it or weigh it.

But as we take a step closer to our own role, the path starts to fade. The wisdom we've gained is complicated and discomfiting in a culture that has only the time to read the headlines. Your own role suggests, *He loves me—as long as I take what he does as love; He loves me more than I love him—or is it that he is stronger, less afraid to risk love than I am?* It says, in effect, that we invent our lives as much as we live them out, and that we are, therefore, responsible to a degree for our own creations.

Those creations result from the choices we make, and sometimes from those we discover we've made. Think of Audrey Hepburn in the pivotal scene of the too-true romantic comedy about marriage, *Two for the Road*. She is sitting at a table across from her lover, on the terrace of the hotel where they have spent the night. Her husband, Albert Finney, has just confronted the two of them, and Audrey has acknowledged to him that, yes, she was unfaithful, she is in love, and she is leaving him.

We know why she is leaving. Audrey and her husband were passionately in love when they married, but he is a vastly self-absorbed charmer who has become less and less attentive to Audrey as he became more and more successful. Finney plays a warm and expansive architect with a huge appetite for every opportunity, from wealth to other women. "I could be anyone," Audrey says to him once, when he celebrates a particularly triumphant evening by reaching out to make love to her.

Audrey is Wife, beautiful background, a fact of his life—but not its emotional center. When she meets her lover for the first time, he looks and sees her—really *sees* her—in a way that Albert Finney was never able to. Of course she falls in love. Of course she is thinking of leaving.

So here Audrey sits, on this gorgeous terrace in the south of France, her husband confronted, her ties cut, and she listens as her lover makes plans for their future together. But as he plans, she pictures, and what she pictures is not their future, but her own past. She sees her husband in her mind's eye—sees their moments together, their history, the times he made her laugh. She recalls a private moment and speaks the punch line aloud, but her lover doesn't get the joke. She sees the fact of their marriage and the fact of their love.

The scene cuts to Albert Finney alone and in agony in his hotel room. The door opens and there is Audrey. She is very serious, but she is there. "I'm back," she says. "I've come back." And we know why she did.

Audrey comes back, though she does not think that Finney will suddenly change, does not imagine that he will now appreciate what he almost lost. Audrey has always known that she was her husband's ballast, known that he could only fly so high because he had such an elegant and unflappable catcher. She knows that he knows, too, and knows he will forget again.

For weeks, we imagine, she has been weighing and measuring these two men, calculating flaws and value. Her lover offers her a lot of what she needs that she does not get from her husband. Her husband, on the other hand, has his own assets. Suddenly, sitting on the terrace, she sees that none of these calculations matter. She doesn't have to decide which is the better man or the better deal, what she would be giving up or what she would be gaining.

She stays because something has become clear. She is attached. And so is her husband. He is her person. She is his. They have chosen each other to love. The fact of that choice has brought something larger into the picture, something that cannot be contained by a list of pros and cons. It may even be something that she cannot quite figure, and certainly something that she would rather not trust. But there it is.

There is really only one simple decision for Audrey to make: will she continue towards love with this man she has chosen, or will she pull away from it? Like the rest of us on the same path, she will make this one decision over and over, throughout their time together. Sometimes she may decide for love, but sometimes not. Sometimes she will wish fervently that she could choose in one direction but find herself unable to.

At rare and difficult crossroads, like the one that Audrey reached, we may be required to choose consciously and deliberately, though most often our choices are mercifully automatic. We may choose for or against love with wholehearted vigor, or with great hesitation.

The choice to move towards or away from loving someone presents itself in so many forms, with such intricate plot twists, disguised as so many other things, that, viewed up close, it appears to be an inextricable maze. So much so that we would trust ourselves to magic rather than believe that we could ever sort our own way through love's convolutions.

But the big picture looks quite different. From this perspective, the decisions that shape our path are as simple to live as to read about. We choose for love, or we choose against it. We have reached a moment in our history that allows us to choose for love without choosing against ourselves. Therefore our choice is simpler: choose love.

In Favor of Love

You know from what you've already read that I have a clear bias. I believe those parts of us still swaddled in the safe small death of dependency must brave the strain of separation. I believe those parts of us that have found sanctuary in that separation need to move beyond it, towards the risks and rewards of loving men.

And I believe the point of all our progress is love. Hard love. The love that is sometimes indistinguishable from hard time. Not the philosophical airy-fairy "love thy neighbor" love. But the other kind, the too-real, too-close, too-strange and difficult and painful other-person kind of love. Our purpose has been to make ourselves strong enough for that love; God knows experience has shown us that it will take what strength we have.

Remember, attachment and separation are two equal forces within us. The best solution to any two opposing pulls has always been the same: seek the golden mean. That was true when Plato prescribed it, and it is as true today. The path to love is that golden mean, and each of us is skewed off center in her own particular way. Up ahead, and in the middle, is love.

As a group, women were shuttled off the path into a dependent attachment, and many of us are still mired there, seeking ourselves, but too constrained by the requirements of a relationship to look very hard.

Most of us, though, have moved beyond these dependent limits, to one degree or another. We've moved beyond them, though we've been married our whole lives and we've moved beyond them through the shock of more than one divorce. We've done it as heterosexuals, and we've done it as lesbian women. We've done it as single women, or we've faced it when we found ourselves widowed. We have focused on ourselves, on stretching ourselves, and required more of ourselves than any women have ever asked of themselves before.

Because we required it of ourselves, because we have such a well of energy and vision, women as a group have gone beyond the limits we once accepted. We have transformed ourselves into something extraordinary. It is our own capacity that has miraculously expanded, our own skills that are multiplying and exploding, our own voices that have begun to be heard, and to be listened to. We are becoming the magic power that we have always been hoping to find in men.

Become it. Just don't stop there. This process was never supposed to be only about us. This was not some giant narcissistic cat stretch, some great clawing leap into new opportunities, harder currency, softer beds, and smug self-congratulations. All those fears we faced, all the self-examination endured, all the screaming, marching, muscle-building, outsmarting, one-upping loneliness we have survived—all that it has taken to get us to who we are today—had a purpose larger than ourselves. Our purpose was to be strong enough, brave enough, resilient enough to love.

Now we are. We need to look up from our well-deserved pride in our progress and take that next step forward. For, though our development certainly has affected our feelings for ourselves, it has not yet moved us closer to loving men. In fact, it has turned many of us away from that middle ground. Oh, we are with men still—we seduce them, depend on them, hire them, have our children with them, marry them, and much more. But so many of us lean away from loving them.

We lean away from love and keep it a secret from ourselves— believing that we *seek* love, but never quite finding that ideal lover; believing that we *do* love, but allowing free rein to our harshest criticisms and then innocently gaping at the damage done to love; and believing that we *would* love, but for some fault, some flaw, some misfortune of timing or circumstance beyond our control, which unfortunately makes our loving impossible.

Some of us lean away quite deliberately, and congratulate ourselves on our capacity to do so. Resisting love does make life simpler. It is quieter and apt to be more under our own control. It may be calmer, freer from strife, exploitation, or disappointment. Life requires far less effort without the burdens for consensus and cooperation that love imposes. And without the threat of love, we require far less strength, because there are fewer powerful emotional pulls to withstand, fewer saps on our spirit.

Leaning away from love—any kind of love—is your option, of course. But I believe you will always be settling for a half-life—however clean or beautiful or self-satisfying or well controlled that half of life may be. Choose love instead, because love puts you in the middle of life, and that's where all the action is. It is messy action, true. It is dirty laundry and hurt feelings, ruined schedules, conflicts of interest, of loyalty, of values, taste, preferences, styles, and sometimes just conflict for its own perverse sake. Choose it anyway. Thicken your plot.

The dream is that love is bliss. The reality is that life is more serene and requires less work if romantic love is not a part of it. That's why we all need breaks from loving, and why we automatically take them, without necessarily recognizing that we have. It is part of why we go numb to our husbands or lovers for long stretches, why we lose interest in dating, why we can have lingering relationships with men for whom we have no love at all.

Loving is both a choice and an ongoing commitment, and every one of us needs time off from both. Loving requires effort to overcome the anger and anxiety that real life delivers as its side dishes. Often the effort is beyond us. We need to pull away, to recoup, to tend to ourselves, stoke ourselves, and restore our sense of self.

Fine. Take the break. Do what you have to. And then—choose love. Choose love, stretch towards it. Surprise yourself. Yes, it seems unlikely or even impossible that you could go from here to love under your current circumstances. Not with this man. Not with this marriage, this unsuitable affair, not under these financial, physical, social, emotional circumstances. Choose love despite it all, because, if you follow your logical course, all you will end up with are your reasons.

Choose love, even when it doesn't make sense, even though you cannot really believe your lover will ever learn to offer it in return. Choose in favor of loving, though you have no idea how you will ever find each other, or rediscover each other after all you've lost.

Choose it anyway. Against all odds. No matter how long the stretch looms between you and loving, between you and feeling loved—stretch towards it. Have faith. Remember: "These are the days of miracle and wonder. This is the long-distance call. . . ."

Choose it because we know the difference between trusting our instincts and pandering to our fears. Our instincts point us towards love. It is our fears that hold us back. Choose love. Then get there by being loving. Along the way, never lose the childhood vision of a perfect and a true love. But deepen your understanding of perfection.

Choose love because we've known it was the right choice ever since we bit the apple. We are on our path, love is our purpose, and that stretch is our next step forward. If not you, then who? If not now, then when? Choose love.

Notes

Chapter One: Temporary Blindness

3 *In shadow, their bodies curve inward* . . . : paraphrased from Roberta Silman, *Beginning the World Again*.

4 *Love is not a woman's only purpose:* It is important to note that, though our vision of love is as a central emotional driver, it is limited and not just by the presence of the many other forces driving women besides the urge towards attachment. The urge towards loving attachment itself is qualified. It is not equally strong at every age; in fact, the urge to be separate and self-sufficient may overwhelm our need to connect at crucial moments. Furthermore, even if the urge towards attachment is operating as a woman's motivational force, that urge is not always satisfied by romantic or erotic love. The hunger to experience and then to savor maternal love can be (and very often is) as compelling and as satisfying at one point in a woman's life as romantic love may be at another. Filial love, platonic love, and altruistic love are each vehicles for the satisfaction of the hunger to connect, and each can be an enormously powerful drive in and of itself. And, as will be noted explicitly later in the text, even when the drive is specifically channeled towards romantic or erotic love, men are not the necessary object of those feelings. For some of us, other women are the magnets that draw our sexual and emotional impulses.

5 *"one's not half two . . .":* "1 × 1" in E. E. Cummings, *Complete Poems 1913–1962*, p. 556.

5 *". . . Honor both Gods":* Thomas Moore, *Soul Mates*, p. 29.

6 *We are ready now:* Chapters one and two of this book make the psychological and social argument for this statement. The observation, however, has been made in a number of different forums. Faye Wattleton's quote is from an article called "Do Women Love Men? *in Esquire*, May 1995, p. 82. In that same forum (p. 784), Nadine Strossen, president of the

ACLU, comments (ruefully, I thought), "The thing is, I spent my whole life working for equal rights for women and yet I get the sense that most women probably care less about that than they do about romance. . . ." She concludes in a more balanced fashion, going beyond the initial ouch of her observation to the optimistic reality of both drives for women, when she says, ". . . women aspire to equality, but they also aspire to love and romance with men." Her assertion of the coexistence of these urges for women, rather than the either/or perspective of earlier feminists, represents the sea-change described in this book. See Naomi Wolf's passionate discussion of this same synthesis, which she calls "powerful feminism" as compared with the previous "victim feminism" in her book *Fire with Fire*, as well as in the *Ms.* magazine piece, "Radical Heterosexuality." Dr. Judith Wallerstein concerns herself with this same question in the opening anecdote of *The Good Marriage*. She notes (p. 4) the duality of "cynicism and hope" that women express when they are discussing the idea of a "good" marriage. Wallerstein cites the knowing laughter that accompanies her request to interview people with a good marriage, a cynicism that lives side by side with the heartfelt congratulations one woman offers another on the news of a daughter's engagement. Wallerstein concludes that along with our open assertion that "there are no happy marriages" lie our "buried images of love and intimacy." She reaches the same conclusion as Wattleton and Strossen when she says (p. 5) that we have a "human need for enduring love and intimacy. . . . We want and need erotic love, sympathetic love, passionate love, tender, nurturing love all of our adult lives."

6 This imaginary scene between the young King Arthur and his tutor, Merlin, was adapted from two sources: T. H. White, "The Sword in the Stone," in *The Once and Future King*, and its screenplay adaptation, *Camelot*, screenplay by Alan Jay Lerner.

10 *relationships depend far less on whom we choose than on who we are:* Stephen Covey, 7 *Habits of Highly Effective People*. This is the core of Covey's book, a statement of philosophy of character-centered rather than personality-centered ethics. He states the point directly on p. 189, but discusses it in depth in part one of his book. What Covey views as a values statement, others have offered as a common piece of our cultural wisdom, cited in sources ranging from George Bernard Shaw— ". . . the difference between a lady and a flower girl . . . is in how she's treated" (*Pygmalion*, act III) to my mother, who frequently reminded me, "People will treat you the way you expect to be treated, dear."

10 *no matter where you happen to be in your lifelong circumnavigation of love:* Woman tend to be defined, and we often define ourselves, by our relationship status. So we come to think of ourselves as "single," "divorced," "married," "widowed," as if these were fixed identity points, rather than

more accurately noting them as the life stages and temporary social address they are. Over our lifetime we are likely to fit two, three, perhaps all four of these categories. Instead of automatically dividing ourselves from each other according to the distinctions in our current circumstances, we would do better to emphasize the commonality of our concerns.

12 *From Freud through Erik Erikson*: Carol Gilligan's ground-breaking work, *In a Different Voice*, reviews these classic models of human development, each of which endorses a natural progression from attachment to separation. Focusing on moral development, Gilligan demonstrates that these traditional models are not models of human development but, rather, of male development, which has been taken as the norm and ideal, and against which females have been measured. In contrast to male development, which emphasizes separation, female development emphasizes attachment. Instead of viewing this focus on attachment as female psychopathology, Gilligan says of her work, ". . . I reframe women's psychological development as centering on a struggle for connection rather than speaking about women in the way that psychologists have spoken about woman—as having a problem in achieving separation" ("Letter to Readers," *In a Different Voice*, p. xv). This freshly positive view of women's desire for attachment, and of our struggles to achieve it, expressed by Gilligan (and by Jean Baker Miller in her equally influential work, *Toward a New Psychology of Women*), is both the theoretical underpinning and the value system on which the thinking in *Loving Men More, Needing Men Less* is based. Gilligan and Miller speak of webs, connections, and attachment, and I am calling all of that our "vision of love." Whichever the label, the perspective on this aspect of female psychology is similar: Women seek love and relationship with others. Far from being a weakness, attachment is a female strength, as long as it is achieved simultaneous to the development of the self, rather than at the cost of the development of the self.

15 *I want the table sitter:* I have confirmed in a telephone conversation with Naomi Wolf that she is indeed the person who made this statement. She believes she said it during a print interview, and neither of us knows where it first appeared in print.

Chapter Two: Loving Him More and Needing Him Less

16 *"I improved"*: Andrew Sarris, "Muriel's Wedding: Throw the Bouquet for this One," *New York Observer.* The correct quote from *Knight's Gambit* (p. 246) is "I have improved."

16 "I do believe that we have crossed the threshold . . .": Faye Wattleton, in "Do Women Really Love Men?," *Esquire*, June 1995, p. 82.

23 *I Ain't Marchin' Any More:* title of song by singer/songwriter Phil Ochs, published by Appleseed Music, 1964.

24 *We still only earn seventy cents:* U.S. Bureau of the Census, 1991, cited in *Welcomat*, Nov. 16, 1994, p. 31.

25 *"I've always liked your anger . . .":* Lillian Hellman, "Julia," in *Pentimento*, p. 140.

26 **Each of these is, in effect, a road map for love:** In *The Seven Habits of Highly Effective People*, Stephen Covey discusses (p. 247) the idea that a map may not only locate what is real—"Maps of *the way things are*"—but also locate our values—"maps of *the way things should be. . . .* The social paradigms under discussion in this chapter are very much maps of the way we assume male and female relationships *should be.*

26 *It happens every so often:* Thomas Kuhn's classic, *The Structure of Scientific Revolutions*, presents the best-known discussion of the conditions under which basic assumptions or paradigms about how the world works are changed when data are discovered for which these basic models cannot account. He describes the crisis atmosphere required before such fundamental changes are even suggested, and the inevitable resistance that they always encounter. When Copernicus showed that the earth was not the center of the universe, he did not meet with instant applause. When women, at a moment of crisis, suggested that men were not the center of the universe, they faced a similarly hostile response.

28 *The Women's Revision:* A more precise name for this model might have been "The Feminist Revision." Unfortunately, feminism is an antagonistic term for many women who feel themselves to have been disenfranchised by its radical proponents. I chose the name "Women's Revision" to remind us that when this model was developed, the base of women who identified with, endorsed, or incorporated the Women's Revision into their lives in some way, was very, very broad.

31 *"Hangin' up my coil . . .":* I believe this to be a song lyric from the mid-seventies, written by a lesbian singer/songwriter whose name I have been unable to discover.

37 *Men take up a lot of space on your hard drive:* paraphrased from a conversation with graphic designer Toby Schmidt Schachman.

Chapter Three: Clearing Your Path

48 *Between Stimulus and Response, There Is You:* In *The Seven Habits of Highly Effective People*, "Habit 1 Be Proactive" (p. 40), Stephen Covey bases much of his thinking on what he describes as "a fundamental principle about the nature of man: Between stimulus and response, man has the free-

dom to choose." In that same chapter, Covey applies this concept of choice specifically to love.

M. Scott Peck adheres to this same model of love as a choice, saying, in *The Road Less Traveled* (p. 83), "Love is an act of will—namely, both an intention and an action. . . . We choose to love. No matter how much we may think we are loving, if we are in fact not loving, it is because we have chosen not to love and therefore do not love despite our good intentions." Peck makes a clear distinction between "falling in love," which we cannot choose, and "loving," which we must choose.

In *Challenge of the Heart*, John Welwood (p. 3) discusses that tradition of thinkers who emphasize the *agape* aspect of love, defining love as "willing the good of the other, regardless of the consequences to oneself," as compared with writers like D. H. Lawrence or Alan Watts, who focus on *eros*, which emphasizes the divine exhilaration of union with the beloved.

The whole argument of chapters two and three—that women can be active as opposed to reactive, that we can influence our emotions as well as be at the mercy of their effect, that between a stimulus and a woman's automatic response she can choose, shape, will, or otherwise influence her emotional reaction—is drawn directly from the tradition of thinking that views love as more of a decision and an action than as pure feeling. ("Love is a verb," said psychoanalyst Erich Fromm, in *The Art of Loving*, and we have been paraphrasing him ever since.)

53 **Refocusing** *shifts* where *you define the locus of the problem:* In *The Dance of Intimacy*, Harriet Goldhor Lerner makes this same point about the overwhelming importance of self-focus. In fact, she goes so far as to say (p. 86) that "change occurs only as we begin thinking about and working on the self—rather than staying focused on and reactive to others." For those interested in a more extensive discussion of the importance of self-focus, as well as in more detailed techniques describing how one might lower emotional reactivity, this is an excellent book.

53 *Reframing shifts* what *you define as the problem:* This term is not original to me. It is a classic-concept family-therapy technique. Also, although he does not use the term "reframing," Albert Ellis' Rational-Emotive Therapy is based on essentially this principle, namely, that how we perceive events contributes more to emotional disturbance than the events themselves. Ellis refers back to one of the earliest observers of this phenomenon, stoic philosopher Epicteus, who said, "People are disturbed, not by things but by their view of things." (Ellis, *Reason and Emotion in Psychotherapy*, p. 54.)

74 **empathy:** Dr. Judith Wallerstein reports finding this quality in her study of happily married couples. In *The Good Marriage* (p. 65) she says, ". . . happily married partners I interviewed not only learned the other per-

son's life story, they kept it in mind at all times. . . . Moreover they tried to modify their demands according to what the other person could tolerate rather than insisting on something the other could not do."

Chapter Four: How Do We Love from Here?

91 *The balance of love and need:* In *The Art of Loving* (p. 34), Erich Fromm makes the following distinction: "Immature love says: 'I love you because I need you.' Mature love says: 'I need you because I love you.' Infantile love follows the principle: 'I love because I am loved.' Mature love follows the principle: 'I am loved because I love.' "

96 ". . . *but he didn't get in my way*": Natalia Makarova won the Tony for Best Actress in *On Your Toes*, in 1983. This quote is from her acceptance speech, which I heard.

97 *We hold in contempt those who marry for money:* In a 1995 survey in *Money* magazine in which one thousand adults were asked what things they would do for money, 93 percent said they wouldn't marry for money.

99 *Emotional Security:* For a fuller discussion of women's need for approval, the idea of basic female shame which approval expiates, and the "code of goodness" generated from these feelings, see Claudia Bepko and Jo-Ann Krestan, *Too Good for Her Own Good.*

99 *In a way, we make a tradeoff with men:* This is the tradeoff so well described in *The Cinderella Complex* by Colette Dowling.

103 *The thing is, even if we get it, it usually goes:* The more secure you are in each other's love, the closer you are as friends, companions, or emotional intimates, the less passion you are likely to feel over time. As intimacy increases, passion decreases. Robert Steinberg of Yale University makes this point in his "Triangle Theory of Love," a theory that might help you think differently about the part enduring passion must play in your vision of love. By contrast, Judith Wallerstein identified one type of couple, "The Romantic Marriage," that does sustain a higher degree of sexual passion than the other types of good marriage. Hence my use of the qualifier "usually." For a complete explication of this very useful way of thinking about love, see Robert Trotter, "The Three Faces of Love."

104 *some women report that an affair strengthened their marriage:* In *The Erotic Silence of the American Wife*, Dalma Heyn discusses the very sensitive, almost taboo subject of what happens to women sexually inside marriage, and how a lover outside the marriage can help some women to rediscover their sexuality. Heyn was not precisely pilloried for reporting this uncomfortable truth, but the phrase "kill the messenger" does come to mind.

112 *"Never do something for somebody else . . .":* Bepko and Krestan, *Too Good,* p. 110.

Chapter Five: A Map of the Middle

127 *"I could not love thee, dear, so much . . .":* "To Lucasta: Going to the Wars," Richard Lovelace, in *Poetry: The Norton Introduction to Literature,* ed. J. P. Hunter (New York: W. W. Norton, 1973), p. 12.

Chapter Six: To Eros Human, To Forgive Divine

157 *To Eros Human, To Forgive Divine:* The author of this phrase, Toby Schmidt Schachman, generously allowed me to use it as the title of this chapter.

158 *those two internal dragons—anger and anxiety:* The idea that anger and anxiety are inevitable in intimate relationships is in no way unique to this book. A recent affirmation of these difficult facts of life is found in Judith Wallerstein's study of *The Good Marriage,* where Dr. Wallerstein observes (p. 67): "Closeness inevitably provokes anxiety and reawakens fears of being laughed at, rejected, abandoned or not loved. . . . Each person is angry about having to yield, about having to share, about having to give up earlier freedom." Wallerstein's recent study of good marriages underscores the fact that anger and anxiety live right alongside love, a fact that still surprises too many of us.

159 *"Keep your eyes on the prize":* African-American freedom song.

173 *try some of the following to help your anger cool:* In *Opening Our Hearts to Men,* Dr. Susan Jeffers suggests these techniques, including adding something positive at the end of every mental complaint (which on p. 118 she calls "Sidestep your negativity). In her chapter "How Do I Judge Thee? Let Me Count the Ways," Dr. Jeffers includes several other "appreciation exercises" which can be helpful tools to assist you in overcoming anger in order to get to love.

186 *"Men are too fragile . . ."* Frank Conroy, "How Sex Feels," *Esquire,* June 1987.

Chapter Seven: The Limits of Love

201 *"Jesus Christ, Why did your name have to be Mervyn?":* Wendy Wasserstein, *The Sisters Rosensweig,* p. 105.

208 The John and Annie Glenn anecdote is from Tom Wolfe, *The Right Stuff,* pp. 310–13.

209 *"We misunderstand love . . ."*: Sam Keen, *The Passionate Life*, p. 4.

Chapter Eight: Lassoing the Moon

215 *". . . I'll throw a lasso around it and pull it down for you"*: Francis Goodrich, Albert Hackett, and Frank Capra, *It's a Wonderful Life: Complete Script in Its Original Form* (New York: St. Martin's Press, 1986), pp. 60–61.

219 *seek the golden mean:* One of the twelve Delphic Maxims, inscribed on the lintel of the Temple of Apollo at Delphi. See William K. Guthrie, *The Greeks and Their Gods.*

222 *"These are the days of miracle and wonder . . ."*: Paul Simon, "The Boy in the Bubble," Warner Brothers, 1986.

Bibliography

The Art of Love and Other Love Books of Ovid. New York: Grosset & Dunlap (Universal Library), 1959.

Barreca, Regina. *Perfect Husbands (& Other Fairy Tales).* New York: Harmony Books, 1993.

Belenky, Mary Field; Clinchy, Blyme McVicker; Goldberger, Nancy Rule; and Tarule, Jill Mahuck. *Women's Ways of Knowing.* New York: Basic Books, 1986.

Bepko, Claudia, and Krestan, Jo-Ann. *Too Good for Her Own Good.* New York: HarperPerennial, 1991.

Brown, Norman O. *Love's Body.* Berkeley: University of California Press, 1966

Cummings, E. E. *Complete Poems 1913–1962.* New York: Harcourt Brace Jovanovich, 1972.

Covey, Stephen R. *The Seven Habits of Highly Effective People.* New York: Simon & Schuster (Fireside), 1990.

Dowling, Colette. *The Cinderella Complex.* New York: Pocket Books, 1990.

Dryden, Windy, and Ellis, Albert. "Rational-Emotive Therapy," in Keith S. Dodson, ed., *Handbook of Cognitive-Behavioral Therapies.* New York: The Guilford Press, 1988.

Ellis, Albert. *Reason and Emotion in Psychotherapy.* New York: Stuart, 1962.

Faulkner, William. *Knight's Gambit.* New York: Random House, 1978.

Friedan, Betty. *The Feminine Mystique.* New York: Dell Publishing, 1962.

Friday, Nancy. "Do Women Really Love Men?" *Esquire*, June 1995, pp. 77–82.

Fromm, Erich. *The Art of Loving.* New York: Bantam Books, 1956.

Gilligan, Carol. *In a Different Voice*. Cambridge, Mass.: Harvard University Press, 1982, 1993.

Guthrie, William K. *The Greeks and Their Gods*. Boston: Beacon Press, 1955.

Heimel, Cynthia. *Get Your Tongue Out of My Mouth, I'm Kissing You Goodbye!* New York: Fawcett Columbine, 1993.

Hellman, Lillian. "Julia," in *Pentimento*. Boston: Little, Brown and Company, 1973.

Heyn, Dalma. *The Erotic Silence of the American Wife*. New York: Turtle Bay Books, 1992.

Jeffers, Susan. *Opening Our Hearts to Men*. New York: Ballantine Books, 1989.

Johnson, Susan, with Hara Estroff Marano. "Love: The Immutable Longing for Contact," in *Psychology Today*, March–April 1994, pp. 32–37.

Kammer, Jack. *Good Will Towards Men*. New York: St. Martin's Press, 1994.

Keen, Sam. *The Passionate Life: Stages of Loving*. New York: HarperCollins, 1984.

Kravitz, Leonard, and Olitzky, Kerry M., eds. *Pirke Avot*. New York: UAHC Press, 1993.

Kuhn, Thomas S. *The Structure of Scientific Revolutions*. Chicago: University of Chicago Press, 1962.

Laing, R. D. *Knots*. New York: Random House, 1970.

Lerner, Harriet Goldhor. *The Dance of Intimacy*. New York: Harper & Row, 1989.

Miller, Jean Baker. *Toward a New Psychology of Women*. Second ed. Boston: Beacon Press, 1986.

Moore, Thomas. *Soul Mates*. Excerpted in *Psychology Today*, March–April, 1994, pp. 27–31.

Peck, M. Scott. *The Road Less Traveled*. New York: Touchstone, 1978.

Sarris, Andrew. "Muriel's Wedding: Throw the Bouquet for This One," *New York Observer*, vol. 1, 10 (March 13, 1995), p. 21.

Schneir, Miriam, ed. *Feminism: The Essential Historical Writings*. New York: Random House, 1972.

Sell, Emily Hilburn ed. *The Spirit of Loving*. Boston: Shambhala Publications, 1995.

Silman, Roberta. *Beginning the World Again*. New York: Viking, 1990.

Steinem, Gloria. *Revolution from Within*. Boston: Little, Brown and Company, 1992.

Trotter, Robert J. "The Three Faces of Love." *Psychology Today*, September 1986, pp. 46–54.

Viorst, Judith. *Necessary Losses*. New York: Ballantine Books, 1986.

Wallerstein, Judith, and S. Blakeslee. *The Good Marriage*. Boston: Houghton Mifflin, 1995.

Wasserstein, Wendy. *The Sisters Rosensweig.* New York: Harcourt Brace & Co., 1993.

Welwood, John, ed. *Challenge of the Heart.* Boston: Shambhala Publications, 1985.

White, Theodore H. "The Sword in the Stone," in *The Once and Future King.* New York: Putnam, 1958.

Williamson, Marianne. *A Woman's Worth.* New York: Random House, 1993.

Wolf, Naomi. *Fire with Fire.* New York: Random House, 1993.

————. "Radical Heterosexuality." *Ms.*, July–Aug. 1992, pp. 29–31.

Wolfe, Tom. *The Right Stuff.* New York: Farrar, Straus, Giroux, 1979.

Index